Decades of Melody: from the 1950s, 6 Music S Your Ultimate Music Time Machine!

Contents

1950s	....	01
Rock 'n' Roll Revolution	....	02
Elvis Presley: The King of Rock	....	09
Jazz and Blues Roots	....	15
Iconic 50s Bands and Duos	....	23
The Birth of Rockabilly	....	29
Women in 50s Music	....	37
Songs of the Decade (1950s)	....	44
1960s	....	53
The British Invasion	....	54
Beatlemania	....	57
Psychedelic Rock Surge	....	69
Bob Dylan: Folk and Protest Songs	....	76

Vietnam War Playlist	88
Motown and Soul Explosion	97
Woodstock	104
The Rolling Stones: Rock's Bad Boys	109
Songs of the Decade (1960s)	119
1970s	122
Disco Fever	122
Led Zeppelin: Hard Rock Pioneers	126
Punk Rock: Anarchy in Music	137
Progressive Rock and Concept Albums	146
Reggae and Rastafarian Influence	158
Queen	168
Glam Rock and Theatricality	181
Fleetwood Mac: A Story of Success and Turmoil	185
Songs of the Decade (1970s)	190
1980s	192
MTV and the Music Video Era	193
Michael Jackson: The King of Pop	196
Live Aid	205
Heavy Metal Mania	211
Hip-Hop and Rap: From the Streets to Mainstream	224

Electronic and Synth-Pop Revolution	....	228
Bonus Sections	....	257
Iconic Music Venues Around the World	....	257
One-Hit Wonders Through the Decades	....	265
Famous Music Festivals Through Time	....	268
Ultimate Countdown of Record-Breaking Album Sales	....	271
Influential Music Producers	....	277
Music in Movies: Iconic Soundtracks	....	281
Iconic Album Covers and Artwork	....	285
Music and Technology: From Vinyl to Digital	....	288
International Music: Influences Across Borders	....	292

Decades of Melody: Trivia Treasures from the 1950s, 60s, 70s, and 80s Music Scene!
Your Ultimate Music Time Machine!

Hey there, music enthusiasts, trivia buffs, and time travelers! Grab your leather jackets, dust off your vinyl records, and let's jive into the heart-thumping, soul-stirring world of music from the fabulous 50s to the electrifying 80s!

Ever wondered what made Elvis's hips swivel, or why The Beatles had such a feverish following? Curious about how a simple guitar riff could start a whole new genre, or why disco balls became the symbol of an era? Well, you're in for a treat!

In this trivia-packed journey, we're not just revisiting the tunes that had us twisting, shouting, and moonwalking - we're diving deep into the stories, scandals, and sock hops behind them. We'll unveil the secrets of the grooviest bands, the catchiest one-hit wonders, and the eyebrow-raising moments that left the world in awe.

From the rock 'n' roll revolution that shook the 50s, through the psychedelic 60s, the disco-divine 70s, and into the bold and brash 80s, this book is your all-access backstage pass. We'll explore iconic music venues, revisit legendary concerts, and even decode the fashion statements that defined each decade.

So, whether you're a die-hard music lover, a casual listener, or just here to find out what your parents (or grandparents!) were raving about, gear up for a ride through the golden ages of music. Trivia, laughter, and perhaps a few "Aha!" moments await.

Welcome to the Fabulous 1950s
The Dawn of a Musical Revolution!

Ah, the 1950s! A decade where music found its rebellious streak and teenagers became the new beatniks of the jukebox. Before we jitterbug into this era, let's rewind a bit. Picture a world where Big Bands and Swing orchestras reigned supreme, Jazz crooners and Blues legends serenaded in smoky bars, and music was a sophisticated, often formal affair. It was a world ripe for revolution.

And then, the 1950s rolled in with a bang! Or should we say, with a rock and a roll? This was the decade that saw a seismic shift - a transition from the polished to the pulsating, from the refined to the raw energy of Rock 'n' Roll. It was like someone had turned up the volume on the jukebox of life, and everyone was ready to dance!

The Rock 'n' Roll Revolution

Before the 1950s, the music scene was a smooth cocktail of Big Band swing, crooning jazz, and rhythm & blues, simmering under a more conservative cultural lid. Then came the 1950s, a decade poised to shake, rattle, and roll the foundations of music forever.

The 1950s didn't just herald a new decade; it launched a cultural tsunami in the form of Rock 'n' Roll. This wasn't just music; it was a rebellion in rhythm, a revolution in melody, a cultural shockwave that said,

"Out with the old, in with the bold!"

The Key Figures of the Revolution

- Elvis Presley: The undisputed king. With gyrating hips and a voice that could soothe souls or electrify a crowd, Elvis wasn't just a singer; he was a phenomenon. "Heartbreak Hotel," "Hound Dog," and "Jailhouse Rock" are just the tip of his musical iceberg.

- Chuck Berry: If Elvis was the king, Chuck Berry was the architect. With his pioneering guitar riffs and energetic stage presence, Berry's classics like "Johnny B. Goode" and "Roll Over Beethoven" became anthems of the era.

- Little Richard: The flamboyant showman, his raw energy and electrifying performances in hits like "Tutti Frutti" and "Long Tall Sally" were crucial in shaping the genre.

- Buddy Holly: With his bespectacled look and unique sound, Holly brought us hits like "That'll Be the Day" and "Peggy Sue," leaving a lasting impact despite his short career.

- Jerry Lee Lewis: Known for his wild piano skills and hits like "Great Balls of Fire," Lewis was a bundle of untamed energy.

Did you know that the term "Rock 'n' Roll" was popularized by DJ Alan Freed, who used it to describe the rhythm and blues records he played?

Elvis Presley's hip-shaking moves were so controversial that when he appeared on the Ed Sullivan Show, he was only shown on camera from the waist up.

Chuck Berry's famous "duck walk" dance move was actually a result of a childhood accident, which made it more comfortable for him to walk in that manner.

"Rock Around the Clock" by Bill Haley & His Comets, often credited with bringing rock 'n' roll to mainstream America, was not initially a hit. It only gained popularity after being featured in the movie "Blackboard Jungle."

Buddy Holly is considered one of the first to use the standard rock band lineup: two guitars, bass, and drums.

The Rock 'n' Roll revolution of the 1950s was more than just a change in musical taste. It was a social movement that broke racial barriers, influenced fashion, challenged conservative norms, and set the stage for the cultural upheavals of the 1960s. The reverberations of this revolution are still felt in music today, making it a defining moment in music history.

Breaking Racial Barriers

The Rock 'n' Roll revolution of the 1950s played a pivotal role in breaking down racial barriers in American society. This era's music was deeply rooted in African American rhythm and blues (R&B), bringing black musicians' sounds into the predominantly white mainstream.

Rock 'n' Roll was one of the first music genres to cross racial lines widely. Artists like Chuck Berry and Little Richard, who were African American, gained immense popularity among white audiences. Similarly, white artists like Elvis Presley drew heavily from R&B, a genre predominantly black. This crossover brought about a shared musical experience that transcended racial boundaries.

Radio DJs, most notably Alan Freed, played a significant role by introducing black artists' music to white audiences. This exposure was crucial in promoting racial integration through music.

Rock 'n' Roll concerts were among the first public events where black and white audiences would mingle. While there was resistance in some areas, with segregation laws still in place, these concerts began to challenge and slowly erode the norms of racial segregation in public spaces.

- The Moondog Coronation Ball, 1952: Did you know that the first major rock 'n' roll concert, promoted by Alan Freed, was one of the earliest events to have a racially integrated audience, even though it ended in chaos due to overcrowding?
- Sister Rosetta Tharpe's Influence: Often called the "Godmother of Rock 'n' Roll," Sister Rosetta Tharpe, a black musician, was a major influence on early rock artists. Her guitar playing style was especially pioneering.
- Integration at the Record Shops: Record stores in the 1950s, initially segregated, began integrating their music sections as the popularity of Rock 'n' Roll blurred racial lines in music preferences.
- The Crossover of "Cover Songs": White artists often covered songs by black musicians, sometimes leading to greater commercial success. This practice highlighted the racial divides in the industry but also brought attention to original black artists.

Influencing Fashion

The 1950s was an era marked by conservatism in fashion, but Rock 'n' Roll brought a rebellious edge to youth fashion. Leather jackets, tight jeans, and T-shirts became synonymous with the Rock 'n' Roll lifestyle, inspired by icons like James Dean and Elvis Presley.

The pompadour hairstyle, famously worn by Elvis and other rock stars, became a fashion statement. Additionally, accessories like bandanas, sunglasses, and Converse sneakers became popular among young fans wanting to emulate their musical heroes.

The energetic dance styles that accompanied Rock 'n' Roll music also influenced fashion. Clothing needed to be more flexible and durable, leading to the popularity of fabrics like denim.

Rock 'n' Roll also played a role in challenging gender norms in fashion. Women in the Rock 'n' Roll scene, like Wanda Jackson, began wearing clothes that were considered bold at the time, such as tighter fitting pants and shorter skirts, signaling a shift in gender-based fashion norms.

- The Circle Skirt Phenomenon: The danceability of Rock 'n' Roll led to the popularity of the circle skirt, ideal for twirling around the dance floor. It became a staple in young women's wardrobes.

- Sneakers as a Fashion Statement: Did you know that Chuck Taylor All-Stars gained immense popularity as a fashion item in the 50s, partly due to their association with the Rock 'n' Roll lifestyle?

- Elvis's Gold Lamé Suit: Designed by Nudie Cohn, Elvis's iconic gold lamé suit was a fashion statement that embodied the flashy, rebellious spirit of Rock 'n' Roll.

- Also known for his extravagant designs, Nudie Cohn created iconic outfits for stars such as Johnny Cash and Elton John, solidifying his reputation as the go-to tailor for music legends.

Questions - The Rock Revolution

Which artist is known as the "Father of Rockabilly"?
a). Johnny Cash
b). Carl Perkins
c). Eddie Cochran

"The Day the Music Died" refers to the tragic plane crash that claimed the lives of several prominent musicians. Which of these artists was not on that plane?
a) Buddy Holly
b) Ritchie Valens
c) Chuck Berry

Which female artist was referred to as the "Queen of Rockabilly"?
a) Patsy Cline
b) Wanda Jackson
c) Brenda Lee

Gene Vincent's biggest hit, "Be-Bop-A-Lula," was released in which year?
a) 1956
b) 1958
c) 1960

Fats Domino is famous for which hit song that became synonymous with the Rock 'n' Roll era?
a) "Blueberry Hill"
b) "Ain't That a Shame"
c) "Tutti Frutti"

Which artist was known as "The Killer" in the Rock 'n' Roll era?
a) Little Richard
b) Jerry Lee Lewis
c) Chuck Berry

Answers

Answer: b) Carl Perkins
- Trivia Snapshot: Carl Perkins, known for his song "Blue Suede Shoes," was a pioneer in the Rockabilly genre, blending country with rhythm and blues.

Answer: c) Chuck Berry
- Trivia Snapshot: The tragic plane crash in 1959 took the lives of Buddy Holly, Ritchie Valens, and J.P. "The Big Bopper" Richardson. Chuck Berry was not involved in this incident.

Answer: b) Wanda Jackson
- Trivia Snapshot: Wanda Jackson, known for her hit "Let's Have a Party," was a groundbreaking female figure in the male-dominated Rockabilly scene.

Answer: a) 1956
- Trivia Snapshot: "Be-Bop-A-Lula" is Gene Vincent's most famous song, showcasing the classic Rock 'n' Roll sound of the mid-50s.

Answer: a) "Blueberry Hill"
- Trivia Snapshot: Fats Domino's "Blueberry Hill" became one of the biggest hits of the 1950s and remains an iconic song in the history of Rock 'n' Roll.

Answer: b) Jerry Lee Lewis
- Trivia Snapshot: Jerry Lee Lewis, known for his wild piano playing and energetic performances, earned the nickname "The Killer" for his ability to "kill" the audience with his dynamic stage presence.

Elvis Presley: The King of Rock

In the landscape of the 1950s music scene, Elvis Presley emerged not just as a singer, but as a cultural icon who would redefine what it meant to be a rock star. With his debut in 1954, Elvis brought an electrifying blend of various music styles – combining country with rhythm and blues, and adding a distinct pop sensibility that was irresistible to a wide audience.

Elvis's early recordings at Sun Records, like "That's All Right," were groundbreaking. They didn't fit neatly into any existing category of music. This was something new, something that felt like the birth of rock 'n' roll. His move to RCA Records in 1956 catapulted him to national fame with hits like "Heartbreak Hotel," "Hound Dog," and "Jailhouse Rock," songs that remain timeless anthems.

It wasn't just his music that made Elvis a legend; it was also his charismatic stage presence. His infamous hip gyrations were considered scandalous, pushing the boundaries of the conservative 50s society. His style, featuring flamboyant outfits, slicked-back hair, and a rebellious snarl, became as iconic as his music.

Elvis's influence extended beyond the music scene into Hollywood. He starred in 31 films, which, while not always critically acclaimed, were hugely popular and helped solidify his status as a cultural icon. Films like "Jailhouse Rock" and "Viva Las Vegas" are classic examples of his on-screen charisma.

In 1958, at the peak of his fame, Elvis was drafted into the U.S. Army, serving for two years. This stint did little to diminish his popularity, and his return to music in 1960 was marked by successful TV specials and hits like "It's Now or Never" and "Suspicious Minds."

Elvis's impact on music and culture is immeasurable. He brought rock 'n' roll to the masses, breaking down barriers between genres, influencing countless artists, and leaving an indelible mark on the 20th century's musical landscape. His untimely death in 1977 was a global tragedy, but the King of Rock 'n' Roll's legacy endures, immortalized in his recordings, movies, and the undying love of his fans

- Elvis's twin brother, Jesse Garon Presley, was stillborn, making Elvis a single child.
- He was a natural blond; Elvis dyed his hair black for that iconic look.
- Elvis never performed outside of North America, with his only three concerts outside the United States being in Canada.
- The famous "Elvis the Pelvis" nickname was something he personally disliked.
- Graceland, his Memphis home, is the second most-visited private home in the United States, after the White House.
- His 1968 television special, known as the '68 Comeback Special, is credited with reviving his career, showcasing him in his element as a live performer.

The King's Greatest Hits

"Heartbreak Hotel" (1956)
This was Elvis's first RCA single and his first to reach No. 1 on the charts. The song's haunting lyrics and Elvis's soulful delivery resonated with a wide audience, announcing his arrival on the big stage.

"Hound Dog" (1956)
Originally recorded by Big Mama Thornton, Elvis's version of "Hound Dog" is a rock 'n' roll classic. His energetic performance, both on record and on TV, made this song a symbol of his raw stage power.

"Jailhouse Rock" (1957)
Featured in the movie of the same name, "Jailhouse Rock" showcases Elvis's ability to blend rock and cinema. The song's catchy beat and memorable lyrics, accompanied by an iconic dance routine, made it a massive hit.

"Love Me Tender" (1956)
A departure from his rockabilly roots, this ballad showed Elvis's versatility as a singer. The song, named after the movie in which he starred, highlighted his softer, more emotional singing style.

"Suspicious Minds" (1969)
Marking his return to the top of the charts after several years, "Suspicious Minds" is often considered one of his greatest comebacks. This song's blend of pop and soul elements showcased a more mature sound.

"Can't Help Falling in Love" (1961)
Featured in his movie "Blue Hawaii," this romantic ballad became one of his most enduring and covered songs. Its gentle melody and heartfelt lyrics have made it a timeless classic.

"All Shook Up" (1957)
This song, blending rock, rhythm and blues, and pop, exemplifies Elvis's unique musical style. Its catchy chorus and upbeat tempo made it an instant hit.

"Blue Suede Shoes" (1956)
Though originally recorded by Carl Perkins, Elvis's version of "Blue Suede Shoes" became a rock standard. His rendition brought a new level of energy and charisma to the song.

"In the Ghetto" (1969)
A song with a social message, "In the Ghetto" marked a significant moment in Elvis's career, showcasing his ability to tackle more serious and contemplative material.

"Burning Love" (1972)
One of his last major hits, "Burning Love" captures the essence of Elvis's later years – vibrant, energetic, and full of life.

Did You Know?

- "Heartbreak Hotel" was inspired by a newspaper article about a man who committed suicide, leaving behind a note saying, "I walk a lonely street."
- "Hound Dog" was performed by Elvis on "The Milton Berle Show," stirring controversy due to his suggestive gyrations.
- "Jailhouse Rock" was one of the first videos to look like what we now consider a music video.
- "Can't Help Falling in Love" is based on the melody of "Plaisir d'amour," a French love song from 1784.
- "Suspicious Minds" was the last of Elvis's singles to reach No. 1 in the U.S. charts during his lifetime.

Elvis Presley Trivia Questions

Elvis's Acting Debut:
In which film did Elvis Presley make his acting debut?
a) Jailhouse Rock
b) Love Me Tender
c) Viva Las Vegas

Military Service:
What year did Elvis Presley enlist in the U.S. Army?
a) 1956
b) 1958
c) 1960

Sun Records Breakthrough:
What was the title of Elvis's first single released on Sun Records?
a) "That's All Right"
b) "Blue Moon of Kentucky"
c) "Heartbreak Hotel"

What color was the leather suit Elvis wore during the iconic '68 Comeback Special?
a) Black
b) White
c) Red

Which TV host nicknamed Elvis as "Elvis the Pelvis"?
a) Ed Sullivan
b) Milton Berle
c) Steve Allen

For which movie did Elvis Presley record the soundtrack album that included "Can't Help Falling in Love"?
a) Blue Hawaii
b) King Creole
c) G.I. Blues

Elvis Presley had several close friends throughout his life, including Joe Esposito, Red West, and Jerry Schilling. These individuals were not only friends but also part of his inner circle, providing support and companionship during various stages of his career and personal life.

Joe Esposito was a close friend and confidant of Elvis Presley. He served as Presley's road manager and also as a member of the "Memphis Mafia,"

Red West was another close friend of Elvis Presley, known for his multifaceted role as a bodyguard, stuntman, and occasional actor.

Jerry Schilling was a close friend of Elvis Presley since their teenage years. He worked as a personal aide and eventually became part of the "Memphis Mafia." Schilling remained a loyal friend and associate of Presley throughout his life.

Answers with Trivia Snapshot

Answer: b) Love Me Tender
- Trivia Snapshot: "Love Me Tender" (1956) was Elvis's acting debut. The title song was a huge hit, showcasing his softer, ballad singing style.

Answer: b) 1958
- Trivia Snapshot: Elvis was drafted in 1958, serving in the U.S. Army until 1960. His service was a significant event, showing his commitment to his country at the height of his fame.

Answer: a) "That's All Right"
- Trivia Snapshot: "That's All Right," recorded in 1954, was Elvis's first single with Sun Records, marking the beginning of his meteoric rise in rock 'n' roll.

Answer: a) Black
- Trivia Snapshot: The '68 Comeback Special featured Elvis in a black leather suit, symbolizing his return to his rock 'n' roll roots and rejuvenating his career.

Answer: b) Milton Berle
- Trivia Snapshot: It was on "The Milton Berle Show" where Elvis's gyrating performances earned him the nickname "Elvis the Pelvis," a moniker he personally disliked.

Answer: a) Blue Hawaii
- Trivia Snapshot: "Blue Hawaii" (1961) featured "Can't Help Falling in Love." The soundtrack album was a huge success, further cementing Elvis's status as a music and movie star.

Jazz and Blues Roots

In the 1950s, the jazz and blues scenes were not just genres of music; they were the bedrock upon which the era's musical revolution was built. This period was a melting pot of sounds, styles, and cultural influences, laying the groundwork for the emergence of rock 'n' roll.

This decade witnessed the evolution of bebop with artists like Charlie Parker and Dizzy Gillespie, who introduced complex harmonies and rhythms, shifting jazz from danceable tunes to a more artistically complex form.

A Tale of Two Sounds

Jazz in the 1950s was a genre in the midst of a remarkable evolution. This decade saw jazz stretch its wings beyond the swing and big band sounds of the previous era, moving towards more complex and artistically ambitious forms.

Bebop emerged as the dominant form of jazz in the 1950s. Pioneered by virtuosos like Charlie Parker and Dizzy Gillespie, bebop was characterized by fast tempos, complex chord progressions, and virtuosic, improvised playing. This era marked a shift from jazz as dance music to a more listener-focused, concert-style experience.

In contrast to bebop's intensity, cool jazz offered a calmer, more measured approach. Artists like Miles Davis and Chet Baker favored smoother sounds and more restrained techniques. The release of Miles Davis's "Kind of Blue" in 1959, one of the best-selling jazz albums of all time, was a seminal moment for this style.

The 1950s also heralded a golden age for vocal jazz. Singers like Ella Fitzgerald and Billie Holiday captivated audiences with their ability to convey deep emotion and storytelling through jazz standards. Fitzgerald's scat singing and Holiday's soul-stirring vocal expression were groundbreaking.

The blues, deeply rooted in African American history, continued to evolve in the 1950s, setting the stage for the birth of rock 'n' roll.

- The Rise of Chicago Blues: The Great Migration saw African Americans move from the rural South to urban centers like Chicago, where the blues took on a new, electrified form. Artists like Muddy Waters and Howlin' Wolf plugged in their guitars, creating a grittier, more urban sound. This electric blues was a direct precursor to the rock 'n' roll sound of the late '50s and '60s.

- Rhythm and Blues (R&B): R&B, a term first used in the late 1940s, gained prominence in the 1950s. This genre blended elements of jazz, blues, and gospel, and was exemplified by artists like Ray Charles and Little Richard. Their music was not only groundbreaking in its sound but also in its appeal, crossing racial divides and gaining a diverse audience.

- Influence on Rock 'n' Roll: The blues provided the fundamental structure for early rock 'n' roll. The 12-bar blues format and the AAB lyrical pattern became staples in the new genre. Chuck Berry, often cited as a key figure in the development of rock 'n' roll, drew heavily on blues patterns and storytelling in his songwriting.

Crossing Paths and Breaking Barriers

The 1950s were not just about musical evolution; they were also about breaking cultural and racial barriers. Jazz clubs and blues bars were often some of the first integrated spaces in America. The music coming out of these genres was a unifying force, bringing together audiences from different backgrounds and playing a crucial role in the early stages of the Civil Rights Movement.

- "Kind of Blue" Release: The 1959 release of Miles Davis's Kind of Blue is often considered one of the greatest jazz albums ever recorded, showcasing the best of cool jazz.
- Jazz at the Philharmonic: Norman Granz's "Jazz at the Philharmonic" series broke racial barriers by featuring racially integrated bands and audiences, a rarity in the 1950s.
- Chicago Blues Goes Electric: The electrification of the blues in Chicago laid the groundwork for rock 'n' roll, influencing countless rock musicians in the following decades.
- Integration of R&B into Mainstream: The mainstream success of R&B artists in the 1950s set the stage for the later widespread acceptance of other African American music forms.

The term "mainstream" refers to the popular and widely accepted styles of music within a culture. In music, it describes the genres, artists, and songs that enjoy broad commercial success and widespread recognition through radio, streaming platforms, and other media channels. Mainstream music often includes genres like pop, rock, hip-hop, and electronic dance music, reflecting the dominant trends in music consumption and cultural expression.

Key Players in 1950s Jazz and Blues

Charlie Parker and Dizzy Gillespie: Pioneers of Bebop

- Charlie Parker: Often referred to as "Bird," Parker was a saxophonist whose innovative approaches to melody, rhythm, and harmony propelled bebop into the spotlight. His work, including the iconic recording "Ko-Ko," redefined jazz improvisation.
- Dizzy Gillespie: A trumpet virtuoso and bandleader, Gillespie was known for his bent trumpet and puffy cheeks. His collaborations with Parker, like the album "Bird and Diz," are considered jazz milestones. Gillespie's influence extended beyond music into the realm of cultural ambassadorship.

Miles Davis and the Cool Jazz Movement

- Miles Davis: A central figure in the cool jazz movement, Davis's album "Kind of Blue" remains a pinnacle of the genre. His style, characterized by a less-is-more approach, left an indelible mark on jazz. Davis continually evolved throughout his career, influencing various jazz sub-genres.

Ella Fitzgerald and Billie Holiday: Voices That Defined an Era

- Ella Fitzgerald: Known as the "First Lady of Song," Fitzgerald was celebrated for her purity of tone, impeccable diction, phrasing, timing, and a "horn-like" improvisational ability. Her series of albums interpreting the Great American Songbook are considered some of the best in vocal jazz.
- Billie Holiday: Holiday's emotive voice and unique phrasing made her one of the most influential jazz singers. Her renditions of songs like "Strange Fruit" and "God Bless the Child" were powerful statements on social issues of the time.

Muddy Waters and Howlin' Wolf: Chicago Blues Innovators

- Muddy Waters: Born McKinley Morganfield, Waters was a key figure in the post-war Chicago blues scene. His hits like "Hoochie Coochie Man" and "Mannish Boy" featured his pioneering electric guitar sound and charismatic vocals, influencing the British blues explosion and rock music.
- Howlin' Wolf: With a booming voice and imposing physical presence, Howlin' Wolf (Chester Arthur Burnett) was a key player in the Chicago blues scene. Songs like "Smokestack Lightnin'" and "Spoonful" have become blues standards, covered by many rock bands.

Ray Charles and Little Richard: Bridging Blues, R&B, and Rock 'n' Roll

- Ray Charles: A versatile musician, Charles was instrumental in the creation of soul music, a blend of R&B, gospel, and blues. Hits like "What'd I Say" and "Georgia on My Mind" showcased his unique sound, earning him the nickname "The Genius."
- Little Richard: Richard Wayne Penniman, known for his electrifying performances and flamboyant persona, was a pioneer in the transition from R&B to rock 'n' roll. His hits "Tutti Frutti" and "Long Tall Sally" were influential in shaping the sound and style of the genre.

Chuck Berry: The Poet Laureate of Rock 'n' Roll

- Chuck Berry: Often considered the father of rock 'n' roll, Berry's songwriting, guitar playing, and stage presence were highly influential. His songs like "Johnny B. Goode" and "Roll Over Beethoven" told stories that resonated with the youth, blending blues with an appealing rock rhythm.

Jazz and Blues Roots Trivia Questions

Bebop Innovator:
Which instrument was Charlie Parker famous for playing?
a) Trumpet
b) Saxophone
c) Piano

Miles Davis' Masterpiece:
In which year was Miles Davis's groundbreaking album "Kind of Blue" released?
a) 1955
b) 1957
c) 1959

The First Lady of Song:
Which jazz standard was NOT recorded by Ella Fitzgerald?
a) "Summertime"
b) "Strange Fruit"
c) "Dream a Little Dream of Me"

Chicago Blues Legend:
Muddy Waters is best known for which influential blues song?
a) "The Thrill Is Gone"
b) "Hoochie Coochie Man"
c) "Crossroads"

Pioneering Soul Musician:
What was Ray Charles' first number one hit on the Billboard R&B chart?
a) "I Got a Woman"
b) "Hit the Road Jack"
c) "Georgia on My Mind"

Answers

Answer: b) Saxophone
Trivia Snapshot: Charlie Parker, known as "Bird," revolutionized jazz music with his virtuosic saxophone playing, becoming a leading figure in the development of bebop.

Answer: c) 1959
Trivia Snapshot: "Kind of Blue," released in 1959, is one of the most acclaimed jazz albums of all time and a defining moment in the cool jazz movement, showcasing Davis's innovative modal jazz style.

Answer: b) "Strange Fruit"
Trivia Snapshot: "Strange Fruit" was famously recorded by Billie Holiday. Ella Fitzgerald, known for her impeccable vocal range and scat singing, recorded numerous jazz standards but not "Strange Fruit."

Answer: b) "Hoochie Coochie Man"
Trivia Snapshot: Muddy Waters' "Hoochie Coochie Man," released in 1954, is a classic of the Chicago blues genre and played a significant role in the development of electric blues.

Answer: a) "I Got a Woman"
Trivia Snapshot: "I Got a Woman," released in 1954, marked Ray Charles' breakthrough into mainstream success, blending gospel with rhythm and blues to create a new sound that would pave the way for soul music.

Iconic 50s Bands and Duos: A Harmonic Revolution

The 1950s saw the rise of numerous bands and duos that would leave an indelible mark on the music industry. This era was characterized by a diverse array of musical styles, ranging from doo-wop and rock 'n' roll to rhythm and blues and pop. These groups not only defined the sound of a decade but also influenced future generations of musicians.

The 1950s saw the rise of doo-wop and vocal harmony groups, whose music became synonymous with the era's sound.

- The Platters: The Platters were a key group in bridging the gap between doo-wop and mainstream pop. Their harmonious blend and romantic ballads, including hits like "Only You" and "The Great Pretender," not only topped the charts but also won them a place in the hearts of millions. Their smooth style and polished performances set them apart in an era rich with vocal talent.

- The Drifters: The Drifters brought a unique blend of doo-wop and R&B to the music scene. With their smooth style and memorable hits like "Save the Last Dance for Me" and "Under the Boardwalk," they created timeless classics that still resonate today. The Drifters' evolving lineup boasted some of the era's most talented vocalists, contributing significantly to the genre's development.

The rock 'n' roll scene was dominated by dynamic duos and bands that defined the era's sound.

The Everly Brothers, known for their close-harmony singing, were a significant influence on rock 'n' roll. Their blend of rockabilly and country, evident in hits like "Bye Bye Love" and "All I Have to Do Is Dream," influenced future generations of musicians. Their harmonious interplay set a standard for vocal duos and groups in rock music.

Buddy Holly's career, both as a solo artist and with The Crickets, though tragically short, had a profound impact on the rock 'n' roll genre. Songs like "That'll Be the Day" and "Peggy Sue" not only became cornerstones of 50s rock music but also influenced the sound and style of future rock musicians. Holly's approach to songwriting and performance left an indelible mark on the music industry.

The rhythm and blues scene of the 1950s laid the groundwork for what would become soul music, led by groundbreaking artists and groups.

Ray Charles, often accompanied by The Raelettes, brought a soulful intensity to rhythm and blues. His fusion of gospel, jazz, and blues was revolutionary, paving the way for the soul music genre. Charles's profound impact on music was evident in his passionate performances and innovative compositions.

Before achieving solo fame, Sam Cooke's tenure with The Soul Stirrers highlighted his extraordinary vocal talent. His time with the group set the stage for his later title as the "King of Soul." Cooke's smooth, emotive voice and charismatic stage presence made him one of the most influential figures in the development of soul music.

Trivia Tidbits

- The Platters' Originality: The Platters were originally managed by Ralph Bass, a famed producer known for his work in rhythm and blues.
- The Drifters' Revolving Door: Over 60 different singers were part of The Drifters over the years, making them one of the most dynamic groups in terms of membership.
- Everly Brothers' Family Ties: The Everly Brothers were influenced by their family's music group, "The Everly Family," where they performed as children.
- Buddy Holly's Glasses: Holly's iconic glasses were initially chosen not for style but because of his nearsightedness, yet they became a fashion statement.
- Ray Charles' Early Start: Ray Charles started losing his sight at the age of 5 and was completely blind by the age of 7, yet he overcame these challenges to become a musical legend.
- Sam Cooke's Transition: Sam Cooke moved from gospel to pop and R&B despite initial resistance from his fan base in the gospel community.
- The Platters' Cinema Connection: The Platters appeared in the film "Rock Around the Clock," showcasing their crossover appeal from music to movies.
- The Drifters' Multiple Iterations: The Drifters had two distinct periods of success with different lineups: the Clyde McPhatter era and the Ben E. King era
- The Everly Brothers' Military Service: Both Don and Phil Everly served in the United States Marine Corps Reserve, adding a unique chapter to their lives.

- Buddy Holly's Unfinished Album: Holly was in the process of recording a new album in New York when he died; the unfinished recordings were released posthumously.

- Ray Charles and Country Music: In 1962, Ray Charles released "Modern Sounds in Country and Western Music," showcasing his versatility across genres.

- Sam Cooke's Pioneering Business Moves: Cooke was one of the first African American artists to found his own record label, SAR Records.

- The Platters' Legal Battles: The Platters faced numerous legal battles over the rights to the band's name, reflecting the tumultuous nature of the music business.

- The Drifters' Stand on Segregation: The Drifters were among the groups that played an important role in breaking down racial barriers in the music industry, particularly in touring and performances.

- The Everly Brothers' Influence on The Beatles: The Beatles cited the Everly Brothers as a major influence, with John Lennon and Paul McCartney initially modeling their vocal harmonies on the duo.

The Everly Brothers began performing professionally at the **Grand Ole Opry** in Nashville, Tennessee, in 1955. They made their debut on January 8, 1955, at the age of 18 and 16, respectively. While not a traditional "club" per se, the Grand Ole Opry was and remains one of the most prestigious venues for country music performance, and it played a pivotal role in launching the Everly Brothers' career.

Questions

The Platters' Film Appearance:
In which pioneering rock 'n' roll film did The Platters make an appearance?
a) The Girl Can't Help It
b) Rock Around the Clock
c) Jailhouse Rock

The Drifters' Unique Lineup:
Approximately how many different singers were part of The Drifters throughout their career?
a) Over 30
b) Over 40
c) Over 60

Everly Brothers' Background:
Before becoming famous, the Everly Brothers performed as part of which family group?
a) The Everly Family
b) The Harmony Brothers
c) The Kentucky Crooners

Buddy Holly's Iconic Look:
What was the initial reason behind Buddy Holly's choice to wear glasses?
a) Fashion statement
b) Nearsightedness
c) Stage fright

Ray Charles' Genre Crossover:
What genre did Ray Charles uniquely blend into his 1962 album "Modern Sounds in Country and Western Music"?
a) Jazz
b) Soul
c) Rhythm and Blues

Answers

Answer: b) Rock Around the Clock
- Trivia Snapshot: The Platters appeared in the 1956 film "Rock Around the Clock," showcasing their versatility and helping to popularize rock 'n' roll in cinema.

Answer: c) Over 60
- Trivia Snapshot: The Drifters saw more than 60 different singers in their lineup over the years, making them one of the most dynamic and evolving groups of the era.

Answer: a) The Everly Family
- Trivia Snapshot: The Everly Brothers started their music journey with "The Everly Family," where they developed their close-harmony singing that later became their trademark in rock 'n' roll.

Answer: b) Nearsightedness
- Trivia Snapshot: Buddy Holly initially wore glasses due to nearsightedness, but they quickly became an iconic part of his rock 'n' roll image.

Answer: b) Soul
- Trivia Snapshot: In his album "Modern Sounds in Country and Western Music," Ray Charles innovatively blended soul with country, showcasing his extraordinary ability to cross musical genres.

Did You Know that before Sam Cooke became known as the "King of Soul," his exceptional vocal talent was first recognized during his time with The Soul Stirrers? As a member of this gospel group, Cooke's powerful voice and emotive delivery set the foundation for his later success in the world of soul music.

The Birth of Rockabilly

Rockabilly emerged in the early 1950s as an exciting blend of rhythm and blues and country music, often seen as the precursor to rock 'n' roll. This genre combined the twang of country with the rhythm of blues, creating a unique sound that resonated with young audiences and paved the way for future music styles.

Key Influences and Characteristics

- Roots in Country and R&B: Rockabilly's roots lay in the Southern United States, where artists mixed the sounds of country, also known as "hillbilly" music, with rhythm and blues. This fusion resulted in a fast-paced, energetic sound characterized by a strong rhythm section, simple chord progressions, and spirited vocal delivery.

- Pioneering Artists: Elvis Presley is often credited with bringing rockabilly to mainstream attention with songs like "That's All Right" and "Heartbreak Hotel." However, other artists like Carl Perkins, with his hit "Blue Suede Shoes," and Johnny Cash with "Folsom Prison Blues," were also instrumental in defining the rockabilly sound.

- The Stand-Up Bass and Slapback Echo: Instrumentation in rockabilly music often included the stand-up bass, which added a distinctive rhythm. The use of slapback echo, a delay effect, in recordings, especially in Sam Phillips' Sun Records productions, became a hallmark of the rockabilly style.

Sam Phillips and Sun Records: Catalysts of Rockabilly

- Sun Records' Foundation: Sam Phillips founded Sun Records in Memphis, Tennessee, in 1952. The label quickly became a beacon for aspiring artists who wanted to break the mold of traditional music genres.

- Discovering Legends: Phillips had an uncanny ability to recognize raw talent. He is credited with discovering several legendary artists who would become synonymous with rockabilly and rock 'n' roll. The most notable among them was Elvis Presley, whose first single, "That's All Right" (1954), recorded at Sun Records, is often considered the first true rockabilly record.

- The "Sun Sound": Sun Records developed a distinctive sound that was essential to the birth of rockabilly. This "Sun Sound" combined elements of blues, country, and pop, resulting in a unique and captivating musical style. The label's slap-back echo, a production technique used by Phillips, became a signature sound of early rockabilly recordings.

- Other Rockabilly Icons at Sun Records: Besides Elvis Presley, Sun Records was home to other rockabilly icons like Johnny Cash, Jerry Lee Lewis, Carl Perkins, and Roy Orbison. Each of these artists brought their own flavor to rockabilly, contributing to the genre's richness and diversity.

Did You Know that the humble headquarters of Sun Records, nestled in Memphis, Tennessee. Located at 706 Union Avenue. This unassuming storefront studio became a melting pot of talent and creativity during the 1950s. It served as a vital hub for emerging artists, offering a platform for experimentation and innovation.

Rockabilly's Impact on Music and Culture

Rockabilly, while a product of the 1950s, had a lasting impact that extended far beyond its initial decade. It set the stage for various subgenres and styles within rock music, influencing the development of musical movements from the British Invasion to psychobilly and punk rock in later years.

In the 1960s, British bands like The Beatles and The Rolling Stones drew heavily from American rockabilly and rock 'n' roll, incorporating these influences into their music. This transatlantic exchange helped to globalize rockabilly's influence and ensured its place in the pantheon of rock history.

The 1970s and 1980s saw a resurgence of interest in rockabilly, often termed as the rockabilly revival. Artists like Stray Cats led the charge, bringing back the classic sound of rockabilly to a new generation. This revival helped to reaffirm the genre's significance and influence in the broader spectrum of rock music.

The raw energy and rebellious spirit of rockabilly also resonated with the punk rock movement. Bands like The Cramps blended punk with rockabilly, creating a unique sound that influenced the alternative rock scene. The DIY ethos and the emphasis on simplicity and energy in rockabilly were key inspirations for many punk bands.

Rockabilly went beyond music to influence fashion and subculture. The classic rockabilly style, including pompadour hairstyles, vintage clothing, and hot rod culture, became iconic and continues to be celebrated in various subcultures around the world. These fashion elements, combined with the music, represent a nostalgic homage to the 1950s while maintaining a timeless appeal.

Trivia Tidbits

- First Rockabilly Record: Many consider Jackie Brenston's "Rocket 88," recorded in 1951 and produced by Sam Phillips, to be the first rockabilly (and arguably the first rock 'n' roll) record.

- Women in Rockabilly: Female artists also contributed to rockabilly, with artists like Wanda Jackson, known as the "Queen of Rockabilly," making significant contributions to the genre.

- Elvis Presley's First Recording: Elvis Presley paid to record his first song, "My Happiness," at Sun Records as a birthday gift for his mother before he became famous.

- Carl Perkins' "Blue Suede Shoes": This song was the first million-selling country song to cross over to both the R&B and pop charts, showcasing the cross-genre appeal of rockabilly.

- Jerry Lee Lewis' "Great Balls of Fire": This iconic song, recorded at Sun Records, became one of the best-selling singles of all time and a defining moment in rockabilly history.

- Johnny Cash's Unique Sound: Cash's early sound, often categorized as rockabilly, was unique for its use of the "Tennessee Three" backing band, which created a simple, rhythmic, and driving sound.

- Link Wray's "Rumble": Although not purely rockabilly, Link Wray's instrumental hit "Rumble" in 1958 is noted for its influence on the rockabilly genre and rock music in general, especially for its pioneering use of power chords.

A **Power Chord** is a cable used to connect an electric guitar to an amplifier or other electronic equipment, allowing the guitar to be powered and amplified for performance.

- Rockabilly in Movies: Rockabilly culture and music were popularized in films like "Jailhouse Rock" starring Elvis Presley, which helped to promote the genre's aesthetic and sound to a wider audience.

- The Influence of African American Music: Rockabilly was heavily influenced by African American music, especially rhythm and blues, which contributed significantly to its rhythmical and vocal style.

- Rockabilly's Influence on The Beatles: Before achieving fame, The Beatles were heavily influenced by rockabilly music, covering songs from artists like Carl Perkins in their early performances.

- Sun Records' "Million Dollar Quartet": This impromptu jam session featuring Elvis Presley, Jerry Lee Lewis, Carl Perkins, and Johnny Cash at Sun Records in 1956 became a legendary moment in rockabilly and music history.

- The Stray Cats' Revival: The Stray Cats, a band formed in the late 1970s, played a significant role in the rockabilly revival, bringing the genre back into the mainstream in the 1980s.

- Rockabilly's Influence on Fashion: The genre influenced 1950s fashion, popularizing styles like the greaser look, which included leather jackets, jeans, and slicked-back hair.

- Hot Rod Culture: Rockabilly music was closely associated with the hot rod car culture of the 1950s, with many songs referencing cars and racing.

- Rockabilly Hall of Fame: The Rockabilly Hall of Fame was established to honor the contributions of artists to this genre and to preserve the legacy of rockabilly music for future generations.

True or False: Rockabilly Artists Trivia

Jerry Lee Lewis' hit "Great Balls of Fire" was initially rejected by radio stations for being too scandalous.
True / False

The term 'rockabilly' was first used in the early 1960s to describe the music style.
True / False

Elvis Presley's "That's All Right" was the first song ever played on "American Bandstand."
True / False

Roy Orbison's first record was produced by Sam Phillips at Sun Records.
True / False

The Beatles' early style was heavily influenced by rhythm and blues, not rockabilly.
True / False

Carl Perkins wrote "Blue Suede Shoes" after seeing a dancer get angry about his shoes being stepped on.
True / False

"The Ed Sullivan Show" refused to book rockabilly acts during the 1950s.
True / False

Link Wray's "Rumble" was banned from several radio stations despite being an instrumental track.
True / False

Sam Phillips founded Sun Records with the primary goal of promoting rockabilly music.
True / False

Johnny Cash's "Folsom Prison Blues" was recorded at Sun Records in 1956.
True / False

Wanda Jackson was initially a country singer before turning to rockabilly.
True / False

Elvis Presley recorded his first song at Sun Records as a birthday gift for his mother.
True / False

The Rockabilly Hall of Fame was established in the 1980s.
True / False

The Stray Cats led the rockabilly revival in the 1950s.
True / False

"American Bandstand" debuted the same year Elvis Presley recorded his first song.
True / False

Answers

True. "Great Balls of Fire" faced initial resistance due to its provocative nature.

False. The term 'rockabilly' was used as early as the mid-1950s.

False. "That's All Right" was not the first song played on "American Bandstand."

True. Roy Orbison's first record was indeed produced at Sun Records.

False. The Beatles were influenced by both rhythm and blues and rockabilly.

True. The inspiration for "Blue Suede Shoes" came from an incident Perkins witnessed.

False. "The Ed Sullivan Show" featured various rockabilly acts, including Elvis Presley.

True. "Rumble" was banned by some stations due to its perceived incitement of juvenile delinquency.

False. Sam Phillips founded Sun Records for broader musical purposes, not exclusively for rockabilly.

True. "Folsom Prison Blues" was recorded at Sun Records.

True. Wanda Jackson started in country music before embracing rockabilly.

True. Elvis recorded "My Happiness" at Sun Records as a gift for his mother.

False. The Rockabilly Hall of Fame was established in 1997.

False. The Stray Cats led the rockabilly revival in the late 1970s and 1980s.

False. "American Bandstand" debuted in 1957, while Elvis recorded his first song in 1953.

Women in 50s Music: Pioneers and Icons

The 1950s was a groundbreaking decade for women in music, marking a time when female artists began to make significant inroads in a previously male-dominated industry. This era saw the rise of numerous talented women who left a lasting impact on various music genres, from rock 'n' roll and pop to jazz and country.

Breaking Barriers and Defining Genres

- Patsy Cline: Patsy Cline emerged as one of the most influential vocalists of the 20th century. Her powerful and emotive voice in songs like "Walkin' After Midnight" set a new standard for female artists in country music and beyond.

- Ella Fitzgerald: Known as the "First Lady of Song," Ella Fitzgerald's influence in jazz is unparalleled. Her impeccable voice, innovative scat singing, and ability to interpret a wide range of material made her one of the most revered singers in jazz history.

- Wanda Jackson: Dubbed the "Queen of Rockabilly," Wanda Jackson was a trailblazer in the rock 'n' roll scene. Her distinctive voice and pioneering attitude opened the door for many female rock artists to come.

- Dinah Washington: Bridging jazz, blues, and R&B, Dinah Washington's unique voice and style earned her the title "Queen of the Blues." Her hit "What a Difference a Day Makes" is a classic example of her versatile talent.

- Ruth Brown: Known as "Miss Rhythm," Ruth Brown's success in R&B helped Atlantic Records establish itself as a major label. Her string of hits in the 1950s laid the groundwork for the future of R&B music.

- Billie Holiday: Though her career peaked in the 1930s and 1940s, Billie Holiday's influence persisted throughout the 1950s. Her emotive, soulful style and unique phrasing continued to inspire jazz and blues artists.

- Rosemary Clooney: An immensely popular singer and actress, Rosemary Clooney's hits like "Come On-a My House" showcased her versatility, spanning jazz, pop, and country genres.

- Sarah Vaughan: With her rich, expressive voice, Sarah Vaughan was a major figure in jazz. Known for her complex bebop-influenced singing style, she remains a key influence for jazz vocalists.

Navigating a Male-Dominated Industry

The 1950s was an era when the music industry was predominantly controlled by men, from record label executives to producers and managers. Women artists of this time faced significant challenges, including gender stereotypes, limited opportunities, and often a lack of recognition for their talents compared to their male counterparts.

Female artists in the 1950s often had to overcome the stereotype that women could not be successful in genres like rock 'n' roll or jazz, which were considered masculine. Their success helped to dispel these notions and opened doors for women in all music genres.

Many female artists struggled for recognition and fair compensation. Despite their talents and contributions, they were often overshadowed by male artists or faced hurdles in getting their music played on the radio.

- Ella Fitzgerald's Grammy Awards: Ella Fitzgerald was the first African American woman to win a Grammy Award, paving the way for future artists of color in the industry.
- Patsy Cline's Car Accident: Patsy Cline survived a near-fatal car accident in 1961, which significantly impacted her career and personal life.
- Wanda Jackson's Rock and Roll Hall of Fame Induction: Wanda Jackson was inducted into the Rock and Roll Hall of Fame in 2009, recognized for her contributions to rock music.
- Dinah Washington's Diverse Discography: Dinah Washington recorded in various styles, including traditional pop, blues, and jazz, showcasing her versatility as an artist.
- Ruth Brown's Activism: Later in life, Ruth Brown became an activist for musicians' rights, helping to establish the Rhythm and Blues Foundation.
- Billie Holiday's Posthumous Accolades: Billie Holiday was inducted into the Grammy Hall of Fame posthumously, honoring her timeless contributions to music.
- Rosemary Clooney's Comeback: After facing personal and professional challenges, Rosemary Clooney made a successful comeback in the 1970s, demonstrating her resilience.
- Sarah Vaughan's Nickname: Sarah Vaughan was affectionately known as "Sassy," a nickname that reflected her confident and vibrant personality.

Questions

What was the title of Patsy Cline's first major hit, released in 1957?
a) "Crazy"
b) "Walkin' After Midnight"
c) "I Fall to Pieces"

Which song did Ella Fitzgerald famously cover in her 1956 album, earning widespread acclaim?
a) "Summertime"
b) "Cheek to Cheek"
c) "Lady Is a Tramp"

Wanda Jackson is known for her rockabilly hit that also became a popular feminist anthem. Which song was it?
a) "Fujiyama Mama"
b) "Let's Have a Party"
c) "Hard Headed Woman"

Dinah Washington's Grammy-winning song 'What a Diff'rence a Day Makes' was released in which year?
a) 1959
b) 1957
c) 1961

Which song is often considered Ruth Brown's signature hit?
a) "(Mama) He Treats Your Daughter Mean"
b) "Teardrops from My Eyes"
c) "5-10-15 Hours"

Did You Know?

The Grammy Awards began in 1959, recognizing outstanding achievements in the music industry, and have since become one of the most prestigious honors in the field.

Billie Holiday's 'Lady Sings the Blues' is both a song and the title of her what?
a) Autobiography
b) Last album
c) Documentary

Rosemary Clooney's hit 'Come On-a My House' was part of which album?
a) "Blue Rose"
b) "The Rosemary Clooney Show"
c) "A Touch of Tabasco"

What style of jazz is Sarah Vaughan particularly known for?
a) Swing
b) Bebop
c) Cool Jazz

Which Wanda Jackson song was later covered by Elvis Presley?
a) "Hard Headed Woman"
b) "Riot in Cell Block"
c) "Stupid Cupid"

Which Patsy Cline song became a jukebox hit in the late 1950s?
a) "She's Got You"
b) "Sweet Dreams"
c) "I Fall to Pieces"

Did You Know

The jukebox was invented in 1889 by Louis Glass and William S. Arnold, both from San Francisco, California, United States

Sarah Vaughan, known as the "Divine One," was not only a remarkable jazz vocalist but also a proficient pianist who had perfect pitch.

Answers

Answer: b) "Walkin' After Midnight"
- Fact: This song marked Patsy Cline's breakthrough in country music and became one of her most enduring hits.

Answer: a) "Summertime"
- Fact: Ella Fitzgerald's rendition of "Summertime" is celebrated for its unique improvisation and vocal range.

Answer: a) "Fujiyama Mama"
- Fact: "Fujiyama Mama" gained popularity in Japan and showcased Wanda Jackson's bold and groundbreaking style.

Answer: a) 1959
- Fact: "What a Diff'rence a Day Makes" brought Dinah Washington mainstream success and a Grammy award.

Answer: a) "(Mama) He Treats Your Daughter Mean"
- Fact: This song solidified Ruth Brown's status as a leading R&B singer of her time.

Answer: a) Autobiography
- Fact: "Lady Sings the Blues" is the title of Billie Holiday's autobiography, reflecting her personal and professional struggles.

Answer: c) "A Touch of Tabasco"
- Fact: "Come On-a My House" was a major hit for Rosemary Clooney and highlighted her versatile vocal talent.

Answer: b) Bebop
- Fact: Sarah Vaughan is renowned for her bebop-influenced singing style, which added complexity and depth to jazz vocals.

Answer: a) "Hard Headed Woman"
- Fact: Elvis Presley's cover of "Hard Headed Woman" is a testament to Wanda Jackson's influence on rock 'n' roll.

Answer: c) "I Fall to Pieces"
- Fact: "I Fall to Pieces" became one of Patsy Cline's most popular songs, showcasing her emotional depth and vocal prowess.

In today's music landscape, numerous women draw inspiration from the trailblazing female musicians of the 1950s, channeling their spirit and influence into contemporary artistry.

Amy Winehouse: Renowned for her soulful voice and retro aesthetic, Winehouse's style echoes the vintage allure of artists like Etta James and Dinah Washington, blending elements of jazz, R&B, and blues into her music.

Adele: With her powerhouse vocals and emotionally resonant songwriting, Adele channels the depth and authenticity of artists like Aretha Franklin and Ella Fitzgerald, infusing her music with timeless soul and passion.

Beyoncé: As a multifaceted performer and cultural icon, Beyoncé pays homage to the empowerment and charisma of legendary figures such as Tina Turner and Diana Ross, embodying their fierce independence and stage presence.

Janelle Monáe: Known for her eclectic style and genre-bending music, Monáe draws inspiration from pioneers like Josephine Baker and Eartha Kitt, incorporating elements of jazz, funk, and sci-fi storytelling into her innovative sound.

Top 10 Songs of the 1950s: A Countdown to the Decade's Greatest Hits

As we roll back the clock to the fabulous 1950s. let's dive into a countdown of the top 10 songs that defined this era. These rankings are based on a combination of chart success, historical significance, and enduring popularity, capturing the spirit and energy of the 1950s.

10. "Sh-Boom" by The Chords (1954)

- Did you know that "Sh-Boom" is considered one of the first doo-wop hits to cross over from the R&B charts to mainstream popularity?
- It was originally recorded by an R&B group, The Chords, and later successfully covered by a Canadian group, The Crew-Cuts.
- The song's catchy, upbeat rhythm made it a favorite in jukeboxes across America.

9. "That'll Be The Day" by Buddy Holly & The Crickets (1957)

- This song marked Buddy Holly's first number one hit and is often cited as a key influence in the development of rock 'n' roll music.
- The title was inspired by a line in the John Wayne film "The Searchers."
- The song's success helped establish The Crickets as one of the leading groups of the rock 'n' roll era.

8. "What'd I Say" by Ray Charles (1959)

- Ray Charles improvised this song during a live concert, and its immediate popularity led to its recording.
- The song's call-and-response style and electric piano intro were groundbreaking at the time.
- "What'd I Say" is often seen as a precursor to soul music, blending R&B, gospel, and blues.

7. "Hound Dog" by Elvis Presley (1956)

- Originally recorded by Big Mama Thornton in 1952, Elvis's version became more widely known and is one of his most recognizable songs.
- Elvis's energetic rendition on "The Milton Berle Show" stirred controversy and excitement.
- The song stayed at number one on the charts for eleven weeks.

6. "Johnny B. Goode" by Chuck Berry (1958)

- This song is considered one of the most iconic rock 'n' roll songs ever recorded.
- Chuck Berry's guitar intro in "Johnny B. Goode" is one of the most famous in rock music history.
- The song's lyrics about a country boy who could "play a guitar just like ringing a bell" were semi-autobiographical.

5. "Rock Around the Clock" by Bill Haley & His Comets (1954)

- Often credited with bringing rock 'n' roll to a mainstream audience, this song was a massive hit worldwide.

- It gained popularity after being featured in the film "Blackboard Jungle."
- "Rock Around the Clock" was the first rock 'n' roll song to top the Billboard charts.

4. "Heartbreak Hotel" by Elvis Presley (1956)

- This was Elvis Presley's first number one hit on the Billboard pop charts.
- The song was inspired by a newspaper article about a man who committed suicide, leaving a note that said, "I walk a lonely street."
- "Heartbreak Hotel" was a significant turning point in Elvis's career, establishing him as a major figure in rock 'n' roll.

3. "Summertime Blues" by Eddie Cochran (1958)

- Eddie Cochran's "Summertime Blues" became an anthem for teenage frustration and yearning.
- The song featured Cochran's distinctive guitar playing and vocal style.
- It has been covered by numerous artists and remains a staple in rock 'n' roll history.

2. "Jailhouse Rock" by Elvis Presley (1957)

- Featured in the movie of the same name, "Jailhouse Rock" is one of Elvis's most famous and energetic performances.
- The song exemplifies the rock 'n' roll spirit and was a huge commercial success.
- "Jailhouse Rock" was one of the first songs to integrate choreographed dance moves into the performance.

1. "All Shook Up" by Elvis Presley (1957)

- Topping our list, "All Shook Up" embodies the essence of the 1950s rock 'n' roll craze.
- The song stayed at number one on the Billboard Top 100 for eight weeks.
- "All Shook Up" perfectly captures the energetic and transformative spirit of the era and Elvis Presley's charisma.

"My hands are shaky and my knees are weak"

Did You Know The song was written by Otis Blackwell, a prolific songwriter known for his contributions to the rock and roll genre. Despite being famously associated with Presley, "All Shook Up" was actually written by Blackwell specifically for Elvis.

In addition to his famous compositions for Elvis Presley, Otis Blackwell wrote several hit songs for other artists.

"Fever": Originally recorded by Little Willie John in 1956, "Fever" became a massive hit after Peggy Lee's sultry rendition in the same year. Otis Blackwell co-wrote this iconic song with Eddie Cooley.

"Great Balls of Fire": This rock and roll classic was made famous by Jerry Lee Lewis in 1957. Otis Blackwell wrote the song under the pseudonym "Jack Hammer."

"Handy Man": Recorded by Jimmy Jones in 1959, "Handy Man" reached the top five on the Billboard Hot 100 chart. Blackwell co-wrote this song with Jimmy Jones.

"Daddy Rolling Stone": This rhythm and blues song was recorded by numerous artists, including Otis Blackwell himself. The song gained popularity after being covered by acts like Derek Martin and The Who.

Lyric Based Multiple Choice Questions

Which song's title was inspired by a line from a John Wayne film?
A) "Johnny B. Goode" by Chuck Berry
B) "That'll Be The Day" by Buddy Holly & The Crickets
C) "Jailhouse Rock" by Elvis Presley

"A man who committed suicide, leaving a note that said, 'I walk a lonely street,' inspired which song?
A) "Heartbreak Hotel" by Elvis Presley
B) "Summertime Blues" by Eddie Cochran
C) "Rock Around the Clock" by Bill Haley & His Comets

Which song is considered one of the first doo-wop hits to cross over from the R&B charts to mainstream popularity?
A) "Sh-Boom" by The Chords
B) "Hound Dog" by Elvis Presley
C) "What'd I Say" by Ray Charles

"The song that became a massive hit worldwide after being featured in the film 'Blackboard Jungle' is:
A) "Rock Around the Clock" by Bill Haley & His Comets
B) "All Shook Up" by Elvis Presley
C) "Johnny B. Goode" by Chuck Berry

Which song's lyrics about a country boy who could "play a guitar just like ringing a bell" were semi-autobiographical?
A) "Heartbreak Hotel" by Elvis Presley
B) "Johnny B. Goode" by Chuck Berry
C) "Jailhouse Rock" by Elvis Presley

"I'll be the roundabout / The words will make you out 'n' out" is from which song?
A) "Aqualung" by Jethro Tull
B) "Lucky Man" by Emerson, Lake & Palmer
C) "Roundabout" by Yes

Which song was improvised by Ray Charles during a live concert, leading to its recording due to immediate popularity?
A) "What'd I Say" by Ray Charles
B) "Sh-Boom" by The Chords
C) "All Shook Up" by Elvis Presley

The song known for introducing choreographed dance moves into the performance is:
A) "Summertime Blues" by Eddie Cochran
B) "Jailhouse Rock" by Elvis Presley
C) "That'll Be The Day" by Buddy Holly & The Crickets

"Originally recorded by Big Mama Thornton, which song became more widely known in x version?
A) "Hound Dog" by Elvis Presley
B) "Heartbreak Hotel" by Elvis Presley
C) "Rock Around the Clock" by Bill Haley & His Comets

Which song was Eddie Cochran's anthem for teenage frustration and yearning?
A) "Summertime Blues" by Eddie Cochran
B) "Sh-Boom" by The Chords
C) "All Shook Up" by Elvis Presley

"There's a starman waiting in the sky / He'd like to come and meet us" is a lyric from which song?
A) "Starman" by David Bowie
B) "Space Oddity" by David Bowie
C) "Rocket Man" by Elton John

The song that remained at number one on the Billboard Top 100 for eight weeks and embodies the essence of the 1950s rock 'n' roll craze is:
A) "Jailhouse Rock" by Elvis Presley
B) "All Shook Up" by Elvis Presley
C) "Rock Around the Clock" by Bill Haley & His Comets

Which song's success helped establish The Crickets as one of the leading groups of the rock 'n' roll era?
A) "That'll Be The Day"
B) "Johnny B. Goode"
C) "Hound Dog"

The song known for its iconic synthesizer riff and futuristic theme is:
A) "Cars" by Gary Numan
B) "West End Girls" by Pet Shop Boys
C) "Sweet Dreams (Are Made of This)" by Eurythmics

Think of a synthesizer like a musical chef's kitchen. Just as a chef uses various ingredients to create delicious dishes, a synthesizer uses different electronic components and techniques to cook up an array of sounds and melodies.

Which song became a signature for Yes, known for its complex arrangements and dynamic shifts?
A) "Lucky Man"
B) "Roundabout"
C) "Watcher of the Skies"

Answers

Answer: B) "That'll Be The Day" by Buddy Holly & The Crickets
- Trivia: The phrase "That'll be the day" that inspired this song was actually spoken by John Wayne in the 1956 film "The Searchers."

Answer: A) "Heartbreak Hotel" by Elvis Presley
- Trivia: The song was inspired by a newspaper article about a man who jumped from a hotel window, leaving a suicide note with the line "I walk a lonely street."

Answer: A) "Sh-Boom" by The Chords
- Trivia: "Sh-Boom" is often heralded as one of the first R&B songs to achieve crossover success on the pop charts, signaling the growing popularity of doo-wop and R&B music among wider audiences.

Answer: A) "Rock Around the Clock" by Bill Haley & His Comets
- Trivia: The song's inclusion in the film "Blackboard Jungle" skyrocketed its popularity, making it a defining anthem of the rock 'n' roll era.

Answer: B) "Johnny B. Goode" by Chuck Berry
- Trivia: Chuck Berry's anthem "Johnny B. Goode" was inspired by his own life, reflecting the aspirations of many aspiring musicians of the time.

Answer: C) "Roundabout" by Yes
- Trivia: The opening acoustic guitar of "Roundabout" was recorded in a single take, showcasing Steve Howe's exceptional musicianship.

Answer: A) "What'd I Say" by Ray Charles
- Trivia: "What'd I Say" was spontaneously composed by Ray Charles during a concert when he had time to fill, turning into one of his biggest hits.

Answer: B) "Jailhouse Rock" by Elvis Presley
- Trivia: The dance sequence in "Jailhouse Rock" is considered one of the first examples of choreography in a rock music video.

Answer: A) "Hound Dog" by Elvis Presley
- Trivia: Elvis Presley's "Hound Dog" was recorded in just 31 takes, and its energetic performance on "The Milton Berle Show" caused a national sensation.

Answer: A) "Summertime Blues" by Eddie Cochran
- Trivia: "Summertime Blues" was innovative for its time, using multitrack recording to layer Cochran's vocal and guitar work.

Answer: A) "Starman" by David Bowie
- Trivia: "Starman" was added to the album "The Rise and Fall of Ziggy Stardust and the Spiders from Mars" at the last minute and became a crucial turning point in Bowie's career.

Answer: B) "All Shook Up" by Elvis Presley
- Trivia: "All Shook Up" was inspired by a fizzy soda incident, translating that effervescent feeling into one of rock 'n' roll's most memorable tracks.

Answer: A) "That'll Be The Day" by Buddy Holly & The Crickets
- Trivia: The success of "That'll Be The Day" catapulted Buddy Holly & The Crickets to international fame and is considered a cornerstone of rock 'n' roll music.

Answer: A) "Cars" by Gary Numan
- Trivia: Gary Numan's "Cars" was one of the first tracks to use electronic music in a way that reached a global audience, pioneering a new sound in pop music.

Answer: B) "Roundabout" by Yes
- Trivia: "Roundabout" was inspired by the band's travels through the Scottish highlands, with its lyrics reflecting the landscapes they encountered.

Welcome to the Swinging 1960s

As we wave goodbye to the fabulous 1950s, with its birth of rock 'n' roll and musical rebellion, we step into the vibrant and transformative era of the 1960s. In the 1950s, music had begun its journey of radical change, challenging norms and setting the stage for even greater evolution. Jazz, blues, and big band sounds had blended into the explosive energy of rock 'n' roll, capturing the spirit of a generation eager for change.

And now, the 1960s! A decade synonymous with cultural, social, and, most importantly, musical revolution. In this era, the jukeboxes and vinyl records continued to spin, but the tunes they played echoed the changing times. The early 60s carried forward the rock 'n' roll beat from its predecessor, but as the decade progressed, the music scene became a kaleidoscope of new styles and experimental sounds.

In the 1960s, music became more than just entertainment; it was a statement, a movement, a way of life. It was an era that saw the convergence of music with cultural, political, and social revolutions, creating a soundtrack that would resonate through history. As we delve into the 1960s, let's tune into the beats, the harmonies, and the revolutionary spirit that defined this incredible decade in music history.

"In the 1960s, music became a mirror reflecting the rapidly changing world, capturing the spirit of a generation searching for love, peace, and freedom."

The British Invasion

The British Invasion, a term famously coined in the mid-1960s, marked an era of profound influence and change in the music industry, particularly in the United States. This phenomenon saw British bands and artists, armed with a fresh take on rock 'n' roll, rhythm and blues, and pop, taking the American music scene by storm. It was more than just a musical shift; it was a cultural exchange that reshaped the global music landscape.

The roots of the British Invasion can be traced back to the post-World War II era in the UK. During this time, American soldiers stationed in Britain brought with them the sounds of jazz, blues, and later, rock 'n' roll. British youth, emerging from the austerity of war, found solace and excitement in these new musical styles. Artists like Chuck Berry, Elvis Presley, and Little Richard became idols for these young music enthusiasts, who began forming bands and experimenting with these sounds.

Before the full-blown rock invasion, there was skiffle – a type of music that combined jazz, blues, and folk. It was simple and could be played with improvised instruments. This genre played a significant role in developing the musical skills of many young artists who would later become key figures in the British Invasion.

In the early 1960s, two youth subcultures emerged in Britain - the Mods and the Rockers. The Mods, stylish and modern, gravitated towards the sophisticated sounds of modern jazz, R&B, and bands like The Who and The Small Faces. The Rockers, with their leather jackets and motorcycles, preferred rock 'n' roll. This cultural backdrop set the stage for the diverse sounds of the British Invasion.

The Beatles were undoubtedly the spearhead of this movement, but they were quickly followed by other bands. The Rolling Stones, with their edgier take on blues and rock, The Kinks with their sharp, observational lyrics, and The Who with their explosive performances, all contributed to the rich tapestry of the invasion.

Impact on American Music
The arrival of British bands in the U.S. was a wake-up call for the American music industry. It challenged American musicians to innovate and adapt, leading to a healthy competition that further spurred the evolution of rock music. The British Invasion bands brought with them a new perspective on the American rock 'n' roll and blues they had grown up idolizing, reinterpreting it with a distinctly British flair.

Television and radio played a crucial role in the success of the British Invasion. Shows like "The Ed Sullivan Show" provided a platform for these bands to reach millions of American viewers. The Beatles' appearance on the show in 1964 is often cited as a seminal moment, not just for the band, but for the entire movement. It catapulted them to unprecedented fame in the U.S. and opened the floodgates for other British bands.

- The Beatles' appearance on the show was highly anticipated, following the incredible success of their hits in the U.S. It is estimated that around 73 million viewers tuned in to watch the show, making it one of the most-watched television events at the time.

- The Beatles performed a total of five songs during their first appearance on the show. They opened with "All My Loving," followed by "Till There Was You" and "She Loves You." After Ed Sullivan's introduction and audience interactions, they concluded with "I Saw Her Standing There" and "I Want to Hold Your Hand."

- The studio audience, filled with screaming fans, reflected the frenzy of Beatlemania that was sweeping the nation.

- The show is remembered not just for the music, but for signifying a generational shift in entertainment and social norms.

The music of the British Invasion was characterized by a unique blend of energetic rock 'n' roll rhythms, catchy melodies, and clever lyrics. Bands often incorporated elements of American blues, R&B, and rockabilly, but added their own twist, whether it was the jangly guitar sound of The Byrds or the bluesy riffs of The Rolling Stones.

- **Did you know** that The Byrds were instrumental in popularizing the 12-string guitar in rock music? Their hit "Mr. Tambourine Man" featured this distinctive jangly guitar sound, which became a defining characteristic of the folk-rock genre. The Byrds' Roger McGuinn was inspired by the Beatles' George Harrison's use of the Rickenbacker 12-string, leading to its prominent use in their music.

- The Rolling Stones, often associated with rebellious rock 'n' roll, initially started as a blues band. They were heavily influenced by American blues artists like Muddy Waters and Howlin' Wolf. In fact, the band's name was inspired by Muddy Waters' song "Rollin' Stone."

The British Invasion's impact lasted well beyond the 1960s. It laid the groundwork for future musical genres and influenced countless artists. The creative exchange between the UK and the US during this period set a precedent for the globalized music industry we see today.

Beatlemania

Beatlemania was a cultural phenomenon that defined the 1960s, marked by intense fan frenzy directed towards the English rock band, The Beatles. This unprecedented craze began in the UK in the early 1960s and quickly spread across the globe, particularly to the United States, following their appearance on "The Ed Sullivan Show."

The Beatles, consisting of John Lennon, Paul McCartney, George Harrison, and Ringo Starr, formed in Liverpool in 1960. Their early performances in clubs in Hamburg, Germany, and the Cavern Club in Liverpool, laid the foundation for their rise to fame.

- The Beatles, initially formed under the name "The Quarrymen" by John Lennon in 1956, went through several lineup changes. Paul McCartney joined in 1957, followed by George Harrison in 1958. Pete Best, the original drummer, was later replaced by Ringo Starr in 1962.

- The Beatles' early performances in Hamburg, Germany, were pivotal in their development. From 1960 to 1962, they played in various clubs, honing their skills and developing a loyal fan base. These Hamburg stints were demanding, often involving long hours of playing, which helped solidify their musical cohesion and stage presence.

- In a twist of fate that would later be considered one of the music industry's biggest blunders, Decca Records rejected The Beatles after an audition in 1962, famously stating that "guitar groups are on the way out."

- First Recording: The Beatles' first ever recording was a backing track for singer Tony Sheridan in 1961, under the name "The Beat Brothers."

- Stuart Sutcliffe: Originally, the band included bassist Stuart Sutcliffe, a close friend of Lennon's from art school. Sutcliffe left the band in 1961 to pursue his art career and tragically passed away a year later.

- Name Origin: The name "Beatles" was a play on the word "beat," reflecting their music style, and an homage to Buddy Holly's band, The Crickets.

- Early Influences: Their early sound was heavily influenced by American rock and roll, R&B, and skiffle music. Artists like Elvis Presley, Chuck Berry, and Little Richard were significant influences.

- First Record Contract: George Martin, a producer at EMI's Parlophone label, signed The Beatles in 1962 after hearing their demo tape, despite the initial skepticism from other executives at the label.

The term 'Beatlemania' was coined by the British press to describe the enthusiastic reactions of fans to The Beatles' performances and public appearances. The phenomenon truly took off after the release of their hit singles "Love Me Do" and "She Loves You."

> *"The Beatles were more than just musicians; they were the architects of a timeless legacy that continues to inspire generations."*

The Fab Four

John Lennon: Known for his rebellious nature and wit, Lennon was a co-founder of the group. He was not only a talented songwriter but also known for his peace activism. Lennon famously said, "Life is what happens to you while you're busy making other plans."

Paul McCartney: McCartney was known for his melodic bass playing and versatile songwriting. His more optimistic and romantic songwriting style provided a balance to Lennon's edginess. McCartney stated, "I don't work at being ordinary."

George Harrison: Often referred to as the "quiet Beatle," Harrison was the lead guitarist, contributing significantly to the band's sound with his distinct guitar style. He later developed a deep interest in Indian music and culture. Harrison remarked, "It's all in the mind."

Ringo Starr: The drummer of the band, Starr was known for his steady and reliable drumming. He also contributed vocals to several Beatles songs. His affable nature made him a beloved figure, and he famously said, "I get by with a little help from my friends."

Shea Stadium Concert (1965) and The Final Live Concert at Candlestick Park (1966)

Shea Stadium Concert (1965): A Landmark in Music History

The Beatles' concert at Shea Stadium in New York on August 15, 1965, was more than just a musical performance; it was a historic event that reshaped the landscape of live music concerts. Here's a deeper look at this iconic concert:

- Unprecedented Scale: The concert broke new ground as one of the first major stadium concerts in history. It was held at Shea Stadium, home to the New York Mets baseball team, and attracted over 55,000 fans. This was unheard of at the time for a music concert.
- Record-Breaking Attendance and Revenue: The event set records for both attendance and revenue, highlighting The Beatles' incredible popularity. The sheer scale of the audience was a testament to the band's ability to draw fans from all walks of life, transcending the typical concert-going experience.
- Technical Challenges and Innovations: Given the technology of the time, the concert presented significant challenges in terms of sound quality and amplification. The Beatles performed on a small stage at second base, with amplifiers that were modest by today's standards, making it difficult for many in the crowd to hear them over the screams of fans.
- Cultural Significance: The Shea Stadium concert became a defining moment in the 1960s and a symbol of Beatlemania at its peak. It showcased the cultural impact The Beatles had on not just music, but on global youth culture.

- Legacy: This concert set the precedent for future stadium tours by other bands and is often cited as the birth of the modern outdoor stadium rock concert.

The Final Live Concert at Candlestick Park (1966): The End of an Era

Just a year after the historic Shea Stadium concert, The Beatles performed their last official live concert at Candlestick Park in San Francisco on August 29, 1966. This event marked a significant turning point for the band:

- The Decision to Stop Touring: Exhausted by the constant touring and the chaos that surrounded their public appearances, The Beatles decided to stop touring after the Candlestick Park concert. This allowed them to focus on their studio work, leading to some of their most innovative music.

- Atmosphere and Performance: The concert had an air of finality, with the band and their fans sensing the end of an era. Despite the bittersweet mood, The Beatles delivered a memorable performance, though the sound limitations and the screaming fans remained a challenge.

- Last Setlist: The Beatles' setlist for their final concert included hits like "Rock and Roll Music," "She's a Woman," and "Yesterday." The last song they performed live as a touring band was "Long Tall Sally."

- Historical Context: This final concert came at a time when The Beatles were evolving both musically and personally. Their subsequent albums, such as "Sgt. Pepper's Lonely Hearts Club Band," would reflect this change, showcasing a more experimental and studio-focused approach.

- Legacy of The Beatles' Live Performances: The end of their touring days did not diminish The Beatles' popularity. Instead, it marked a new chapter where they would continue to influence the music industry and pop culture through their innovative studio recordings.

Both the Shea Stadium concert and the final show at Candlestick Park are etched in history as pivotal moments in The Beatles' career. They highlight the band's journey from live performance icons to studio innovators, illustrating their profound impact on the music world.

- First U.S. Visit: The Beatles' first trip to the U.S. in 1964 was greeted with unprecedented fanfare, with over 3,000 fans at JFK airport.

- Massive Record Sales: During Beatlemania, The Beatles dominated the music charts, at one point occupying the top five spots on the Billboard Hot 100.

- Innovative Merchandise: Beatlemania spawned a wide range of merchandise, including dolls, clothing, and even branded shampoo.

- "A Hard Day's Night": The 1964 film captured the essence of Beatlemania and was both a critical and commercial success.

- Royal Variety Performance: Their performance before the Queen in 1963 catapulted them to national fame in the UK.

- Historic Shea Stadium Concert: Their 1965 concert at Shea Stadium set records for attendance and was a landmark event in the history of live performances.

- Global Impact: Beatlemania was a worldwide phenomenon, affecting countries beyond the UK and the U.S., including Japan, Australia, and the Soviet Union.

- Innovative Use of Stadium PA System: The Shea Stadium concert was one of the first to use the stadium's PA system for a concert.

- Philanthropic Concerts: The Beatles' 1963 concert at the Winter Gardens in Morecambe, UK, was one of their first concerts for a charitable cause.

- Beatles' Haircuts: Their iconic haircuts, initially a source of controversy, became a fashion trend.

- Fainting Fans: Beatlemania concerts often saw numerous fans fainting due to excitement.

- Fan Letters: The Beatles received thousands of fan letters daily at the height of Beatlemania.

- Impact on Tourism: Liverpool became a tourist hotspot due to Beatlemania, with fans wanting to see the birthplace of The Beatles.

- Cancellation of Concerts: Some concerts had to be canceled due to safety concerns arising from the overwhelming crowds.

More Popular Than Jesus

In 1966, John Lennon made a controversial statement in an interview with the London Evening Standard, where he remarked, "We're more popular than Jesus now." This comment was part of a larger conversation about the declining influence of religion and the growing fame of The Beatles. At the time in the UK, the comment didn't stir much controversy, perhaps due to the increasingly secular nature of British society at that time.

However, when this interview was republished in the American teen magazine "Datebook" several months later, the reaction was starkly different. The United States, having a stronger religious sentiment, took great offense to Lennon's words. The comment sparked widespread outrage, especially in the Southern states, where The Beatles were denounced on radio stations, and their records were publicly burned. Several radio stations banned Beatles music, and the band faced threats and boycotts.

The controversy reached its peak during The Beatles' 1966 US tour. The band, especially Lennon, was subjected to intense scrutiny and backlash. Fearing for their safety, The Beatles' management arranged for a press conference in Chicago where Lennon was compelled to explain his statement. He clarified that his words were not meant to be boastful but were a comment on the waning influence of religion.

> "I wasn't saying The Beatles are better than God or Jesus... I said 'Beatles' as those other Beatles like other people see us. I'm not saying that we're better or greater, or comparing us with Jesus Christ as a person... I just said what I said and it was wrong. Or it was taken wrong. And now it's all this."

Despite Lennon's apology, the damage was done. The "More popular than Jesus" controversy marked a turning point in The Beatles' career, contributing to their decision to stop touring. It also highlighted the cultural divide between the UK and the US and the immense influence and scrutiny that The Beatles were under as global icons.

The Beatles' Refusal to Play Segregated Venues

In the mid-1960s, at the height of their fame, The Beatles took a stand against racial segregation in the United States, a move that spoke volumes about their values and the social consciousness they brought to their unprecedented popularity.

During the 1960s, America was deeply divided by racial issues, with segregation still prevalent, especially in the South. The Civil Rights Movement was in full swing, fighting against these racial divides. Amidst this backdrop, The Beatles, a band from Liverpool, England, found themselves touring the United States, a country whose racial tensions were vastly different from what they were accustomed to at home.

Prior to their 1966 U.S. tour, The Beatles discovered that the audience in their Jacksonville, Florida concert would be segregated. Upon learning this, they were appalled and immediately took a stand, insisting they would not perform if the audience was divided based on race. Their contract for the tour was subsequently amended to include a clause stating that they would not play to segregated audiences.

The Beatles' concert in Jacksonville went ahead with a non-segregated audience, marking a significant moment not only in their careers but also in the broader context of the Civil Rights Movement in America. Their stance was a bold move, especially considering the potential backlash in the deeply segregated South.

- In retrospect, this stand against segregation is seen as one of the many ways The Beatles influenced not just music but also social attitudes.

- This decision was a reflection of the changing attitudes of the younger generation, whom The Beatles represented, against the backdrop of a society grappling with major social and political changes.

Beatles Trivia Questions
What was the first Beatles song to be recorded using four-track technology?
a) "A Hard Day's Night"
b) "I Want to Hold Your Hand"
c) "Help!"

Which Beatles song was inspired by a circus poster John Lennon bought?
a) "Lucy in the Sky with Diamonds"
b) "Being for the Benefit of Mr. Kite!"
c) "Yellow Submarine"

Which song did Paul McCartney write in response to racial tensions in the United States?
a) "Come Together"
b) "Let It Be"
c) "Blackbird"

Which Beatles song was the first to feature a sitar?
a) "Norwegian Wood (This Bird Has Flown)"
b) "Within You Without You"
c) "Tomorrow Never Knows"

What was the last song recorded collectively by all four members of The Beatles?
a) "The End"
b) "Let It Be"
c) "Abbey Road Medley"

Did You Know that each member of The Beatles had a successful solo career after the band's breakup? It's almost as if they were trying to prove that they really didn't need anybody! Here are some of their biggest solo hits:

John Lennon - **"Imagine"**: Released in 1971 as the title track of his album, "Imagine" is widely regarded as one of the greatest songs of all time. Its lyrics envision a world of peace and harmony, resonating with audiences around the globe.
Paul McCartney - **"Maybe I'm Amazed"**: Released in 1970 on his debut solo album "McCartney," "Maybe I'm Amazed" is a deeply personal love song dedicated to McCartney's wife, Linda. The raw emotion in McCartney's vocals, combined with the soulful melody and heartfelt lyrics, make it a standout track in his solo catalog.
George Harrison - **"My Sweet Lord"**: Released in 1970, "My Sweet Lord" became George Harrison's first solo number one hit. The song's uplifting melody and spiritual lyrics, inspired by Harrison's exploration of Hindu philosophy, struck a chord with listeners worldwide. Despite controversy over its similarities to the Chiffons' "He's So Fine," "My Sweet Lord" remains one of Harrison's most enduring and beloved solo works.
Ringo Starr - **"Photograph"**: Released in 1973 as a single from his album "Ringo," "Photograph" is one of Ringo Starr's most successful solo songs. Co-written with George Harrison, the song reflects on lost love and nostalgia, with poignant lyrics and a memorable melody.

Answers

Answer: b) "I Want to Hold Your Hand"
- Trivia: This song marked a technological leap for The Beatles, showcasing a richer, more vibrant sound and setting a new standard for their recordings.

Answer: b) "Being for the Benefit of Mr. Kite!"
- Trivia: Lennon's inspiration for this song came from a 19th-century circus poster he purchased. The song is known for its vivid imagery and carnival-like atmosphere.

Answer: c) "Blackbird"
- Trivia: McCartney wrote "Blackbird" as a metaphorical response to the U.S. Civil Rights Movement, using the bird as a symbol of hope and freedom.

Answer: a) "Norwegian Wood (This Bird Has Flown)"
- Trivia: This song featured George Harrison playing the sitar, introducing a distinct Indian flavor to Western pop music, and marking the beginning of The Beatles' experimentation with world music sounds.

Answer: a) "The End"
- Trivia: "The End," part of the Abbey Road Medley, is notable for its harmonic structure and features the only drum solo by Ringo Starr as a Beatle. It symbolically represents the final collective studio effort of the band.

Did you know that Oasis, alongside iconic acts like Pink Floyd, Adele, and Radiohead, have also recorded at Abbey Road Studios in London? This historic recording studio was built in 1931 and has been a landmark in the music industry ever since.

Psychedelic Rock Surge

Following the tidal wave of the British Invasion, a colorful and mind-bending genre began to unfurl across the music scene of the 1960s: Psychedelic Rock. This musical style was an audible echo of the counterculture movement, capturing the zeitgeist of exploration, both geographical and psychological, that characterized the era. Psychedelic Rock was not just a genre but an experience, seeking to replicate and enhance the altered states of consciousness that were being explored through psychedelic substances.

Psychedelic Rock was characterized by its experimental sounds, extended compositions, lyrical references to personal and spiritual introspection, and an eagerness to push the boundaries of conventional music production. It often incorporated new recording techniques and effects, such as distortion, reverb, and phasing, to create an otherworldly auditory experience. This genre's emergence was a sonic rebellion against the straightforward pop and rock 'n' roll of the early '60s, inviting listeners on a journey through abstract and often surreal soundscapes.

The 1960s were a time of significant social upheaval, with the youth challenging the status quo and advocating for peace, love, and personal freedom. Psychedelic Rock became the soundtrack to this movement, intertwined with the era's artistic and literary expressions. It reflected the desire for a deeper connection with the mind, the universe, and the shared human experience.

"Psychedelic rock: a sonic journey into the unknown."

Biggest Artists of the Psychedelic Rock Scene:

The Grateful Dead: Known for their eclectic style and improvisational live performances, The Grateful Dead became one of the defining bands of the Psychedelic Rock genre. Their music was an auditory tapestry that weaved together elements of folk, blues, jazz, and more, creating a loyal following known as "Deadheads."

Jefferson Airplane: With hits like "White Rabbit" and "Somebody to Love," Jefferson Airplane was pivotal in bringing Psychedelic Rock into mainstream consciousness. Their music often tackled themes of rebellion and social change, becoming anthems for the counterculture movement.

Jimi Hendrix: A virtuoso on the electric guitar, Jimi Hendrix was a trailblazer in the Psychedelic Rock scene. His innovative use of guitar effects and amplification made him a legendary figure, with performances that were both visually and sonically mesmerizing.

Pink Floyd: Beginning as a Psychedelic Rock band with a penchant for spacey, extended musical compositions, Pink Floyd evolved into one of the most influential bands in rock history. Their album "The Dark Side of the Moon" is a testament to their mastery of the genre and its possibilities.

The Doors: Fronted by the enigmatic Jim Morrison, The Doors' music was a fusion of rock, blues, and psychedelia, often exploring themes of existentialism and the human psyche. Songs like "Light My Fire" and "Riders on the Storm" remain iconic in the Psychedelic Rock canon.

Did You Know Jim Morrison, the legendary frontman of The Doors, was born in Melbourne, Florida?

Lyrical Depth

Lyrics often addressed themes of spiritual awakening, existential pondering, and a quest for deeper truth, differing from the more straightforward love themes of early rock 'n' roll. Symbolic and abstract lyricism invited listeners to find personal meaning, often inspired by literature, philosophy, and the visual arts.

Live shows became multisensory experiences with the integration of liquid light shows, avant-garde art, and theater performances. These 'happenings' were more than concerts; they were gatherings that blurred the lines between performers and the audience, aiming to create a shared, immersive experience.

Psychedelic Rock influenced fashion, with vibrant colors, paisley patterns, and bell-bottom jeans becoming synonymous with the 'hippie' movement. It also impacted graphic design, with album covers, posters, and other visual media adopting the swirling, kaleidoscopic aesthetic that defined the psychedelic art style.

The 1960s were an era where musical boundaries were pushed and often completely redrawn. Psychedelic Rock served as a perfect embodiment of this spirit of experimentation and innovation. Musicians began to view the studio as an instrument in itself, a place where sound could be manipulated and expanded to reflect the rapidly changing consciousness of the era.

Moving away from the predictable patterns of mainstream music, Psychedelic Rock artists started crafting songs that were almost narrative in nature. These compositions often took the listener on a journey, sometimes meandering through various musical themes and motifs without ever returning to a traditional hook or refrain. This approach to songwriting mirrored the free-form, exploratory nature of a psychedelic experience, eschewing structure in favor of a more organic flow.

Studio Technology

Pioneers of Psychedelic Rock began to experiment with new studio techniques that would alter the texture of their music. Tape loops created repeating motifs that could sound otherworldly. Feedback, once considered a nuisance, was embraced for its edgy, immersive qualities. The Leslie speaker, originally designed for organs, was repurposed to give guitars and vocals a swirling, vibrato effect, further enhancing the trippy feel of the music.

The incorporation of Eastern musical influences marked a significant shift in the sound palette of Western musicians. The sitar, with its resonant, droning strings, and the tabla, with its complex rhythms, brought a new dimension to rock music. Artists like George Harrison of The Beatles studied with Indian musicians such as Ravi Shankar, bridging two musical worlds and introducing a broader range of sonic possibilities. Albums like "Revolver" and "Sgt. Pepper's Lonely Hearts Club Band" stand as testaments to this melding of Eastern and Western sounds.

Did You know?

- The Velvet Underground's "Banana" Album: Did you know that The Velvet Underground's debut album featured a peelable banana sticker on the cover, designed by pop artist Andy Warhol? This album is considered one of the most influential in the Psychedelic Rock genre, despite its initial poor sales.

- The Origin of 'Psychedelic': The term 'psychedelic' was coined by psychiatrist Humphry Osmond in 1957 and means "mind-manifesting," which became a perfect descriptor for the music that sought to evoke an altered state of consciousness.

- The First Use of a Synthesizer: Did you know that The Doors were one of the first bands to use a Moog synthesizer on a rock record? The song "Strange Days" features this groundbreaking sound.

- Jimi Hendrix's "Star-Spangled Banner": At Woodstock in 1969, Jimi Hendrix performed a rendition of the U.S. national anthem on his guitar that mimicked the sounds of bombs and gunfire, making a powerful anti-war statement.

- Pink Floyd's Name Homage: Did you know that Pink Floyd's name was derived from two blues musicians, Pink Anderson and Floyd Council? Syd Barrett combined the names to form the band's unique title.

- Grateful Dead's Sound System: The Grateful Dead were pioneers in live sound engineering. They created the "Wall of Sound," a massive, innovative PA system that reduced feedback and allowed for clearer music at their concerts.

- Janis Joplin's Psychedelic Porsche: Janis Joplin famously drove a Porsche that was hand-painted in a psychedelic mural, reflecting the aesthetic of the era.

- The Beatles' Backward Tracks: Did you know that The Beatles were one of the first to use backward vocals and guitar solos in their music, notably in songs like "Rain" and "Tomorrow Never Knows"?

- The First Outdoor Rock Festival: Before Woodstock, the Monterey Pop Festival in 1967 was the first major outdoor rock festival and included performances by Jimi Hendrix, Janis Joplin, and The Grateful Dead, helping to solidify the psychedelic rock genre.

- The Creation of FM Radio: The rise of Psychedelic Rock coincided with the creation of FM radio, which allowed for better sound quality and longer playing time for tracks, perfect for the extended jams of Psychedelic Rock.

True or False Questions: Psychedelic Rock Surge

True or False: The Grateful Dead's "Wall of Sound" was the first instance of on-stage monitors being used during live performances.

True or False: Jimi Hendrix's famous Woodstock performance included a cover of Bob Dylan's "All Along the Watchtower."

True or False: Pink Floyd's original frontman Syd Barrett named the band after his favorite color and the English word for an inflated sense of self.

True or False: The Doors' song "Light My Fire" was one of the first rock singles to exceed seven minutes on the radio version.

True or False: Jefferson Airplane's "White Rabbit" was the first song ever to discuss the topic of Alice in Wonderland in rock music.

True or False: The Leslie speaker was named after the inventor, Donald Leslie, who initially marketed it to Hammond Organ users.

True or False: The Velvet Underground's debut album cover was a plain black sleeve with no banana sticker or any other design.

True or False: The Monterey Pop Festival of 1967 was a three-day concert event that was free to the public.

True or False: FM radio was developed to improve the quality of rock music broadcasts, specifically to enhance the sound of Psychedelic Rock.

Answers with Trivia Snapshot

False. The "Wall of Sound" was indeed revolutionary, but it was not the first to use on-stage monitors. However, it was one of the largest and most complex sound systems ever built, allowing the band to hear their music clearly without feedback.

False. Hendrix's performance did not include "All Along the Watchtower." However, his rendition of the "Star-Spangled Banner" became a historic moment of the festival, symbolizing the counterculture's anti-war stance.

False. Pink Floyd was named after two blues musicians, Pink Anderson and Floyd Council. Syd Barrett combined these names to create the band's title, paying homage to his blues influences.

True. "Light My Fire" originally exceeded seven minutes, and its length was unusual for the time. The radio edit was shorter, but the full version's success helped to break the typical radio constraints.

False. "White Rabbit" was not the first song to discuss Alice in Wonderland, but it was notable for its overt references to the book and for its commentary on the drug experience.

True. The Leslie speaker was indeed named after its inventor, Donald Leslie, and it became integral to the psychedelic sound for its unique effect on instruments and vocals.

False. The Velvet Underground's debut album, "The Velvet Underground & Nico," featured a distinctive Andy Warhol banana sticker that listeners could peel off, revealing a flesh-colored banana underneath.

False. The Monterey Pop Festival was not free to the public; tickets were sold for the event. It was, however, one of the first festivals to bring together artists from multiple musical genres.

True. FM radio was developed for its high-fidelity sound quality, which allowed for a better listening experience.

Bob Dylan: Folk and Protest Songs

Bob Dylan, born Robert Allen Zimmerman in 1941, emerged as one of the most influential figures in the 20th-century music scene. His work, particularly in the 1960s, marked a departure from the existing norms of popular music, both in terms of lyrical depth and musical innovation. Here's a dive into the trivia trove of Bob Dylan's contributions to folk and protest music:

Folk Revival Catalyst

Bob Dylan's arrival in New York City in 1961 and his performances at venues like Gerde's Folk City spotlighted him as a leading figure in the folk revival. His early albums, filled with traditional folk songs and his own compositions, resonated with authenticity and rawness that captured the essence of folk's storytelling tradition. His acoustic guitar, harmonica, and distinct vocal style became symbols of the folk movement, inspiring countless artists to follow his lead.

Protest Anthems Creator

Dylan's knack for capturing the zeitgeist of the 1960s America culminated in songs that voiced the concerns and hopes of a generation. "Blowin' in the Wind" questioned the social injustices of the time, while "The Times They Are a-Changin'" became a call to action for change and is often linked to the Civil Rights Movement. His lyrics were direct yet poetic, and their universal appeal made them timeless anthems of protest and hope.

Electric Controversy

At the 1965 Newport Folk Festival, Dylan performed with an electric band for the first time, signaling a shift from traditional folk to a rock-infused sound. This performance was met with mixed reactions; some fans felt betrayed, while others were exhilarated by the fusion of genres.

This pivotal moment not only marked Dylan's artistic evolution but also reflected the changing landscape of popular music, where electric instruments became the new norm in rock and folk music. Dylan's subsequent album, "Highway 61 Revisited," fully embraced this electric direction, featuring the iconic hit "Like a Rolling Stone" and solidifying his place in rock history.

Here, we explore the most iconic tracks from Dylan's storied career, each a testament to his profound impact on the world of music and culture. From poetic reflections to anthems of change, these songs are the pillars of Dylan's enduring legacy.

"Mr. Tambourine Man"
- Although famously covered by The Byrds, Dylan's original version on "Bringing It All Back Home" (1965) is a poetic ode to escapism and has been interpreted as an allegory for artistic inspiration or a drug-induced journey.

"Subterranean Homesick Blues"
- A landmark track from "Bringing It All Back Home," this 1965 song was Dylan's foray into electric music and is notable for its rapid-fire, stream-of-consciousness lyrics. It was also featured in a famous early music video precursor, with Dylan flipping cue cards.

"Desolation Row"
- This epic 11-minute track from "Highway 61 Revisited" (1965) is a surreal journey through a series of allegorical scenes and characters, showcasing Dylan's unique storytelling ability.

"A Hard Rain's A-Gonna Fall"
- Featured on "The Freewheelin' Bob Dylan" (1963), this song's apocalyptic imagery and haunting melody were interpreted as a reflection on the Cuban Missile Crisis, although Dylan suggested it was more broadly about the state of the world.

"Just Like a Woman"
- From "Blonde on Blonde" (1966), this song's delicate melody contrasts with its complex lyrics that explore themes of love, betrayal, and femininity, and remains one of Dylan's most debated songs.

"The Times They Are A-Changin'"
- This anthem from the album of the same name (1964) captured the spirit of social change in the 1960s and became an enduring call for progress and understanding.

"Blowin' in the Wind"
- Perhaps Dylan's most famous song, from "The Freewheelin' Bob Dylan," it became an anthem for civil rights and anti-war movements. Its questioning lyrics still resonate as a powerful call for peace and justice.

"Like a Rolling Stone"
- Hailed as one of the greatest rock songs of all time, this 1965 release from "Highway 61 Revisited" marked a significant shift in Dylan's musical style and was a breakthrough in its lyrical depth and complexity.

"Knockin' on Heaven's Door"
- Written for the soundtrack of the film "Pat Garrett and Billy the Kid" (1973), this song's simple, plaintive chorus has made it one of Dylan's most covered songs, transcending genres and generations.

Bob Dylan, known for his enigmatic and sometimes unpredictable character, has many amusing anecdotes attached to his name.....

When Dylan Met Sandberg....

As the tale goes, Dylan decided to pay a visit to the renowned poet and writer Carl Sandburg. Sandburg, then in his 80s, was living in North Carolina, and Dylan, a fan of his work, spontaneously decided to drop by unannounced. With no prior appointment, Dylan, accompanied by a friend, drove to Sandburg's house and knocked on his door.

Sandburg, unaware of who Dylan was, answered the door. Dylan introduced himself and explained that he was a musician and a great admirer of Sandburg's poetry. Intrigued but still slightly confused, Sandburg welcomed them in. Dylan, known for his love of privacy and tendency to avoid the media spotlight, decided not to reveal his full identity or fame to Sandburg.

The visit was both awkward and endearing. Dylan brought along a box of expensive cigars as a gift, not knowing that Sandburg had recently quit smoking on doctor's orders. They chatted for a while, with Dylan mostly asking questions and Sandburg sharing his poetic wisdom. The conversation was a bit stilted, as Sandburg was still unsure about who this young visitor was.

As they were leaving, Sandburg's wife, who had recognized Dylan, exclaimed, "Do you know who that was? That was Bob Dylan!" To which Sandburg reportedly replied, "Who's Bob Dylan?"

The story, humorous in its encounter of two vastly different generations and personalities, is often cited as an example of Dylan's spontaneous nature and his deep respect for his literary heroes. It also highlights the cultural gap between the old literary world and the emerging new world of popular music, a gap that Dylan himself was instrumental in bridging.

Weird Dylan

Bob Dylan's perception as "weird" by some people can be attributed to a combination of his unique artistic traits, enigmatic personality, and unconventional approach to his career and public image. Here are a few aspects that contribute to this perception:

- Idiosyncratic Vocal Style: Dylan's singing voice is distinctive and unconventional. He doesn't have a traditionally melodic voice, and his nasal tone, phrasing, and sometimes mumbled delivery stand in stark contrast to the polished vocal performances prevalent in popular music. This uniqueness, while endearing to many, can be off-putting to others who are accustomed to more standard vocal styles.

- Cryptic and Abstract Lyrics: Dylan is known for his profound and often cryptic lyrics. His songwriting is deeply metaphorical, filled with abstract imagery and allusions that can be challenging to interpret. This complexity, while celebrated for its poetic depth, can be perplexing to those who prefer more straightforward and literal songwriting.

- Unpredictable Public Persona: Dylan has a reputation for being elusive and unpredictable in his public appearances and interviews. He often gives enigmatic responses and has been known to shy away from straightforward answers, creating a sense of mystery around his persona.

- Artistic Evolution and Reinvention: Over the decades, Dylan has continually reinvented his music and image, often defying fans' and critics' expectations. From folk to electric, from gospel to standards, his willingness to explore and change his style has sometimes been seen as unconventional or strange, especially when these changes have been abrupt or unexpected.

- **Reclusive Nature:** Dylan's reclusive nature and reluctance to embrace the trappings of fame contribute to his perception as an outsider. Unlike many celebrities who actively seek the spotlight, Dylan has often shunned it, preferring a more private life. This aloofness can sometimes be interpreted as odd or eccentric.

- **On-Stage Persona:** Dylan's on-stage performances are known for their lack of interaction with the audience and his focus on the music rather than on showmanship. This has sometimes been seen as odd, especially in a genre where performers are often expected to engage actively with their audience.

The Covers

The phenomenon of Bob Dylan's songs being covered by other artists, often leading to those versions becoming more popular than his originals, is a testament to the versatility and universal appeal of his songwriting. Artists like Rod Stewart, Jimi Hendrix, The Byrds, and many others have found success with their renditions of Dylan's songs. Here's why this happens:

- "All Along the Watchtower" by Jimi Hendrix: Perhaps the most famous Dylan cover, Hendrix transformed this song into a searing, electric anthem. His version, released in 1968, is now more widely recognized than Dylan's original 1967 recording, thanks to Hendrix's groundbreaking guitar work and intense vocal delivery.

- "Mr. Tambourine Man" by The Byrds: The Byrds' 1965 rendition of this song, with its jangly 12-string Rickenbacker guitar and harmonious vocals, turned Dylan's folk tune into a pop-rock classic, reaching the top of the charts and introducing Dylan's songwriting to a broader audience.

- "Make You Feel My Love" by Adele: While Dylan's original 1997 version was poignant, Adele's soulful and emotive interpretation in 2008 brought a new depth to the song, resonating strongly with a global audience and becoming a staple of romantic playlists.

- "Knockin' on Heaven's Door" by Guns N' Roses: This rock ballad cover, released in 1990, became a staple of Guns N' Roses' live performances. Their hard rock version added a new dimension to the song, distinguishing it from Dylan's more subdued original.

- "Forever Young" by Rod Stewart: While Dylan's original is reflective and folky, Rod Stewart's 1988 version has a more anthemic rock feel. Stewart's rendition, with its uplifting melody and grand arrangement, brought a different kind of energy to the song.

- "Blowin' in the Wind" by Stevie Wonder: Stevie Wonder added a soulful touch to this classic in his 1966 cover. His version, infused with Motown's rhythmic vibrancy, offered a new perspective on Dylan's lyrics, emphasizing the song's universal message.

- "It Ain't Me Babe" by Johnny Cash and June Carter: This country rendition by Johnny Cash and June Carter in 1965 took Dylan's song into a new genre, adding a playful duet dynamic that highlighted the song's narrative of love and independence.

"Bob Dylan's impact on music is unparalleled. He not only reinvented the medium, but he also continues to inspire generations with his timeless artistry."

Dylan's lyrics are poetic, profound, and often open to interpretation, allowing other artists to bring their own perspective and emotional depth to the songs. This adaptability makes his music appealing to artists across various genres.

Dylan's unique vocal style is one of his signatures, but it's not universally appealing. When artists with different vocal qualities cover his songs, they can bring a new level of musicality and appeal to a broader audience.

Some artists who cover Dylan's songs have a more mainstream or commercial sound, which can make their versions more accessible to the general public Cover artists often experiment with different instruments and arrangements. This innovation can breathe new life into Dylan's songs, appealing to listeners who might not be as familiar with or appreciative of the folk and rock blend that characterizes much of Dylan's work.

At times, a cover version becomes popular because it aligns well with the cultural or musical trends of the time. The artist covering the song might be at the peak of their popularity, thereby introducing Dylan's work to a new generation or demographic.

"The answer, my friend, is blowin' in the wind The answer is blowin' in the wind."

"May you have a strong foundation When the winds of changes shift"

"I was so much older then, I'm younger than that now."

Questions

Which famous musician said that hearing Bob Dylan's "Blowin' in the Wind" for the first time was a pivotal moment in his life?
a) Eric Clapton
b) John Lennon
c) Bruce Springsteen

Bob Dylan's "Like a Rolling Stone" was a significant shift in his musical style. How long is the original studio version of the song?
a) 3 minutes and 45 seconds
b) 4 minutes and 20 seconds
c) 6 minutes and 13 seconds

Which Bob Dylan song was originally written for the soundtrack of the film "Pat Garrett & Billy the Kid"?
a) "Knockin' on Heaven's Door"
b) "Lay, Lady, Lay"
c) "Things Have Changed"

Dylan's song "Mr. Tambourine Man" was famously covered by The Byrds. However, which instrument is not prominently featured in The Byrds' version?
a) Guitar
b) Drums
c) Tambourine

Which of the following is a novel that Bob Dylan claimed had an influence on his songwriting?
a) "Moby-Dick" by Herman Melville
b) "On the Road" by Jack Kerouac
c) "The Great Gatsby" by F. Scott Fitzgerald

Bob Dylan was awarded the Nobel Prize in Literature in 2016. For which aspect of his work was he recognized?
a) For his impact on folk music
b) For creating new poetic expressions within American song tradition
c) For his political activism through music

In which city did Bob Dylan famously 'go electric' at the Newport Folk Festival, causing a stir among folk music purists?
a) New York
b) San Francisco
c) Newport

Which Beatles song was directly inspired by Bob Dylan's lyrical style?
a) "Lucy in the Sky with Diamonds"
b) "Norwegian Wood (This Bird Has Flown)"
c) "Help!"

Bob Dylan's original name is Robert Allen Zimmerman. At which university did he start his music career?
a) Harvard University
b) University of Minnesota
c) Columbia University

Which famous poet did Bob Dylan visit unannounced, leading to an amusingly awkward encounter?
a) Allen Ginsberg
b) Carl Sandburg
c) Robert Frost

Answers

Answer: c) Bruce Springsteen
- Trivia Snapshot: Bruce Springsteen has spoken about the profound impact Dylan's music, especially "Blowin' in the Wind," had on him during his formative years as a musician.

Answer: c) 6 minutes and 13 seconds
- Trivia Snapshot: "Like a Rolling Stone" broke the norm of the typical radio single length, and its success helped redefine the boundaries of popular music in the mid-1960s.

Answer: a) "Knockin' on Heaven's Door"
- Trivia Snapshot: This song, written for the 1973 film, has since become one of Dylan's most famous and frequently covered songs.

Answer: c) Tambourine
- Trivia Snapshot: Despite its title, The Byrds' version of "Mr. Tambourine Man" doesn't feature a tambourine, focusing instead on the 12-string guitar.

Answer: b) "On the Road" by Jack Kerouac
- Trivia Snapshot: Dylan has cited Kerouac's novel as a major influence on his songwriting and view of America.

Answer: b) For creating new poetic expressions within American song tradition
- Trivia Snapshot: Dylan's Nobel Prize recognized his groundbreaking approach to songwriting, blending poetry with popular music.

Answer: c) Newport
- Trivia Snapshot: Dylan's electric performance at the 1965 Newport Folk Festival is a historic moment in music history, marking his transition from acoustic folk to electric rock.

Answer: b) "Norwegian Wood (This Bird Has Flown)"
- Trivia Snapshot: John Lennon admitted that Dylan's lyrical style influenced him in writing "Norwegian Wood," especially in its storytelling approach.

Answer: b) University of Minnesota
- Trivia Snapshot: Dylan began exploring folk and rock music while attending the University of Minnesota before dropping out and moving to New York.

Answer: b) Carl Sandburg
- Trivia Snapshot: The visit to Carl Sandburg, a poet Dylan admired, was an example of his respect for literary figures and his often unpredictable behavior.

So, Bob Dylan, ever the rebel, dropped out of the University of Minnesota, where he was supposed to study English. Joining the ranks of musical dropouts, we've got...

Kanye West - Chicago State University
Mick Jagger - London School of Economics
Lady Gaga - New York University
Jon Bon Jovi - Seton Hall University
Alicia Keys - Columbia University
John Lennon - Liverpool College of Art
Stevie Nicks - San Jose State University
Tom Morello - Harvard University
Billy Joel - Columbia University
Paul Simon - Queens College, New York
Eddie Vedder - San Diego State University

Vietnam War Playlist

The 1960s was a decade marked by significant cultural, social, and political upheavals, with the Vietnam War being one of the defining elements. The conflict, which lasted from 1955 to 1975, with the most direct U.S. involvement between 1965 and 1973, deeply influenced the music of the era. Artists used their songs to reflect the sentiments of a generation caught in the turmoil of war, civil rights struggles, and the growing counterculture movement.

Context of the Vietnam War in the 1960s

The U.S. involvement in Vietnam escalated significantly under President Lyndon B. Johnson's administration, particularly after the Gulf of Tonkin Resolution in 1964. This led to a substantial increase in U.S. military personnel in Vietnam.

This major military campaign by the North Vietnamese and Viet Cong forces marked a turning point in the war. Despite being a military failure for the North, it significantly weakened U.S. public support for the war effort.

The Vietnam War was the first war to be extensively televised. Graphic images and reports from the battlefield were broadcasted into American homes, playing a crucial role in shaping public opinion and growing anti-war sentiment.

The war influenced all facets of American culture, including music, literature, and films. It inspired a wave of anti-war music and protest songs, and later, movies that critically examined the war and its effects.

The 1960s were also the peak years of the Civil Rights Movement. Many African Americans and other minority groups saw the Vietnam War as an extension of their struggle for civil rights and equality, as they were disproportionately drafted into the war.

The war fueled the rise of the counterculture movement, with young people protesting not only against the war but also against traditional societal norms and values, advocating for peace, love, and communal living.

Large-scale protests, such as the Moratorium to End the War in Vietnam and the subsequent National Mobilization Committee to End the War in Vietnam, organized some of the largest demonstrations in American history.

The war had a lasting impact on the returning veterans, many of whom faced physical injuries, psychological trauma, and a lack of support and recognition from the government and society.

The Vietnam War era gave rise to a spectrum of music that not only directly addressed the conflict and its implications but also songs that, while not explicitly about the war, have become associated with it through their use in movies and media. These songs capture the mood of the time and have been used extensively to represent the Vietnam War era in popular culture:

- Eve of Destruction" by Barry McGuire (1965): A raw and direct protest song that captured the fear and frustration of the era.

- "Machine Gun" by Jimi Hendrix (1970): Hendrix's visceral protest against the war, with guitar sounds mimicking gunfire and bombs.

- "I-Feel-Like-I'm-Fixin'-to-Die Rag" by Country Joe and the Fish (1967): A satirical anti-war anthem performed memorably at Woodstock.

- "Ohio" by Crosby, Stills, Nash & Young (1970): Written in response to the Kent State shootings, where National Guardsmen shot unarmed students protesting the war.

- "Fortunate Son" by Creedence Clearwater Revival (1969): A protest anthem criticizing the military draft and the socio-political divide it revealed.

- "Blowin' in the Wind" by Bob Dylan (1963): Though written earlier, this song became an anthem for peace and civil rights, resonating with the anti-war movement.

- "Give Peace a Chance" by John Lennon (1969): A rallying cry for peace, it became synonymous with anti-war protests.

- "War" by Edwin Starr (1970): A direct and powerful protest against the war, with its famous line, "War, what is it good for? Absolutely nothing!"

- "The Times They Are A-Changin'" by Bob Dylan (1964): Captured the spirit of change and protest that defined the era.

Songs Associated with the Vietnam Era

- "These Boots Are Made for Walkin'" by Nancy Sinatra (1966): Used in "Full Metal Jacket" (1987), capturing the dichotomy of the era's pop culture and the harsh reality of war.

- "Paint It Black" by The Rolling Stones (1966): Although not explicitly about Vietnam, its dark tones and themes of loss made it a fitting representation of the war's impact.

- "We Gotta Get out of This Place" by The Animals (1965): Became an unofficial anthem for U.S. troops in Vietnam, expressing their desire to return home.

- "All Along the Watchtower" by Jimi Hendrix (1968): Featured in several Vietnam War movies, including "Watchmen" (2009), capturing the era's turmoil and chaos.

- "Gimme Shelter" by The Rolling Stones (1969): Its sense of foreboding and anxiety has made it a popular choice for films depicting the Vietnam War era.

- "Run Through the Jungle" by Creedence Clearwater Revival (1970): Used in movies like "Tropic Thunder" (2008), it's often associated with the dense Vietnamese jungles and the conflict.

- "For What It's Worth" by Buffalo Springfield (1967): Often used in films to evoke the spirit of protest and unrest of the 60s, though it was originally about the Sunset Strip curfew riots.

Vietnam Music and Movies

"Forrest Gump" (1994):
- Music Usage: The soundtrack features a wide array of 1960s music, including songs directly associated with the Vietnam War.
- Impact: Songs like "Fortunate Son" and "For What It's Worth" play during scenes depicting Forrest's service in Vietnam and the anti-war protests, encapsulating the conflicting sentiments of patriotism and disillusionment prevalent during the war.

"Apocalypse Now" (1979):
- Music Usage: This film famously opens with "The End" by The Doors, paired with visuals of napalm explosions and the jungles of Vietnam.
- Impact: The haunting and psychedelic tone of "The End" sets a foreboding atmosphere, symbolizing the mental disintegration and moral ambiguities of the war. "Ride of the Valkyries" plays during a helicopter attack, ironically juxtaposing classical music with the horrors of war, highlighting the absurdity and chaos of the conflict.

"Good Morning, Vietnam" (1987):
- Music Usage: The film features a soundtrack filled with upbeat 60s hits, contrasting sharply with the grim realities of the war.
- Impact: Songs like "Nowhere to Run" and "I Got You (I Feel Good)" are used in Robin Williams' radio broadcasts, providing a stark contrast between the energetic pop culture back home and the tense atmosphere in Vietnam.

"Platoon" (1986):
- Music Usage: Samuel Barber's "Adagio for Strings" is used effectively to underscore the emotional and tragic aspects of the war.
- Impact: The mournful and solemn tone of the music enhances the film's poignant scenes, reflecting the soldiers' despair and the senselessness of the conflict.

"Full Metal Jacket" (1987):
- Music Usage: The use of Nancy Sinatra's "These Boots Are Made for Walkin'" during a scene set in a Vietnamese brothel adds a layer of irony and dark humor.
- Impact: The juxtaposition of a pop song against the backdrop of war highlights the cultural and moral dissonance experienced by American soldiers.

"Born on the Fourth of July" (1989):
- Music Usage: Features a soundtrack that includes classic 60s songs, reflecting the protagonist's journey through the decade.
- Impact: The music parallels the main character's transformation from patriotic enthusiasm to anti-war activism, mirroring the changing American sentiment regarding the Vietnam War.

Questions

Who originally sang the protest song "Eve of Destruction"?
a) Bob Dylan
b) Barry McGuire
c) John Lennon

"Fortunate Son" by Creedence Clearwater Revival is known for its criticism of:
a) The Summer of Love
b) The military draft
c) The British Invasion

Which song by The Animals became an unofficial anthem for U.S. troops in Vietnam?
a) House of the Rising Sun
b) We Gotta Get out of This Place
c) Don't Let Me Be Misunderstood

"Paint It Black" by The Rolling Stones was featured in which Vietnam War film?
a) Apocalypse Now
b) Platoon
c) Full Metal Jacket

"The Times They Are A-Changin'" by Bob Dylan was a call for:
a) Love and peace
b) Social change and understanding
c) The end of the war

"Blowin' in the Wind" became an anthem for:
a) The Civil Rights Movement
b) The Summer of Love
c) Woodstock

"Gimme Shelter" by The Rolling Stones captures the feeling of:
a) Joy and celebration
b) Anxiety and foreboding
c) Romantic love

Jimi Hendrix's "Machine Gun" is best described as:
a) A love ballad
b) A protest against the Vietnam War
c) An instrumental jazz piece

"I-Feel-Like-I'm-Fixin'-to-Die Rag" by Country Joe and the Fish is known for its:
a) Satirical take on the Vietnam War
b) Romantic lyrics
c) Psychedelic sound

"All Along the Watchtower" by Jimi Hendrix is featured in which film?
a) Good Morning, Vietnam
b) Watchmen
c) Born on the Fourth of July

Good Morning, Vietnam

- The film is set in Saigon during the Vietnam War and follows the unorthodox and irreverent radio DJ, Adrian Cronauer, played by Robin Williams. Cronauer brings humor and morale to the troops through his unconventional broadcasts, but clashes with military bureaucracy and censorship.
- Robin Williams' portrayal of Adrian Cronauer earned him critical acclaim and a Golden Globe Award for Best Actor in a Motion Picture – Musical or Comedy
- It highlighted the power of humor in times of adversity and shed light on the complexities of the Vietnam War. The film's soundtrack, featuring iconic 1960s hits juxtaposed with wartime realities

Answers

b) Barry McGuire
Trivia Snapshot: "Eve of Destruction," released in 1965, was one of the earliest and most powerful protest songs of the 1960s, capturing the fears and frustrations of the era.

b) The military draft
Trivia Snapshot: "Fortunate Son" is a vehement protest against the Vietnam War draft, particularly targeting the unfairness of the wealthy and privileged avoiding conscription.

b) We Gotta Get out of This Place
Trivia Snapshot: This song became symbolic of the longing and desperation felt by American soldiers in Vietnam, yearning to return home.

c) Full Metal Jacket
Trivia Snapshot: "Paint It Black" was used effectively in Stanley Kubrick's "Full Metal Jacket," adding to the film's stark portrayal of the Vietnam War.

b) Social change and understanding
Trivia Snapshot: Dylan's song became an anthem for social change during the turbulent 1960s, embodying the era's spirit of protest and transformation.

a) The Civil Rights Movement
Trivia Snapshot: "Blowin' in the Wind" is one of Bob Dylan's most famous songs, serving as a poignant anthem for civil rights and social change.

b) Anxiety and foreboding
Trivia Snapshot: "Gimme Shelter" captures the tumultuous and uncertain atmosphere of the late 1960s, particularly reflecting on the Vietnam War's impact.

b) A protest against the Vietnam War
Trivia Snapshot: Jimi Hendrix's "Machine Gun" is a powerful anti-war statement, with its visceral soundscapes mimicking the horrors of war.

a) Satirical take on the Vietnam War
Trivia Snapshot: This song, performed at Woodstock, is a satirical and critical take on the Vietnam War, capturing the absurdity and tragedy of the conflict.

b) Watchmen
Trivia Snapshot: "All Along the Watchtower" was featured in the film "Watchmen," where its themes of chaos and change complemented the movie's complex narrative.

Quick Context: The military draft, or conscription, is a governmental policy that mandates individuals to serve in the armed forces during times of war or national emergency. It has been a contentious issue throughout history, often sparking debates over individual rights, patriotism, and the morality of war. Famous individuals who refused to participate in the military draft have made headlines for their principled stands against conscription, whether due to moral objections, political beliefs, or conscientious objection to war.

- **Muhammad Ali:** The legendary boxer refused to be drafted into the United States Army during the Vietnam War, citing religious and moral reasons.

- **Joan Baez**: The folk singer and activist was arrested multiple times for her anti-war activism during the Vietnam War.

- **Clint Eastwood:** The actor and filmmaker was deemed medically unfit for military service during the Korean War, but he has voiced his views against the military draft.

Motown and Soul Explosion

The Motown and Soul Explosion of the 1960s was a vibrant and influential period in music history, marked by a surge of soulful rhythms, captivating melodies, and powerful vocals that resonated deeply with audiences across the United States and beyond. This era was not just about music; it was a cultural movement that reflected the social changes and aspirations of the time.

Origins and Impact

Founded by Berry Gordy in 1959, Motown Records, based in Detroit, became the epicenter of this musical revolution. Gordy's vision was to produce music that appealed to both black and white audiences, breaking down racial barriers in the music industry.

Motown's sound, often referred to as "The Sound of Young America," blended elements of soul, R&B, gospel, and pop. This unique combination created a universally appealing sound that was both sophisticated and accessible.

The appeal of Motown and soul music extended far beyond the United States, influencing artists and music styles around the world, and paving the way for future genres like disco and funk.

Key Artists and Contributions

- The Supremes: One of Motown's most successful acts, The Supremes, led by Diana Ross, delivered a string of hits like "Stop! In the Name of Love" and "Where Did Our Love Go," showcasing the label's crossover appeal.

- Marvin Gaye: A versatile artist, Marvin Gaye's music ranged from romantic ballads to socially conscious tracks like "What's Going On," reflecting the complexity and depth of soul music.

- Stevie Wonder: A child prodigy, Stevie Wonder's innovative compositions and exceptional musicianship made him one of the most influential figures in Motown and soul music.

- Aretha Franklin: Known as the "Queen of Soul," Aretha Franklin's powerful voice and emotive performances, especially in songs like "Respect" and "I Say a Little Prayer," made her an icon of soul music.

- James Brown: Often referred to as the "Godfather of Soul," James Brown's energetic performances and unique vocal style were influential in the development of funk music.

- The Temptations: Known for their smooth choreography and harmonious vocals, The Temptations delivered classics like "My Girl" and "Papa Was a Rolling Stone," contributing significantly to the soul genre.

- Smokey Robinson and the Miracles: With hits like "The Tracks of My Tears," Smokey Robinson's silky voice and poignant songwriting were instrumental in shaping the Motown sound.

Key Regions and Their Impact

- Detroit, Michigan: As the birthplace of Motown Records, Detroit was the epicenter of this musical revolution. The city's vibrant musical scene, fueled by a large African American community and an influx of talent from the South, provided the perfect environment for the development of the Motown sound. The label's success turned Detroit into a music powerhouse, earning it the nickname "Motor City" or "Motown."

- Memphis, Tennessee: Memphis played a crucial role in the development of soul music, particularly through Stax Records. Stax, known for its rawer, grittier sound compared to Motown, was home to artists like Otis Redding and Isaac Hayes. Memphis' Beale Street and its rich blues heritage also significantly influenced the soul music emerging from the city.

- Chicago, Illinois: Chicago's contribution to soul music was marked by the presence of labels like Chess Records and Vee-Jay Records. These labels, although initially focused on blues and jazz, became important players in the soul music scene, with artists like Etta James and The Dells.

- Philadelphia, Pennsylvania: Philadelphia soul, also known as "Philly Soul," developed a bit later, in the late 1960s and 1970s, with producers like Kenny Gamble and Leon Huff. This style was characterized by lush orchestration and a smoother, more polished sound. The city's musical scene contributed significantly to the evolution of soul music.

- New York City, New York: While not as central as Detroit or Memphis, New York City's diverse musical culture and media influence helped propel soul music to national and international fame. The city's performance venues, such as the Apollo Theater in Harlem, were crucial platforms for soul and Motown artists to reach wider audiences.

- Southern States: The Southern United States, particularly regions like Georgia, Alabama, and Louisiana, with their deep roots in gospel, blues, and R&B, were fertile grounds for the growth of soul music. Many soul artists originated from the South and brought elements of their musical heritage to the genre.

Cultural and Racial Integration

The widespread appeal of Motown and soul music across these diverse regions played a significant role in cultural and racial integration during a time of significant social change in the United States. The music transcended racial barriers, bringing together black and white audiences in a shared appreciation for the genre. This was especially significant in the Southern states, where racial tensions were high during the Civil Rights Movement.

Which Motown group was known for their hit "Papa Was a Rolling Stone"?
a) The Four Tops
b) The Temptations
c) The Jackson 5

Marvin Gaye's groundbreaking album that addressed social issues was titled:
a) "Let's Get It On"
b) "I Want You"
c) "What's Going On"

Before becoming a solo star, Diana Ross was the lead singer of which group?
a) The Marvelettes
b) The Supremes
c) Martha and the Vandellas

Stevie Wonder's first No. 1 hit, released when he was just 13 years old, was:
a) "Uptight (Everything's Alright)"
b) "Superstition"
c) "Fingertips"

Aretha Franklin's song "Respect" was originally recorded by:
a) Otis Redding
b) Sam Cooke
c) Herself

James Brown was famously known as:
a) The King of Pop
b) The Godfather of Soul
c) The Prince of Motown

Smokey Robinson was not only a singer but also:
a) A Motown Records executive
b) A choreographer
c) A movie actor

Which of these instruments is Stevie Wonder renowned for playing?
a) Guitar
b) Drums
c) Harmonica

Marvin Gaye's duet partner on hits like "Ain't No Mountain High Enough" was:
a) Tammi Terrell
b) Diana Ross
c) Mary Wells

The Temptations' "My Girl" was written and produced by:
a) Holland-Dozier-Holland
b) Smokey Robinson
c) Barry Gordy

Did You Know that The Temptations' "My Girl" was featured in the 1997 film Good Will Hunting?

Answers

Answer: b) The Temptations
Trivia Snapshot: "Papa Was a Rolling Stone" won three Grammy Awards and is known for its iconic bassline and socio-political lyrics.

Answer: c) "What's Going On"
Trivia Snapshot: This 1971 album marked a departure for Gaye, with its themes of drug abuse, poverty, and Vietnam War, representing a significant shift in Motown's direction.

Answer: b) The Supremes
Trivia Snapshot: The Supremes were Motown's most commercially successful act, with 12 No. 1 singles on the Billboard Hot 100.

Answer: c) "Fingertips"
Trivia Snapshot: "Fingertips" was a live recording and hit No. 1 on the Billboard Hot 100 in 1963, making Stevie Wonder the youngest artist to top the chart.

Answer: a) Otis Redding
Trivia Snapshot: Aretha Franklin's version of "Respect," originally by Otis Redding, became an anthem for the feminist movement in the late 1960s.

Answer: b) The Godfather of Soul
Trivia Snapshot: James Brown's dynamic stage presence and hits like "I Got You (I Feel Good)" solidified his title as the "Godfather of Soul."

Answer: a) A Motown Records executive
Trivia Snapshot: Smokey Robinson was not only a successful artist but also served as Vice President of Motown Records, contributing significantly to its artistic direction.

Answer: c) Harmonica
Trivia Snapshot: Stevie Wonder's proficiency with the harmonica is showcased in many of his songs, adding a unique dimension to his music.

Answer: a) Tammi Terrell
Trivia Snapshot: The Marvin Gaye and Tammi Terrell duets are some of Motown's most beloved recordings, known for their chemistry and emotional depth.

Answer: b) Smokey Robinson
Trivia Snapshot: "My Girl," released in 1964, was the first No. 1 hit for The Temptations and is one of Motown's most iconic songs.

Stevie Wonder, born Stevland Hardaway Morris, is a legendary musician and songwriter known for his exceptional talent, versatility, and influential contributions to the music industry. Wonder was born prematurely in Saginaw, Michigan, in 1950. Complications from his premature birth resulted in retinopathy of prematurity (ROP), leading to his blindness shortly after birth. Despite his visual impairment, Wonder showed a remarkable aptitude for music from a young age, learning to play various instruments, including the piano, harmonica, and drums, by ear.

Blind musicians often excel in music due to their heightened sensory awareness, emotional expression, and creative adaptability. Here are some notable blind musicians:

Ray Charles: Pioneer of soul music
Jose Feliciano: Virtuoso guitarist and singer-songwriter
Andrea Bocelli: Internationally renowned operatic tenor
Diane Schuur: Grammy-winning jazz vocalist and pianist

Woodstock

Woodstock, officially known as the Woodstock Music & Art Fair, was a music festival that became a symbol of the 1960s counterculture movement. It was held from August 15 to 18, 1969, on a dairy farm in Bethel, New York, owned by Max Yasgur. The festival is widely regarded as one of the greatest and most pivotal moments in music history.

Woodstock epitomized the era of peace, love, and music. It was initially conceived as a profit-making venture and billed as "Three Days of Peace and Music," but it turned into something much larger than that. The festival became a cultural landmark that embodied the spirit of the counterculture era, which included anti-Vietnam War sentiment, the civil rights movement, and a general sense of rebellion against the established norms.

Over 400,000 people gathered at Woodstock, making it one of the largest and most legendary music festivals ever. The festival was marked by its sense of community and peaceful coexistence, despite the adverse conditions, including food shortages, inadequate sanitation, and bad weather.

The Lineup

Richie Havens: Opened the festival; known for his impromptu performance of "Freedom."

Santana: Their performance, particularly the song "Soul Sacrifice," was a breakout moment for the band.

Janis Joplin: Delivered a powerful, bluesy set in her trademark raspy voice.

The Grateful Dead: Known for their psychedelic music, though their set was marred by technical difficulties.

Creedence Clearwater Revival: Played a high-energy set that included "Bad Moon Rising" and "Proud Mary."

Jefferson Airplane: Performed early in the morning; memorable songs included "Somebody to Love" and "White Rabbit."

The Who: Performed songs from their rock opera "Tommy."

Joe Cocker: His passionate rendition of "With a Little Help from My Friends" was a highlight.

Jimi Hendrix: Closed the festival with an iconic performance that included his rendition of "The Star-Spangled Banner

The Abbie Hoffman Incident

The Who's set at Woodstock is famous not just for their music but for an unexpected interruption by political activist Abbie Hoffman. In the middle of their performance, Hoffman, known for his activism and founding of the Youth International Party (Yippies), took advantage of a brief pause in the music. He jumped onto the stage to deliver a political message.

Hoffman grabbed a microphone and began speaking about the imprisonment of White Panther Party co-founder John Sinclair, who was jailed for possession of marijuana. He implored the audience to rally for Sinclair's release, seizing the moment to make his cause known to the massive crowd.

However, The Who's guitarist Pete Townshend was not amused by this unscheduled interruption. In a moment of frustration and surprise, Townshend shouted at Hoffman to get off the stage, using some choice words, and reportedly swung his guitar at him. Hoffman was quickly ushered off the stage, allowing The Who to resume their performance.

The "Brown Acid" Announcement
One of the most humorous, yet important, moments at Woodstock didn't come from a musical act but rather an announcement made to the audience. As the festival progressed, many attendees partook in psychedelic substances, which was a common occurrence in the counterculture of the 1960s. However, not all substances circulating at the festival were safe.

During the festival, there were reports of a "bad batch" of LSD, commonly referred to as "brown acid," causing adverse effects among some festival-goers. To address this, the festival organizers decided to make a public announcement, warning people about the potentially harmful substance.

The announcement, made from the stage, became one of the most iconic moments of Woodstock. It went something like this: "To get back to the warning that I've received, you may take it with however many grains of salt you wish, that the brown acid that is circulating around us is not specifically too good. It's suggested that you do stay away from that. Of course, it's your own trip, so be my guest."

What makes this story amusing and memorable is the way the announcement was made. The announcer's tone was calm and nonjudgmental, fitting the festival's laid-back and inclusive atmosphere. It was a practical and caring message, delivered in a way that resonated with the audience's values and experiences.

Please Force
Wavy Gravy, born Hugh Romney, was a well-known figure in the counterculture community and played a unique role at Woodstock. As the leader of the Hog Farm, a commune-like collective, he and his group were initially hired to set up some food booths. However, their role quickly expanded to something much more significant.

Wavy Gravy and the Hog Farm ended up being in charge of the "Please Force," a whimsical name for the security team at Woodstock. The name was a playful take on the traditional police force, emphasizing their approach of using non-violence and humor to handle potential conflicts.

Did You Know

- Woodstock was originally expected to attract around 50,000 people. The final attendance of over 400,000 was completely unexpected, causing a logistical and infrastructural overload.

- Free Festival: After the overwhelming influx of attendees made it impossible to collect tickets, Woodstock turned into a free event, contrary to its initial plan as a ticketed festival.

- Births and Deaths: Amidst the chaos and celebration, two births were reported during the festival, and unfortunately, there were also three deaths, two from accidental causes and one from insulin-related complications.

- No Show Acts: Several big names in music at the time, like The Beatles, The Doors, Joni Mitchell, and Led Zeppelin, were either invited and didn't show up, or declined the invitation to perform at Woodstock.

- Helicopter Rides: Due to the massive traffic jams, many artists had to be flown in by helicopter to the festival site to ensure they could perform as scheduled.

- Iconic Album Cover: The album cover of the Woodstock soundtrack features a photograph of a couple wrapped in a blanket. This couple, Bobbi Kelly and Nick Ercoline, are still together and married.

- Improvised Performances: Many performances were improvised and extended due to the need to fill time

- Lack of Facilities: The festival faced a severe shortage of toilets and medical facilities, leading to unsanitary conditions, yet it remained remarkably peaceful and orderly given the circumstances.

- Last-Minute Venue Change: The festival's location was moved to Max Yasgur's dairy farm just weeks before it was scheduled to take place, after the original venue in Wallkill, New York.

- Environmental Clean-Up: After the festival, the cleanup operation was enormous. Max Yasgur, the farmer who provided the land, faced both praise and criticism from his neighbors and had to deal with significant property damage.

Jimi Hendrix,decides to grace Woodstock with his presence. But here's the kicker - he doesn't hit the stage until a whopping 9:00 AM on Monday morning, long after the festival was meant to wrap up. Anyway, when he finally got going, his setlist included.

"Message to Love"
"Spanish Castle Magic"
"Red House"
"Lover Man"
"Foxy Lady"
"Jam Back at the House"
"Izabella"
"Fire"
"Voodoo Child (Slight Return)"
"Star Spangled Banner"
"Purple Haze"
"Woodstock Improvisation" (also known as "Villanova Junction")
"Hey Joe"

The Rolling Stones: Rock's Bad Boys

The Rolling Stones, often portrayed as the rebellious counterparts to The Beatles, emerged in the early 1960s to become one of the most enduring and influential rock bands of all time. Their music, style, and attitude defined the essence of rock 'n' roll's raw, untamed spirit.

The Rolling Stones were formed in London in 1962 by Brian Jones, Mick Jagger, Keith Richards, Bill Wyman, Charlie Watts, and Ian Stewart. Initially influenced by blues and early rock 'n' roll, their raw sound set them apart from the more polished pop bands of the time.

Their rise to fame was marked by hit singles like "Satisfaction," "Paint It Black," and "Jumpin' Jack Flash." The Stones quickly gained a reputation for their edgy, blues-infused rock and their rebellious image, contrasting with The Beatles' cleaner public persona.

The dynamic duo of Jagger and Richards, known as "The Glimmer Twins," became the driving creative force of the band. Jagger's charismatic and energetic stage presence, combined with Richards' innovative guitar riffs, defined the band's signature sound.

The Rolling Stones were often embroiled in controversies, enhancing their 'bad boy' image. Their lyrics and lifestyle embodied the sex, drugs, and rock 'n' roll ethos, attracting both criticism and adulation.

Over the decades, The Rolling Stones have evolved musically, experimenting with various genres while maintaining their fundamental rock roots. Albums like "Beggars Banquet," "Let It Bleed," and "Exile on Main St." are considered classics.

Mick Jagger: As the unmistakable lead singer of The Rolling Stones, Jagger is renowned for his electrifying stage presence and distinctive voice. A master of performance, he has captivated audiences for decades with his unique blend of charisma and energy. Mick Jagger, reflecting on his career, once mused, "Anything worth doing is worth overdoing."

Keith Richards: The quintessential rock guitarist, Richards is celebrated for his innovative riffs and the raw, gritty essence he brings to the band's music. His partnership with Jagger in songwriting has produced some of the most memorable rock songs ever. Embodying the spirit of rock 'n' roll, Richards declared, "Music is a language that doesn't speak in particular words. It speaks in emotions."

Charlie Watts: The drummer, known for his jazz-influenced style, has been the bedrock of the band's rhythm section. Watts, with his understated yet masterful approach, provides the solid foundation upon which the Stones' music thrives. He has been the epitome of cool and collected, famously saying, "I don't know what showbiz is and I've never watched MTV. There are people who just play instruments, and I'm pleased to know that I'm one of them."

Ronnie Wood: Joining the band in the mid-70s, Wood brought a fresh energy and versatility with his guitar skills and backing vocals. His synergy with Richards added an extra layer to the Stones' signature sound. Wood, reflecting on his role, humorously noted, "The first time I saw Keith, he was playing guitar, and I thought, 'That's it. That's what I want to do with my life.'"

Bill Wyman: The band's original bassist until 1993, Wyman's playing was key to the Stones' rhythm and blues-rooted sound. His quiet, stoic presence on stage was a stark contrast to the more flamboyant members. Speaking about his time with the Stones, Wyman once said, "I was lucky enough to have lived through the best era of our times musically."

Brian Jones: A founding member, Jones was instrumental in the band's early years, contributing not just as a guitarist but also on a variety of other instruments. His eclectic style helped shape the Stones' initial sound. Jones, known for his adventurous spirit in music, once expressed, "I want people to know that I am just trying to play as many kinds of music as I can."

Ian Stewart: Often dubbed as "The Sixth Stone," Stewart was initially in the band but later transitioned to a supportive role. His contributions, especially on the piano, remained a vital part of the Stones' music. Keith Richards aptly summed up Stewart's impact, saying, "Stu might not have been on too many Rolling Stones records, but he was a Rolling Stone."

Altamont Free Concert

The Altamont Free Concert, held on December 6, 1969, at the Altamont Speedway in Northern California, stands as one of the most controversial and infamous events in rock history. It was organized by The Rolling Stones as a free concert and intended to be a grand finale to their 1969 U.S. tour. The event, however, descended into chaos and violence, starkly contrasting the peace and love sentiment of the era. Here are some key details about the Altamont Free Concert

The concert was planned in haste as a response to criticism of high ticket prices for Rolling Stones concerts. It was initially set to be held at Golden Gate Park and then Sears Point Raceway, but due to various logistical issues, the location was changed to the Altamont Speedway just days before the event.

In a decision that proved to be disastrous, the Hells Angels motorcycle club was hired to provide security for the event. They were reportedly paid in beer and had little experience in managing a crowd of this size.

An estimated 300,000 people attended the concert, drawn by a lineup that included, besides The Rolling Stones, acts like Jefferson Airplane, Crosby, Stills, Nash & Young, and the Grateful Dead. The sheer number of attendees and inadequate facilities contributed to a tense and unruly atmosphere.

he concert was plagued by violence almost from the start. There were numerous scuffles and incidents throughout the day, many involving the Hells Angels. The situation escalated during The Rolling Stones' performance, culminating in the death of Meredith Hunter, a young African American man, who was stabbed by a member of the Hells Angels after he reportedly pulled out a gun. Hunter's death was captured on film and is one of the defining moments of the festival.

The tragic events of Altamont, captured in the documentary "Gimme Shelter," remain a poignant and dark chapter in the history of rock music, serving as a cautionary tale about the dangers of poor planning and inadequate security at large-scale events.

"(I Can't Get No) Satisfaction" (1965)
- Trivia: This song, with its famous riff and critical lyrics about consumer culture, was one of the Stones' first major hits, helping to establish their image as rock's bad boys. Keith Richards famously came up with the riff in his sleep and recorded a rough version on a tape recorder.

"Sympathy for the Devil" (1968)
- Trivia: Featured on the album "Beggars Banquet," this song's samba-like rhythm and controversial lyrics, narrated from the devil's perspective, showcase the Stones' willingness to push musical and thematic boundaries.

"Gimme Shelter" (1969)
- Trivia: Known for its brooding tone and themes of war and apocalypse, this song was influenced by the turmoil of the late 1960s. Merry Clayton's powerful backing vocals, recorded while she was pregnant, are a standout feature.

"Paint It Black" (1966)
- Trivia: Featuring a distinctive sitar played by Brian Jones, this song's dark and enigmatic lyrics reflect the band's foray into more experimental and psychedelic sounds.

"Jumpin' Jack Flash" (1968)
- Trivia: This song marked a return to the Stones' blues roots after their brief experimentation with psychedelic music. Its energetic rhythm and catchy riff made it a huge hit and a staple in their live performances.

"Angie" (1973)
- Trivia: A departure from their usual hard rock style, this ballad from the album "Goats Head Soup" features an emotional vocal performance by Mick Jagger. The song's subject and inspiration have been the subject of much speculation.

"Wild Horses" (1971)
- Trivia: Recorded at Muscle Shoals Sound Studio in Alabama, this country-inflected tune is known for its poignant lyrics and was supposedly written about Marianne Faithfull, Jagger's then-girlfriend.

"Brown Sugar" (1971)
- Trivia: Opening the album "Sticky Fingers," this song is famous for its controversial lyrics and driving beat. It was recorded in just a few takes at Muscle Shoals.

"Honky Tonk Women" (1969)
- Trivia: This song was a return to the band's rock and roll roots and was released just after Brian Jones' departure from the band. The cowbell intro and raunchy lyrics have made it a rock classic.

"Start Me Up" (1981)
- Trivia: A hit from the album "Tattoo You," this song is known for its iconic opening riff and became one of the Stones' most recognizable and enduring songs. It was originally recorded in 1978 but was not released until 1981.

Did You Know ?

Did you know?... The Rolling Stones were named after the Muddy Waters song "Rollin' Stone." Brian Jones suggested the name during a phone call with a jazz magazine editor, who asked the name of his band.

Did you know?... Mick Jagger and Keith Richards were childhood friends who lost touch but reconnected on a train in 1961. Richards noticed Jagger carrying records by Chuck Berry and Muddy Waters, which reignited their friendship and led to the formation of the band.

Did you know?... The Rolling Stones' first-ever gig was at the Marquee Club in London on July 12, 1962. At this point, the group had a much different lineup and were performing mainly covers of blues and R&B songs.

Did you know?... In 1967, members of the band, including Mick Jagger and Keith Richards, were famously arrested for drug possession, which many considered to be a targeted attack on their rebellious image. Their brief imprisonment sparked a significant public outcry.

Did you know?... The Rolling Stones' iconic tongue and lips logo, first used in 1971, was designed by John Pasche, a student at the Royal College of Art in London. It's one of the most recognizable logos in music history.

Did you know?... "Exile on Main St.," considered one of their best albums, was largely recorded in a villa in the South of France while the band was living abroad as tax exiles.

Did you know?... Charlie Watts, the band's drummer, had a background in jazz and was known for his impeccable dress sense. He often sketched every hotel room he stayed in, a hobby he maintained throughout his touring life.

Did you know?... Mick Jagger studied at the London School of Economics and is known for his astute business acumen, which helped the Stones become one of the wealthiest bands in the world.

Did you know?... In 2002, the Rolling Stones' "A Bigger Bang" tour became the highest-grossing tour of all time, earning a staggering $558 million.

Did you know?... Keith Richards' distinctive guitar sound is partly due to his use of "open tunings," a technique he picked up from blues musicians. He often removed the sixth string from his guitar, as heard in the song "Brown Sugar."

Guess the Song Lyric

"War, children, it's just a shot away, it's just a shot away."
a) "For what it's worth"
b) "Paint It Black"
c) "Gimme Shelter"

"Goodbye, x , who could hang a name on you?"
a) "Angie"
b) "Ruby Tuesday"
c) "Hey Jude"

"I see a red door ."
a) "Back in Black"
b) "Paint It Black"
c) "Black Magic Woman"

"but if you try sometimes, you just might find, you get what you need."
a) "Let It Be"
b) "You Can't Always Get What You Want"
c) "Satisfaction"

"Please allow me to introduce myself, I'm a man of wealth and taste."
a) "Sympathy for the Devil"
b) "Stairway to Heaven"
c) "Bohemian Rhapsody"

Mick Jagger, the frontman of The Rolling Stones, is known for his charismatic stage presence and iconic voice, but when it comes to songwriting, he often collaborates with the band's guitarist. The majority of The Rolling Stones' songs are credited to Jagger/Richards, indicating the joint effort between the two.

Answers

"War, children, it's just a shot away, it's just a shot away."
Answer: c) "Gimme Shelter"
Trivia: "Gimme Shelter" was partly inspired by the Vietnam War, reflecting the band's response to the chaotic and violent times of the late 1960s. Its haunting lyrics and Merry Clayton's powerful backing vocals make it a timeless classic.

"Goodbye, Ruby Tuesday, who could hang a name on you?"
Answer: b) "Ruby Tuesday"
Trivia: "Ruby Tuesday" features a melancholic melody and lyrics about the fleeting nature of relationships and freedom. The song's title character remains an enigma, with various theories about her identity.

"I see a red door and I want it painted black."
Answer: b) "Paint It Black"
Trivia: "Paint It Black" is known for its Eastern-influenced sound, particularly the sitar played by Brian Jones. The song's themes of grief and loss are universal, making it one of the Stones' most enduring hits.

"You can't always get what you want, but if you try sometimes, you just might find, you get what you need."
Answer: b) "You Can't Always Get What You Want"
Trivia: This song was recorded with the London Bach Choir, adding a unique choral element to the Stones' sound. It's often interpreted as a commentary on the end of the idealistic 1960s.

Established in 1876, the London Bach Choir is a prestigious choral ensemble based in the heart of London. Renowned for its captivating performances, the choir showcases choral masterpieces spanning from the timeless works of Johann Sebastian Bach to contemporary compositions.

"Please allow me to introduce myself, I'm a man of wealth and taste."
Answer: a) "Sympathy for the Devil"
Trivia: The recording of "Sympathy for the Devil" was documented in the film "Sympathy for the Devil" by Jean-Luc Godard, showcasing the song's evolution and the band's creative process.

Ronnie Wood

Did you know that before joining The Rolling Stones, Ronnie Wood was a member of The Faces, a British rock band formed in 1969? The Faces, which included Rod Stewart as the lead vocalist, were known for their raucous live performances and their fusion of rock, blues, and folk music. Wood played guitar and occasionally bass, contributing significantly to the band's distinctive sound.

Ronnie Wood's tenure with The Faces coincided with Rod Stewart's rise to solo stardom, and they enjoyed considerable success together. Wood's ability to complement Stewart's vocal style and his skill at blending various musical influences played a crucial role in the band's popularity. The Faces were well-regarded for hits like "Stay with Me" and "Ooh La La," and their albums were critically acclaimed.

Wood's time with The Faces was marked by a similar hard-living lifestyle that he would continue with The Rolling Stones. His creative chemistry with Rod Stewart in The Faces helped establish him as a talented musician in his own right, paving the way for his eventual entry into The Rolling Stones in 1975, following Mick Taylor's departure. This transition marked a significant step in Wood's career, bringing his distinctive style to one of the world's greatest rock bands.

Top 10 Songs of the 1960s

Let's explore the top 10 songs that not only topped the charts but also captured the essence of this transformative era.

10. "I Want to Hold Your Hand" by The Beatles (1963)
- Marking The Beatles' first major success in the United States, this song ignited Beatlemania.
- The catchy melody and fresh sound symbolized the new wave of British pop music.
- Its massive popularity helped The Beatles become a global phenomenon.

9. "My Girl" by The Temptations (1964)
- A timeless classic, "My Girl" is known for its soulful melody and romantic lyrics.
- The song showcased the unique sound of Motown and its impact on the music industry.
- Its simple, yet profound lyrics and melody continue to resonate with audiences.

8. "Blowin' in the Wind" by Bob Dylan (1963)
- Bob Dylan's "Blowin' in the Wind" emerged as one of the most significant protest songs of the 1960s, asking poignant questions about peace, war, and freedom.
- Its simple yet powerful lyrics became an anthem for the civil rights movement and an emblem of the era's social consciousness.
- The song's mix of folk and protest elements made it a landmark in the evolution of folk music, influencing countless artists and becoming a staple in the repertoire of protest music.

7. "Hey Jude" by The Beatles (1968)
- One of The Beatles' most beloved and successful songs, "Hey Jude" is known for its gradual build-up and emotional depth.
- The song's lengthy outro, featuring a sing-along chorus, became a hallmark of its era.
- "Hey Jude" symbolizes the band's musical maturity and enduring legacy.

6. "A Hard Day's Night" by The Beatles (1964)
- The title track of their third album, this song epitomized Beatlemania's height.
- Its distinctive opening chord and upbeat tempo made it instantly recognizable.
- The song's success further solidified The Beatles' influence in the music world.

5. "Satisfaction" by The Rolling Stones (1965)
- Topping our list, "Satisfaction" is emblematic of the raw energy and rebellious spirit of the 60s rock scene.
- The song's iconic guitar riff and Mick Jagger's provocative lyrics captured the youth's restlessness.
- "Satisfaction" not only defined The Rolling Stones' sound but also left an indelible mark on the landscape of rock music.

4 "Respect" by Aretha Franklin (1967)
- Aretha Franklin's powerful rendition transformed this song into an anthem for female empowerment and the civil rights movement.
- Her unforgettable vocal performance added depth and intensity to the song's message.
- "Respect" remains an iconic song in the genre of soul and R&B.

3. Good Vibrations" by The Beach Boys (1966)
- Regarded as a masterpiece of pop music, "Good Vibrations" showcased The Beach Boys' innovative use of the studio as an instrument.
- The song's complex harmonies and use of unconventional instruments marked a significant evolution in the sound of pop music.
- It stands as a testament to the experimental spirit of the 60s.

2. "I Want to Hold Your Hand" by The Beatles (1963)
- Marking The Beatles' first major success in the United States, this song ignited Beatlemania.
- The catchy melody and fresh sound symbolized the new wave of British pop music.
- Its massive popularity helped The Beatles become a global phenomenon.

1. "California Dreamin'" by The Mamas & The Papas (1965)
- A quintessential anthem of the 60s, "California Dreamin'" captured the longing for a warmer, idyllic climate.

"California Dreamin'" has been covered by numerous artists since its original release, spanning various genres and styles. Here are some notable covers:
- **Bobby Womack** (Year: 1968) - His soulful rendition adds a bluesy flavor to the song.
- **Diana Krall** (Year: 1996) - The jazz pianist and vocalist offers a smooth and sophisticated interpretation.
- **The Carpenters** (Year: 1973) - Their soft rock version adds a gentle touch to the iconic melody.
- **Sia** (Year: 2015) - Sia's pop rendition adds a modern twist while retaining the song's essence.
- **The Beach Boys** (Year: 1986) - Their rendition infuses the song with their signature surf-rock sound.
- **José Feliciano** (Year: 1968) - His unique Latin jazz style brings a fresh interpretation to the song.

Welcome to the Seventies
A Decade of Disco, Punk, and Rock Innovation!

Dive into the 1970s, a decade where music became a vibrant tapestry of groundbreaking styles and genres. From the glittering allure of disco's dance floors to the rebellious roar of punk rock, the seventies unfurled a panorama of sounds that defined an era of bold experimentation and cultural expression. As the echoes of the sixties' psychedelia faded, a new wave of musical diversity took center stage, painting the decade with an array of unforgettable melodies and rhythms.

Disco Fever

In the 1970s, a new rhythm took over the airwaves and dance floors, creating a cultural phenomenon known as Disco Fever. This vibrant era of glitter balls, bell-bottoms, and electrifying dance music left an indelible mark on the music industry and popular culture.

The Birth of Disco

Disco's roots can be traced back to the urban nightlife of cities like New York and Philadelphia. It emerged from a melting pot of funk, soul, and Latin beats, catering to a diverse crowd seeking liberation and fun on the dance floor. Clubs like Studio 54 in New York City became the epicenters of this new wave, attracting celebrities, socialites, and ordinary people alike, all united by the infectious beat of disco music.

What set disco apart was its relentless, upbeat tempo, typically between 100-130 beats per minute, perfect for non-stop dancing. The music was characterized by a steady four-on-the-floor beat, rich basslines, and a lavish use of synthesizers and orchestral elements. Songs often featured soaring vocals and catchy choruses that resonated with a wide audience.

Disco wasn't just about the music; it was a full-fledged fashion statement. The dance floors were a dazzling display of sequins, satin, and shimmer. Platform shoes, tight-fitting clothes, and flamboyant outfits became synonymous with disco nights, embodying the era's exuberance and flair.

Disco was more than just a music genre; it was a social movement. It broke down barriers, bringing together people of different races, ethnicities, and sexual orientations. The disco scene was particularly significant for the LGBTQ+ community, offering a space of freedom and acceptance.

However, disco also faced its share of backlash. The "Disco Sucks" movement of the late 70s, culminating in the infamous Disco Demolition Night in 1979, highlighted the genre's polarizing nature in American culture. Critics viewed disco as overly commercial and artistically shallow, leading to its dramatic decline as the 80s approached.

The Legacy of Disco

Despite its eventual fade from the mainstream, disco's influence is undeniable. It paved the way for future genres like house, techno, and dance-pop. Elements of disco can still be heard in modern music, a testament to its enduring appeal and impact.

In retrospect, Disco Fever was more than a fleeting fad. It was a vibrant chapter in the history of music, reflecting the spirit of an era that championed freedom, inclusivity, and, above all, the joy of dancing. The disco ball might have stopped spinning, but the legacy of this glittering era continues to resonate in the hearts of music lovers around the world.

Bee Gees
- "Stayin' Alive": A defining anthem of the disco era, known for its catchy beat and the Gibb brothers' distinctive falsettos.
- "Night Fever": Another quintessential Bee Gees hit, capturing the essence of disco with its infectious rhythm and smooth vocals.

Donna Summer
- "I Feel Love": A groundbreaking track known for its pioneering use of synthesizers, offering a futuristic sound that was ahead of its time.
- "Last Dance": A classic disco ballad, showcasing Summer's dynamic vocal range, and often played as the closing song in discotheques.

Chic
- "Le Freak": A smash hit famous for its catchy hook and funky bassline, embodying the stylish and upbeat nature of disco.
- "Good Times": Known for its bass riff, later sampled in many other songs, epitomizing the carefree and joyful spirit of the disco scene.

The Village People
- "Y.M.C.A.": An iconic song recognized for its catchy chorus and distinctive dance moves, becoming a staple at parties and events.
- "Macho Man": A celebration of flamboyant masculinity set to an energetic disco beat, further popularizing the group's unique style.

Gloria Gaynor
- "I Will Survive": An empowering anthem with a strong message of resilience and independence, resonating well beyond the disco era.

Disco Demolition Night in 1979

Disco Demolition Night, held on July 12, 1979, stands as one of the most infamous events in music history, symbolizing the backlash against the disco era. This event took place at Comiskey Park in Chicago, Illinois, during a doubleheader baseball game between the Chicago Red Sox and Detroit Tigers.

The event was orchestrated by Steve Dahl, a popular rock DJ who had recently lost his job when his station switched to an all-disco format, a change that was happening at many radio stations across the United States due to disco's rising popularity. Dahl's anti-disco sentiment resonated with many rock fans who felt alienated by the disco craze.

The promotion involved inviting fans to bring their disco records to the game in exchange for a discounted ticket price. Between the games of the doubleheader, the collected records were to be blown up in a large crate in center field.

However, the event didn't go as smoothly as planned. The explosion damaged the field and created a large fire. Moreover, the situation escalated when thousands of fans, fueled by anti-disco sentiment (and likely alcohol), stormed the field. They set additional fires, destroyed the batting cages, and vandalized the stadium. The chaos led to the second game of the doubleheader being forfeited due to the unplayable and unsafe conditions.

While on the surface it was a promotional stunt playing on the disco vs. rock rivalry, it also had underlying elements of racism and homophobia, as disco was closely tied to the African American, Latino, and gay communities.

The event marked a turning point for disco music. Although disco remained popular for a while after, Disco Demolition Night is often cited as a symbol of the genre's decline in the late 1970s and the rise of other musical genres,

Led Zeppelin: Hard Rock Pioneers

Led Zeppelin, formed in 1968, London. They emerged as one of the most influential and pioneering bands of the hard rock genre, leaving an indelible mark on the music scene of the 1970s. Their sound, a potent mix of blues, rock, and folk music, coupled with their legendary live performances, cemented their status as icons of hard rock.

The band was formed by guitarist Jimmy Page, who sought to create a group that would surpass the success of his previous band, The Yardbirds. He recruited vocalist Robert Plant, drummer John Bonham, and bassist/keyboardist John Paul Jones. This lineup would remain constant throughout the band's history, a rarity in the rock world.

Led Zeppelin's music was characterized by its heavy use of blues and folk influences, innovative guitar work by Page, and Plant's powerful and distinctive vocal style. They were known for their experimental approach to music, not confining themselves to the standard structures of rock and blues. Songs like "Whole Lotta Love" and "Kashmir" showcase their unique fusion of different genres and sounds.

The band's self-titled debut album, "Led Zeppelin," released in 1969, made a significant impact with its raw sound and fusion of blues and rock. This was followed by "Led Zeppelin II," "Led Zeppelin III," and the untitled fourth album, often referred to as "Led Zeppelin IV." This fourth album featured one of their most famous songs, "Stairway to Heaven," which became a staple of FM radio despite never being released as a single.

Led Zeppelin was renowned for their energy and improvisation during live performances, often extending their songs with lengthy solos and jams. Bonham's powerful drumming and Jones' versatile musicianship added depth to their live shows. Their concerts were legendary, drawing huge crowds and solidifying their reputation as one of the greatest live bands of all time.

Jimmy Page: As the founder and lead guitarist of Led Zeppelin, Page was the driving force behind the band's sound. Renowned for his innovative guitar playing, including the use of alternate tunings and bowing techniques, he created some of rock's most memorable riffs. Page once stated, "I believe every guitar player inherently has something unique about their playing. They just have to identify what makes them different and develop it."

Robert Plant: The charismatic frontman and vocalist of Led Zeppelin, Plant's powerful and emotive voice became a defining element of the band's music. Known for his onstage energy and mystical lyrics, he brought a unique blend of blues and folk influences to the group. Reflecting on his career, Plant said, "Music is for every single person that walks the planet."

John Paul Jones: As the bassist and keyboardist, Jones was the band's multi-instrumentalist, contributing heavily to their distinctive sound. His musical versatility and skills in arrangement were crucial in the creation of the band's complex compositions. Jones observed, "I like to think that my instruments have a certain soul and character to them."

John Bonham: Widely regarded as one of the greatest drummers in rock history, Bonham's powerful and innovative drumming style was a key component of Led Zeppelin's sound. His speed, power, and feel for the groove were unparalleled, setting new standards for rock drumming. Bonham once noted, "The drummer is the backbone of any band. Our job is to keep the time and the spirit of the song alive."

Trivia Tidbits

- Band Name Origin: The name "Led Zeppelin" originated from a joke made by The Who's drummer Keith Moon and bassist John Entwistle, who said that a supergroup containing them and Jimmy Page would go down like a "lead balloon."
- Logo Design: The band's iconic logo, featuring each member's individual symbol, was first used on the cover of their untitled fourth album. Each symbol was chosen by the band members to represent themselves.
- No Singles in the UK: Led Zeppelin famously refused to release singles in the UK, wanting their albums to be experienced as a whole.
- "Stairway to Heaven" Live Debuts: Despite its popularity, "Stairway to Heaven" was never released as a single. It made its live debut at the Ulster Hall in Belfast in 1971.
- Record-Breaking Concerts: The band broke the world record for the largest attendance at a solo indoor attraction in 1973 when they played to 56,800 fans at Tampa Stadium.
- Innovative Recording Techniques: Led Zeppelin was known for pioneering recording techniques, including the use of backward echo on "Whole Lotta Love."
- "Black Dog" Naming: The song "Black Dog" was named after a black labrador retriever that wandered around the Headley Grange studio during recording.
- First Album's Quick Creation: Their debut album, "Led Zeppelin I," was recorded in just 36 hours.
- Album Covers: None of their album covers include the band's name or the album title, a rare practice for the time.

- "When the Levee Breaks" Recording: The distinctive drum sound in "When the Levee Breaks" was achieved by recording John Bonham's drumming at the bottom of a stairwell at Headley Grange.
- No Synthesizers: Until their seventh album, "Presence," Led Zeppelin did not use synthesizers, a contrast to many bands of that era.
- "Immigrant Song" Inspiration: "Immigrant Song" was inspired by the band's concert in Iceland and is filled with Viking imagery and references to Norse mythology.
- Album Sales: Despite receiving mixed reviews from critics initially, their albums have sold over 300 million copies worldwide.
- Live Aid Reunion: The band briefly reunited for Live Aid in 1985 with Phil Collins and Tony Thompson filling in for the late John Bonham on drums.
- Kennedy Center Honors: In 2012, Led Zeppelin was honored at the Kennedy Center Honors, celebrating their contribution to American culture and the arts.

Led Zeppelin's Greatest Songs

"Stairway to Heaven" (1971)
- Often cited as one of the greatest rock songs of all time, "Stairway to Heaven" is known for its progressive structure, moving from a gentle, acoustic beginning to a powerful, electrifying climax.

"Whole Lotta Love" (1969)
- A hallmark of hard rock with one of the most famous guitar riffs in rock history, this song showcases the band's raw energy and innovative use of studio effects.

"Kashmir" (1975)
- Featuring a distinctive, driving rhythm and orchestral arrangement, "Kashmir" is celebrated for its epic scope and blending of Eastern and Western musical influences.

"Rock and Roll" (1971)
- A tribute to the roots of rock music, this high-energy track is characterized by its classic rock 'n' roll rhythm and a standout drum performance by John Bonham.

"Black Dog" (1971)
- Known for its complex, intertwining rhythms and memorable vocal lines, "Black Dog" demonstrates the band's ability to blend blues and hard rock.

"Immigrant Song" (1970)
- This song is marked by its driving beat, wailing vocals, and lyrics inspired by Norse mythology, encapsulating the band's adventurous and exploratory musical spirit.

"When the Levee Breaks" (1971)
- A blues cover transformed into a hard rock classic, this song is famous for its distinctive, powerful drumming and harmonica playing, creating an intense and brooding atmosphere.

The Mysterious Case of the Stolen Sharkk
In the wild world of rock and roll, few bands have stories as legendary or as outlandish as Led Zeppelin.

| Among the many tales, one stands out for its sheer absurdity and humorous undertones - the curious incident involving a shark.

The story takes us back to the early 1970s, a time when Led Zeppelin was at the height of their fame, touring across the United States and living the quintessential rock star lifestyle. The band, known for their love of extravagance and mischief, often stayed at the ritzy Edgewater Inn in Seattle, famous for its fishing right out of the hotel windows.

One evening, following a particularly energetic concert and an after-party that was equally lively, the band, along with their entourage, found themselves back at the Edgewater Inn. Among the group was a young woman, a fan who had managed to charm her way into the exclusive circle for the night.

As the night progressed, the party moved to one of the hotel rooms. In a moment of rock and roll madness, a member of the band's crew decided it would be hilarious to do some fishing. To the amusement of everyone, he managed to catch a small shark (or, as some versions of the story claim, a large mudshark) from the window.

Now, this is where the tale takes a turn into the surreal. The caught shark, which was still very much alive and flipping, became the centerpiece of an impromptu and bizarre prank. The details of what happened next vary, with some versions suggesting the shark was used in a lewd act with the young fan, while others imply it was merely a prop in a series of jokes.

The truth behind the shark episode remains murky. Over the years, the story has been exaggerated, downplayed, and outright denied by those involved. It has become a part of Led Zeppelin folklore, a tale that blurs the line between reality and myth.

What's not in doubt, however, is the band's penchant for wild behavior and their ability to leave a lasting impression, whether through their groundbreaking music or their off-stage antics. The shark incident, whether fully true, partly true, or entirely fabricated, represents the peak of rock and roll excess and the kind of story that could only involve a band as iconic as Led Zeppelin.

Popular Culture

Led Zeppelin, with their groundbreaking music and larger-than-life persona, didn't just shape the world of rock; they left a profound imprint on popular culture that extends well beyond music. Their influence permeates various aspects of art, fashion, film, and even lifestyle, making them one of the most significant cultural icons of the 20th century.

Led Zeppelin epitomized the quintessential rock star image. Their flamboyant fashion, characterized by tight jeans, flowing shirts, and iconic hairstyles, became a template for rock musicians and fans alike. They personified the sex, drugs, and rock 'n' roll lifestyle, a trope that many bands would aspire to emulate. This image wasn't just about appearance; it was a symbol of rebellion and nonconformity that resonated with the youth of the era.

Musically, Led Zeppelin's fusion of blues, rock, and folk, along with their innovative use of recording techniques, set a new standard in the music industry. Their style influenced a plethora of artists across various genres, from hard rock and heavy metal to alternative and indie music. Bands like Aerosmith, Guns N' Roses, and later, Nirvana and The White Stripes, have cited Led Zeppelin as a major influence.

Led Zeppelin's live performances, known for their energy and improvisation, revolutionized the concert experience. They turned live shows into a theatrical spectacle, complete with elaborate light shows, extended solos, and on-stage antics. This approach transformed expectations for live music, influencing the way concerts were staged and experienced.

Their music has been a staple in film soundtracks, used to evoke intensity, nostalgia, or a sense of rebellion.

Thor: Ragnarok" (2017)
- Song: "Immigrant Song"
- Used during major battle scenes, fitting perfectly with the film's Norse mythology theme.

"School of Rock" (2003)
- Song: "Immigrant Song"
- Featured in a scene where Jack Black's character teaches his students about rock history.

"Shrek the Third" (2007)
- Song: "Immigrant Song"
- Used humorously in a scene where Snow White summons animals to attack the guards.

"Almost Famous" (2000)
- Song: "Misty Mountain Hop," "The Rain Song," "Bron-Yr-Aur," "Tangerine"
- Multiple songs are featured throughout this film about a young journalist touring with a rising rock band in the 1970s.

"Argo" (2012)
- Song: "When the Levee Breaks"
- Played during the opening sequence to set the tone for the 1979 Iranian hostage crisis.

"The Fighter" (2010)
- Song: "Good Times Bad Times"
- Used to underscore the main character's struggles and triumphs.

"It Might Get Loud" (2008)
- Song: Various Led Zeppelin songs
- This documentary about electric guitars prominently features Jimmy Page and includes several Led Zeppelin tracks.

"The Song Remains the Same" (1976)
- Song: Various Led Zeppelin songs
- A concert film featuring live performances by Led Zeppelin, including fantasy sequences for each band member.

Questions

1. What unusual instrument did John Paul Jones play on the track "The Rain Song"?**
   A) Mellotron
   B) Theremin
   C) Moog synthesizer

2. Which Led Zeppelin song features lyrics inspired by J.R.R. Tolkien's "The Lord of the Rings"?
   A) "Over the Hills and Far Away"
   B) "Ramble On"
   C) "Immigrant Song"

3. Led Zeppelin's "No Quarter" is known for its distinctive keyboard solo. Where was this song first recorded?
   A) Headley Grange
   B) Electric Lady Studios
   C) Island Studios

4. Which city's music scene inspired the creation of "Kashmir"?
   A) Marrakech
   B) Bombay
   C) London

5. Before settling on the name Led Zeppelin, what was one of the band's initial names?
   A) The New Yardbirds
   B) The Noble Zeppelins
   C) The Atomic Blimps

6. "Going to California" was written about which famous female singer?
   A) Janis Joplin
   B) Joni Mitchell
   C) Grace Slick

Answers

1. Answer: A) Mellotron
   - Trivia Snapshot: The Mellotron used in "The Rain Song" added a symphonic texture to the track, showcasing John Paul Jones' versatility and the band's willingness to experiment with different sounds.

2. Answer: B) "Ramble On
   - Trivia Snapshot: "Ramble On" references characters and places from Tolkien's universe, reflecting Robert Plant's fascination with fantasy literature and its influence on his songwriting.

3. Answer: A) Headley Grange
   - Trivia Snapshot: "No Quarter" was recorded at Headley Grange, a Victorian house where the band used the building's natural acoustics to create the song's haunting atmosphere.

4. Answer: A) Marrakech
   - Trivia Snapshot: The trip to Marrakech provided Jimmy Page and Robert Plant with new musical inspiration, directly influencing the creation of "Kashmir" with its Middle Eastern musical scales and themes.

5. Answer: A) The New Yardbirds
   - Trivia Snapshot: The band initially performed under the name The New Yardbirds to fulfill previously booked gigs for Page's former band, The Yardbirds, before adopting the name Led Zeppelin.

6. Answer: B) Joni Mitchell
   - Trivia Snapshot: "Going to California" was inspired by Joni Mitchell, with whom both Robert Plant and Jimmy Page were enamored. The song reflects the band's softer, acoustic side and showcases Plant's lyrical admiration for Mitchell's artistry.

Punk Rock: Anarchy in Music

Punk Rock emerged in the mid-1970s as a defiant, high-energy counterpoint to mainstream music, embodying a raw, unfiltered expression of youth rebellion. Characterized by its simplicity, aggressive sound, and anti-establishment ethos, punk rock became a cultural phenomenon that reshaped music, fashion, and attitudes.

Punk's roots can be traced back to garage rock and proto-punk bands like The Stooges, The MC5, and The New York Dolls. These bands laid the groundwork with their raw sound and rebellious attitude. However, it was in the gritty streets of New York City and London where punk truly found its voice.

New York Scene

In New York, clubs like CBGB became the breeding ground for punk. Bands like The Ramones, Television, and Patti Smith Group pioneered a fast, stripped-down sound that contrasted sharply with the era's progressive rock and disco. The Ramones, especially, with their short, rapid-fire songs, leather jackets, and jeans, epitomized the punk ethos.

London Scene

Across the Atlantic, punk resonated with the UK's disaffected youth. The Sex Pistols, led by the provocative Johnny Rotten, and managed by the enigmatic Malcolm McLaren, became the face of British punk. Their 1977 single "God Save the Queen" was a scathing critique of the British monarchy and society, encapsulating punk's spirit of anarchy and dissent.

Sex Pistols
- "Anarchy in the U.K.": A quintessential punk anthem, capturing the spirit of rebellion and dissatisfaction with the status quo. Its aggressive sound and provocative lyrics made it a defining song of the punk movement.
- "God Save the Queen": Infamous for its controversial lyrics, this song exemplified the punk ethos of challenging authority and convention, becoming a symbol of the punk rock movement.

The Clash
- "London Calling": A politically charged song that reflects the anxieties of the era, blending punk with reggae influences. Its iconic opening line and driving beat make it a timeless punk classic.
- "Should I Stay or Should I Go": Known for its catchy riff and dynamic tempo shifts, this song showcases the band's ability to blend punk energy with a more mainstream sound.

Ramones
- "Blitzkrieg Bop": With its simple, repetitive lyrics and frenetic pace, this song encapsulated the raw, stripped-down essence of punk rock.
- "I Wanna Be Sedated": A fast-paced track that combines humor with the band's signature punk sound, reflecting the Ramones' influence on the punk genre.

Dead Kennedys
- "Holiday in Cambodia": A song that mixes dark humor with biting social commentary, showcasing the band's more hardcore punk style.
- "California Über Alles": A satirical take on California politics, this track is known for its sharp lyrics and energetic punk rhythm.

The Stooges
- "I Wanna Be Your Dog": A raw and primal song that predated and influenced the punk movement, known for its minimalist approach and Iggy Pop's intense vocal performance.
- "Search and Destroy": Featuring a gritty guitar riff and confrontational lyrics, this track is often cited as a significant influence on the development of punk rock.

Punk's influence extended beyond music. It created a distinct fashion style, characterized by torn clothing, safety pins, Mohawks, and Doc Martens. This DIY aesthetic was a rebellion against the era's prevailing fashion norms and a visual representation of punk's anti-conformist message.

Punk's DIY ethos encouraged a generation to create their own music, fashion, and fanzines, independent of mainstream industry controls. This approach democratized music production and laid the groundwork for the indie and alternative scenes of the 80s and 90s.

While the initial wave of punk was relatively short-lived, its impact was profound. It influenced the post-punk, new wave, and later the grunge movements. Bands like The Clash, who blended punk with reggae, and The Dead Kennedys, with their politically charged lyrics, carried punk's legacy forward.

Punk rock, with its raw energy, anti-establishment message, and transformative cultural impact, was more than just a music genre. It was a movement that gave voice to a generation's frustration and desire for change, leaving an indelible mark on music and popular culture.

Did You Know that Doc Martens started as work boots but became famous for their durability and style?

Trivia Tidbits

- CBGB: The New York club CBGB, where many punk bands started, stands for "Country, Bluegrass, and Blues."
- The Ramones' Uniform: The Ramones adopted their iconic uniform of leather jackets and ripped jeans to unify their image.
- "Blitzkrieg Bop" Chant: The "Hey! Ho! Let's go!" chant in "Blitzkrieg Bop" by The Ramones became a rallying cry in punk music.
- Patti Smith's Poetry: Patti Smith, often called the "punk poet laureate," blended rock and poetry in her music.
- Sex Pistols' Original Name: The Sex Pistols were originally called 'The Strand.'
- Malcolm McLaren's Influence: Malcolm McLaren, manager of the Sex Pistols, was pivotal in creating the band's image and was previously involved with the New York Dolls.
- The Clash's Diverse Influences: The Clash were known for incorporating reggae, ska, and funk into their punk music.
- Iggy Pop's Stage Antics: Iggy Pop of The Stooges was known for his outrageous stage antics, including self-mutilation and stage diving.

One of the most notorious aspects of Iggy Pop's performances was his penchant for self-mutilation. In a time when rock performances were relatively tame, his actions were shocking and unprecedented. During concerts, he would cut himself with broken glass or expose himself to the audience, turning the stage into a space of visceral self-expression. This extreme behavior was more than just shock value; it was a form of performance art that expressed the raw, unfiltered emotion of his music. It also symbolically broke down barriers between performer and audience, making his shows a cathartic experience for those who witnessed them.

Stage diving and crowd surfing were other hallmarks of Iggy Pop's performances. He was one of the first performers to make leaping into the audience a regular part of his act. This not only energized the crowd but also created a sense of unity and participation. His fearless dives into the audience were expressions of trust and a breaking down of the traditional separation between artist and spectator. This act, now a staple in rock and punk shows, was revolutionary at the time and added an element of danger and excitement to his performances.

Iggy Pop's wild stage antics were integral to the identity of The Stooges and the ethos of punk rock that followed. His uninhibited expression and physicality on stage challenged conventional norms and inspired a generation of performers to embrace a more raw and authentic form of self-expression.

- The Sex Pistols' U.S. Tour: The Sex Pistols' 1978 U.S. tour was chaotic and marked by numerous cancellations and controversies.
- The Ramones' Debut Album: The Ramones' debut album was recorded in just seven days.
- Johnny Rotten's Real Name: Johnny Rotten of the Sex Pistols was born John Lydon.
- The Clash's Political Lyrics: The Clash's lyrics often addressed social and political issues, distinguishing them from many contemporary punk bands.
- MC5's Political Activism: The MC5 were heavily involved in left-wing political activism, influencing the punk movement's anti-establishment stance.
- Dead Kennedys' Name Origin: The Dead Kennedys chose their name to reflect the death of the American Dream.
- The Stooges' Raw Power: "Raw Power" by The Stooges, produced by David Bowie, is often considered one of the first punk albums.

- Punk Fashion Icon: Designer Vivienne Westwood played a significant role in creating the punk fashion style.
- The New York Dolls' Look: The New York Dolls were known for their androgynous style, wearing platform shoes and tight, flamboyant clothing.
- "God Save the Queen" Controversy: The Sex Pistols' "God Save the Queen" was banned by the BBC but still reached number two on the UK charts.

"God Save the Queen" by the Sex Pistols remains one of the most controversial songs in rock history, epitomizing the spirit of punk rock in its direct challenge to British social and political norms. Released in 1977, the timing was provocative – it coincided with Queen Elizabeth II's Silver Jubilee, marking 25 years on the throne.

The song's lyrics, penned by vocalist Johnny Rotten, were a scathing critique of the British monarchy and the wider establishment. Lines like "God save the queen / The fascist regime" and "She ain't no human being" were direct and confrontational, reflecting the punk movement's disdain for authority and tradition. The artwork for the single, featuring the Queen's image defaced with a safety pin and bold, anarchic text, added to the uproar.

The BBC deemed the song inappropriate for airplay, banning it from their channels. Despite this, or perhaps because of it, the song became an anthem for disaffected British youth. Its anti-establishment message resonated with a generation experiencing economic hardship and societal upheaval, mirroring punk's broader themes of rebellion and disenfranchisement.

The controversy surrounding "God Save the Queen" only fueled its popularity. It quickly climbed the UK music charts, but its ascent was shrouded in further controversy. There were widespread rumors that the song's chart position was being manipulated to prevent it from reaching number one during the Jubilee week, a claim bolstered by the fact that the chart for that week left the number one spot blank.

The song's success and the furore it created were emblematic of the Sex Pistols' impact on the music scene and British culture. It challenged societal norms, questioned authority, and gave a powerful voice to punk's raw, rebellious ethos. The band, already notorious for their chaotic live performances and rebellious image, became symbols of the punk movement, with "God Save the Queen" as their rallying cry.

- The Ramones' Fast Songs: The Ramones' songs were famously short and fast; their debut album has 14 tracks but is only 29 minutes long.
- The Clash's "London Calling" Cover: The cover of "London Calling" by The Clash pays homage to Elvis Presley's debut album cover.
- Patti Smith's "Horses" Album: Patti Smith's debut album "Horses" is considered a landmark in the evolution of punk rock.
- Dead Kennedys' Satirical Lyrics: The Dead Kennedys were known for their biting satire and political commentary.

One of the most notable examples of their satirical approach is the song "Holiday in Cambodia." Released in 1980, it targets privileged Western youth who are oblivious to the harsh realities of life in other parts of the world. The lyrics juxtapose the comfortable, naive life of a typical American college student with the brutal regime of Pol Pot and the Khmer Rouge in Cambodia.

Lines like "It's a holiday in Cambodia / Where people dress in black" and "You'll work harder with a gun in your back for a bowl of rice a day" starkly contrast the complacency of Western society with the suffering under totalitarian regimes. This song exemplifies the Dead Kennedys' ability to use irony and exaggeration to make a political statement.

Another significant song, "California Über Alles," serves as a scathing critique of then-California Governor Jerry Brown and, by extension, the entire American political system. The song imagines a dystopian future where Brown's liberal policies have led to a fascist state. Lyrics like "I am Governor Jerry Brown / My aura smiles and never frowns" satirize Brown's progressive image, while "Zen fascists will control you" highlights the band's view of the potential dangers of unchecked political power. The song's title itself, a play on the Nazi anthem "Deutschland Über Alles," underscores its message about the slippery slope from well-intentioned policies to authoritarianism.

"Kill the Poor," another track from their debut album, uses hyperbole to criticize apathy towards the underprivileged and the disparities in wealth and power. The song sarcastically suggests using neutron bombs to eliminate poverty by eradicating the poor themselves, a grotesque exaggeration to highlight society's neglect of the less fortunate. Lyrics like "Efficiency and progress is ours once more / Now that we have the neutron bomb" mock the idea of progress at the expense of humanity and empathy.

- Iggy Pop's "Lust for Life": Iggy Pop's "Lust for Life" was co-written with David Bowie during their time in Berlin.
- Television's "Marquee Moon": Television's debut album "Marquee Moon" is considered one of the greatest rock albums for its guitar work and complex songwriting.

- The Stooges' Induction into the Rock and Roll Hall of Fame: The Stooges were inducted into the Rock and Roll Hall of Fame in 2010.
- Sex Pistols' Short Lifespan: The Sex Pistols effectively ended with Sid Vicious' death in 1979, making their career span less than three years.
- Ramones' Induction into the Rock and Roll Hall of Fame: The Ramones were inducted into the Rock and Roll Hall of Fame in 2002.
- Punk Zines: Punk culture popularized DIY 'zines, which were crucial in the spread of punk music and culture.
- Sid Vicious' Stage Name: Sid Vicious of the Sex Pistols got his stage name from a pet hamster owned by Johnny Rotten.

In various movies, the influence and legacy of these iconic artists and bands have been celebrated or referenced, showcasing their impact on music and culture:

- Trainspotting" (1996) features Iggy Pop's "Lust for Life," setting an energetic tone for the film.
- Television's influential album "Marquee Moon" has left its mark on filmmakers and musicians, with their music appearing in soundtracks and documentaries exploring the 1970s New York music scene.
- The Stooges' induction into the Rock and Roll Hall of Fame in 2010 is recognized in documentaries like "Gimme Danger" (2016), directed by Jim Jarmusch, which delves into the band's rise and impact.
- Films such as "Sid and Nancy" (1986) depict the Sex Pistols' brief but impactful career, including the tragic story of Sid Vicious and Nancy Spungen against the backdrop of punk rock's emergence.
- The Ramones' pioneering role in punk music is celebrated in films like "Rock 'n' Roll High School" (1979), featuring the band's high-energy performance.

Progressive Rock and Concept Albums

The 1970s marked a golden era for progressive rock, a genre characterized by its ambitious, often experimental approach to music. This decade saw the rise of concept albums - records that unified their songs under a central theme, story, or idea, offering listeners a complex and immersive experience. These albums not only showcased musical virtuosity but also pushed the boundaries of what rock music could be.

One of the most prominent bands in this genre was Pink Floyd, whose 1973 album "The Dark Side of the Moon" became one of the best-selling albums of all time. This concept album explored themes of mental illness, greed, and the passage of time, using innovative sound effects and studio techniques to create a vivid auditory landscape. Its seamless flow of songs and use of synthesizers and sound effects set a new standard for musical storytelling and production quality in rock music.

Another key player in the progressive rock scene was Yes, known for their intricate compositions, complex arrangements, and technical proficiency. Their 1972 album "Close to the Edge" is often cited as one of the greatest progressive rock albums ever made. It featured just three songs, each a suite of interconnected sections, blending rock with classical, jazz, and folk influences. The title track, spanning 18 minutes, is an epic journey through various musical landscapes, showcasing the band's skill in composing and performing extended pieces.

Genesis, yet another titan of the genre, embraced the concept album with "The Lamb Lies Down on Broadway" in 1974. This double album narrated a surreal story about a young man named Rael, incorporating themes of identity and transformation. Genesis' blend of poetic lyrics, theatrical stage performances, and complex musical compositions made them standouts in the progressive rock genre.

The 1970s' progressive rock and concept albums represented a pinnacle of artistic ambition in rock music. These works were not just collections of songs but cohesive artistic statements, offering listeners rich and often challenging musical experiences. They reflected the era's spirit of experimentation and the desire to push the boundaries of popular music, leaving a lasting impact on the rock genre.

Ten of the biggest concept albums of the era

Pink Floyd - "The Dark Side of the Moon" (1973)
- The album explores the themes of conflict, greed, time, death, and mental illness.
- It remained on the Billboard charts for 741 weeks from 1973 to 1988, making it one of the longest-charted albums in history.
- The iconic album cover, a prism dispersing light, was designed by Storm Thorgerson and became one of the most recognizable in rock music.
- The album is known for its pioneering use of analog synthesizers and sound effects, including the sound of a cash register on "Money."

Genesis - "The Lamb Lies Down on Broadway" (1974)
- This double album tells the surreal story of Rael, a Puerto Rican street tough from New York City.
- It was the last Genesis album to feature Peter Gabriel as the lead vocalist.
- The album's cover art, designed by Hipgnosis and Betty Swanwick, features a surreal scene fitting the album's narrative.

- Live performances of the album were known for their theatricality, with elaborate costumes and stage effects.

Yes - "Close to the Edge" (1972)
- The album consists of just three songs, with the title track lasting over 18 minutes.
- The album's artwork was created by Roger Dean, who designed many of Yes's covers, contributing to the band's visual identity.
- "Close to the Edge" was composed through a collaborative effort, with each band member contributing to the extended pieces.
- The album is often considered a masterpiece of progressive rock for its intricate musicianship and complex song structures.

David Bowie - "The Rise and Fall of Ziggy Stardust and the Spiders from Mars" (1972)
- The album tells the story of Ziggy Stardust, a bisexual alien rock superstar.
- It combined glam rock with narrative storytelling, creating a unique concept album experience.
- The song "Starman" was the album's hit single and played a key role in popularizing Bowie.
- The album's cover, showing Bowie standing in a London street, has become iconic in the world of rock music.

Jethro Tull - "Thick as a Brick" (1972)
- Initially presented as a single continuous piece of music, the album satirizes the concept of the concept album.
- The album's lyrics were credited to a fictitious child poet named Gerald Bostock.
- Its album cover was designed as a spoof of a local newspaper, complete with humorous articles and advertisements.

- "Thick as a Brick" was a response to critics who labeled the band's previous album, "Aqualung," as a concept album.

The Who - "Quadrophenia" (1973)
- The album narrates the story of a young mod named Jimmy and his struggle with a split personality.
- "Quadrophenia" is a double album and the group's second rock opera after "Tommy."
- The title is a play on the word schizophrenia and the band's use of quadrophonic sound.
- The album was adapted into a successful film in 1979, which became a cult classic.

Rush - "2112" (1976)
- The title track "2112" takes up the entire first side of the album, telling a dystopian story set in the year 2112.
- The album marked Rush's commercial breakthrough and is one of their most popular works.
- The story was influenced by the works of Ayn Rand, particularly her novella "Anthem."
- Despite its science fiction themes, the album is considered a pivotal moment in the evolution of progressive rock.

Supertramp - "Crime of the Century" (1974)
- While not a narrative concept album, it thematically deals with themes of loneliness and mental stability.
- The album produced the hit singles "Dreamer" and "Bloody Well Right."
- Its cover art, showing a pair of handcuffs in a beam of light, is striking and symbolic.
- "Crime of the Century" is often considered Supertramp's greatest work.

Pink Floyd - "Wish You Were Here" (1975)
- The album serves as a tribute to former band member Syd Barrett and his struggle with mental health.
- The song "Shine On You Crazy Diamond" is explicitly about Barrett.
- The album cover, featuring two businessmen shaking hands with one on fire, was designed by Storm Thorgerson.
- "Wish You Were Here" explores themes of absence, the music industry, and the band's own feelings of alienation.

Electric Light Orchestra - "Eldorado" (1974)
- A concept album about a dreamer's journey in search of Eldorado, a mythical golden city.
- The album mixes rock with orchestral arrangements, creating a distinctive sound.
- It includes the popular track "Can't Get It Out of My Head," which became the band's first top 10 single in the USA.
- The album's overture is often praised for its cinematic quality and sets the tone for the entire album.

Trivia Tidbits

- Pink Floyd's Original Name: Before settling on Pink Floyd, the band performed under names like "The Pink Floyd Sound" and "The Tea Set."
- Yes's Rotating Lineup: Over the years, Yes has had a constantly evolving lineup, with over 19 different members being part of the band at various times.
- Genesis and The Farm: Genesis owned a piece of property known as The Farm, where they wrote and rehearsed much of their music from the 1980s onward.

- David Bowie's Alter Egos: Besides Ziggy Stardust, Bowie adopted several other personas during his career, including Aladdin Sane and The Thin White Duke.
- Jethro Tull's Unique Name Origin: The band is named after Jethro Tull, an 18th-century agriculturist, chosen randomly from a history book.
- The Who's Record for Loudest Concert: In 1976, The Who entered the Guinness Book of World Records for playing the loudest performance of any rock band.
- Rush's Neil Peart as a Primary Lyricist: Drummer Neil Peart was the primary lyricist for Rush, joining the band after their first album.
- Supertramp's Breakfast in America Cover: The cover of "Breakfast in America" features a waitress named Libby posed as the Statue of Liberty.
- Roger Waters' Departure from Pink Floyd: Roger Waters left Pink Floyd in 1985, leading to legal battles over the use of the band's name and material.
- Yes's "Owner of a Lonely Heart" Success: Despite their 70s fame, Yes's only number one hit was "Owner of a Lonely Heart" in 1983.
- Genesis's "Invisible Touch": Genesis's most successful album, "Invisible Touch" (1986), was released long after their progressive rock phase.
- David Bowie's Acting Career: Bowie was also an accomplished actor, starring in films like "The Man Who Fell to Earth" and "Labyrinth."
- Jethro Tull's Grammy Controversy: In 1989, Jethro Tull won the first-ever Grammy for Best Hard Rock/Metal Performance, controversially beating Metallica.
- The Who's Rock Operas: Besides "Quadrophenia," The Who are famous for another rock opera, "Tommy," which was later adapted into a film and Broadway musical.

- Rush's "Moving Pictures": Rush's 1981 album "Moving Pictures" is one of their most successful, featuring the hit "Tom Sawyer."
- Supertramp Co-Founders: Supertramp was co-founded by Rick Davies and Roger Hodgson, who had contrasting songwriting styles.
- Syd Barrett's Influence on Pink Floyd: Syd Barrett, a founding member of Pink Floyd, was a major influence on the band's early sound and style.
- Chris Squire's Legacy with Yes: Chris Squire was the only member of Yes to appear on every studio album, known for his distinctive bass playing.
- Phil Collins' Genesis and Solo Career: Phil Collins, drummer and later lead vocalist for Genesis, achieved significant success as a solo artist.
- Bowie's "Berlin Trilogy": David Bowie's "Berlin Trilogy" of albums ("Low," "Heroes," and "Lodger") were critical favorites, showcasing his experimental and avant-garde side.

Lyric Based Multiple-Choice Questions

"And through the window in the wall / Come streaming in on sunlight wings / A million bright ambassadors of morning" refers to which song?
A) "Firth of Fifth" by Genesis
B) "Shine On You Crazy Diamond" by Pink Floyd
C) "And You and I" by Yes

"A tolling bell / I hear it echo in my mind" is from which song?
A) "Eldorado" by Electric Light Orchestra
B) "Tubular Bells" by Mike Oldfield
C) "The Lamb Lies Down on Broadway" by Genesis

"The words of the prophets are written on the subway walls" comes from?
A) "Karn Evil 9" by Emerson, Lake & Palmer
B) "The Spirit of Radio" by Rush
C) "Sound of Silence" by Simon & Garfunkel

"I'll be the roundabout / The words will make you out 'n' out" is from which song?
A) "Aqualung" by Jethro Tull
B) "Lucky Man" by Emerson, Lake & Palmer
C) "Roundabout" by Yes

"There's a starman waiting in the sky / He'd like to come and meet us" is a lyric from which song?
A) "Rocket Man" by Elton John
B) "Starman" by David Bowie
C) "Space Oddity" by David Bowie

"So you ride yourselves over the fields / And you make all your animal deals" is from which song?
A) "Animals" by Pink Floyd
B) "Watcher of the Skies" by Genesis
C) "Thick as a Brick" by Jethro Tull

"The music is reversible but time is not / Turn back, turn back, turn back" is from?
A) "Time" by Pink Floyd
B) "Back in NYC" by Genesis
C) "Turn of the Century" by Yes

"The heat's hot and the ground's dry / But the air is full of sound" is from which track?
A) "Desert Song" by Def Leppard
B) "A Horse with No Name" by America
C) "Kashmir" by Led Zeppelin

"Selling England by the pound" is a lyric from which Genesis song?
A) "The Cinema Show"
B) "Dancing with the Moonlit Knight"
C) "Firth of Fifth"

"I've looked at life from both sides now / From up and down, and still somehow" is from?
A) "The Logical Song" by Supertramp
B) "Life on Mars?" by David Bowie
C) "Both Sides, Now" by Joni Mitchell

"Do you remember a guy that's been / In such an early song" is a line from which song?
A) "Life on Mars?" by David Bowie
B) "Starman" by David Bowie
C) "Ashes to Ashes" by David Bowie

"If I were a swan, I'd be gone" is the opening line of which song?
A) "Bourée" by Jethro Tull
B) "Nights in White Satin" by The Moody Blues
C) "Lucky Man" by Emerson, Lake & Palmer

"The words of the prophets are written on the studio wall, concert hall" echoes in which song?
A) "Tom Sawyer" by Rush
B) "Limelight" by Rush
C) "Spirit of Radio" by Rush

"And the man in the back said everyone attack " is from?
A) "Rebel Rebel" by David Bowie
B) "Rock and Roll Part 2" by Gary Glitter
C) "Ballroom Blitz" by Sweet

"Ticking away the moments that make up a dull day" is from which Pink Floyd song?
A) "Wish You Were Here"
B) "Time"
C) "Money"

David Bowie was known for his insightful and often candid interviews throughout his career. In these interviews, he discussed a wide range of topics, including his music, influences, creative process, and personal life. Bowie's interviews often revealed his intellectual curiosity, artistic experimentation, and willingness to challenge conventions in both music and society. He was also known for his charismatic and enigmatic personality, which captivated audiences and fans around the world. Overall, Bowie's interviews provided valuable insights into his multifaceted persona and creative genius.

- Painter and Art Collector: Bowie was a talented painter and enthusiastic art collector, amassing a significant collection of modern and contemporary art.
- Internet Pioneer: He was one of the first major artists to embrace the internet, launching his own internet service provider called BowieNet in 1998.
- Acting Career: Bowie had a successful acting career, starring in films like "The Man Who Fell to Earth" and "Labyrinth."
- Innovative Music Videos: He was a pioneer in music videos, creating groundbreaking visuals for songs like "Ashes to Ashes" and "Space Oddity."
- Business Ventures: Bowie established his own record label, ISO Records, in 2000, giving him greater creative control over his music.
- Hidden Talents: Bowie was skilled in mime, having studied under Lindsay Kemp, and also dabbled in fashion design, creating his own stage costumes and fashion line.

Answers

Answer: B) "Shine On You Crazy Diamond" by Pink Floyd
Trivia Snapshot: The song is a tribute to former band member Syd Barrett, whose unexpected visit to the studio during recording deeply moved the band.

Answer: C) "The Lamb Lies Down on Broadway" by Genesis
Trivia Snapshot: This album was a pioneering concept work in progressive rock, telling a surreal story that showcased Genesis's narrative ambition.

Answer: C) "Sound of Silence" by Simon & Garfunkel
Trivia Snapshot: This song marked a turning point for the duo, becoming a defining anthem of the 60s' folk-rock movement.

Answer: C) "Roundabout" by Yes
Trivia Snapshot: "Roundabout" became a signature song for Yes, known for its complex arrangements and dynamic shifts.

Answer: B) "Starman" by David Bowie
Trivia Snapshot: This song introduced the concept of Ziggy Stardust, a central figure in Bowie's work, blending rock music with futuristic storytelling.

Answer: B) "Watcher of the Skies" by Genesis
Trivia Snapshot: The song's Mellotron intro set a new standard for the use of keyboard textures in progressive rock.

Answer: A) "Time" by Pink Floyd
Trivia Snapshot: Known for its use of clocks and alarms as instruments, "Time" explores the theme of mortality in an innovative way.

Answer: B) "A Horse with No Name" by America
Trivia Snapshot: This song's simplicity and evocative lyrics captured the essence of the American desert landscape.

Answer: B) "Dancing with the Moonlit Knight" by Genesis
Trivia Snapshot: The song critiques commercialism in England, weaving complex musical motifs with lyrical depth.

Answer: C) "Both Sides, Now" by Joni Mitchell
Trivia Snapshot: Mitchell's introspective lyrics and innovative guitar tunings made this song a timeless piece of folk music.

Answer: C) "Ashes to Ashes" by David Bowie
Trivia Snapshot: This song revisited the character of Major Tom, reflecting on Bowie's career and changes in his artistic direction.

Answer: C) "Lucky Man" by Emerson, Lake & Palmer
Trivia Snapshot: Written by Greg Lake when he was just 12 years old, this song became a defining moment in ELP's early success.

Answer: C) "Spirit of Radio" by Rush
Trivia Snapshot: Celebrating the joy of FM radio, this song showcases Rush's ability to blend complex musicianship with accessible rock.

Answer: C) "Ballroom Blitz" by Sweet
Trivia Snapshot: Inspired by an actual event where the band was driven off stage by an unruly crowd, the song became an anthem of glam rock.

Answer: B) "Time" by Pink Floyd
Trivia Snapshot: Featuring the iconic sound of ticking clocks, "Time" is a philosophical meditation on life's passage, highlighted by Gilmour's guitar solos.

Did You Know Joni Mitchell is indeed Canadian, and she was born in Fort Macleod, Alberta, Canada, on November 7, 1943.

Reggae and Rastafarian Influence

In the 1970s, reggae music, deeply intertwined with Rastafarian culture, emerged from Jamaica to captivate a global audience. This genre's distinctive rhythm and socially conscious lyrics had a profound impact on music and popular culture, going far beyond its Caribbean origins.

Reggae developed from earlier genres like ska and rocksteady, but it brought a slower, steadier beat. This sound was reflective of the social and political climate in Jamaica, often conveying messages about love, social justice, and resistance. The music was as much about rhythm and dance as it was a vehicle for commentary and storytelling.

Bob Marley is synonymous with reggae music. His profound connection to Rastafarianism, a spiritual and cultural movement that arose in Jamaica in the 1930s, heavily influenced his music. Marley's songs often incorporated Rastafarian beliefs, which include the spiritual use of cannabis, the sacredness of nature, and the idea of a promised homeland in Africa. Hits like "No Woman, No Cry," "Redemption Song," and "One Love" remain timeless classics, blending smooth melodies with powerful messages of unity and resistance.

Marley, together with his band, The Wailers, played a pivotal role in popularizing reggae globally. Other significant reggae artists include Peter Tosh and Bunny Wailer, who were originally part of The Wailers, along with artists like Burning Spear, Gregory Isaacs, and Lee "Scratch" Perry, each bringing their unique style to the genre.

Rastafarianism's influence on reggae is evident in its themes of anti-colonialism, the quest for freedom and identity, and the longing for return to an African homeland (Zion). The Rastafarian colors – green, gold, and red – became symbols within the genre, often seen on album covers, clothing, and concert stages.

By the late 1970s, reggae had spread worldwide, influencing various music genres, including rock, hip-hop, and punk. Artists like The Clash and The Police incorporated reggae rhythms into their music. Reggae's laid-back rhythm and association with political activism resonated with audiences globally, making it more than just a musical genre but a voice for social change.

Reggae's influence in the 1970s is a testament to its power as a voice of the marginalized, a unifying force, and a catalyst for social and political awareness. Its legacy continues to inspire and influence music and culture around the world.

Bob Marley & The Wailers - "No Woman, No Cry" (1974)
- An anthem of resilience and comfort, the song's live version from the "Live!" album became more famous than the studio recording.
- It showcases Marley's talent for writing deeply emotional and universally relatable lyrics.
- The song helped establish Bob Marley as a global icon of reggae and a voice for the oppressed.

Peter Tosh - "Legalize It" (1976)
- A provocative song advocating for the legalization of cannabis, aligning with Rastafarian beliefs.
- Tosh's defiant lyrics and smooth rhythm made it an anthem for cannabis legalization movements worldwide.
- The song is known for its straightforward and controversial stance, reflecting Tosh's reputation as a bold and uncompromising artist.

Burning Spear - "Marcus Garvey" (1975)
- The song pays tribute to the Black nationalist leader Marcus Garvey, echoing Rastafarian reverence for him.
- Its powerful lyrics and militant rhythm made it a landmark song in the roots reggae genre.
- Burning Spear's passionate delivery and the song's historical relevance resonated deeply with listeners.

Bob Marley & The Wailers - "Redemption Song" (1980)
- One of Marley's most poignant works, featuring just his voice and an acoustic guitar, highlighting its heartfelt message.
- The song's lyrics, inspired by a speech by Marcus Garvey, call for emancipation from mental slavery.
- It's often regarded as a global anthem for freedom and redemption.

Jimmy Cliff - "The Harder They Come" (1972)
- The title track for the film of the same name, in which Cliff starred, bringing reggae to international audiences.
- A song about perseverance and defiance, it has become an enduring symbol of reggae's rebellious spirit.
- The soundtrack, largely featuring Cliff, was pivotal in popularizing reggae across the world.

Toots and the Maytals - "Pressure Drop" (1970)
- A classic track that combines reggae with elements of ska and rocksteady.
- The song gained international fame after being covered by The Clash, showcasing reggae's influence on punk.
- Its infectious rhythm and memorable chorus made it a staple of the reggae genre.

Bunny Wailer - "Blackheart Man" (1976)
- The title track from his debut album, it's a deeply spiritual song that draws on Rastafarian teachings and folklore.
- Bunny Wailer's introspective lyrics and roots reggae sound exemplify the genre's depth and cultural roots.
- The album "Blackheart Man" is considered a seminal work in reggae music.

Lee "Scratch" Perry - "Roast Fish and Cornbread" (1978)
- A showcase of Perry's innovative production style, blending reggae with dub elements.
- The song is known for its catchy rhythm and experimental sound, typical of Perry's work.
- Lee "Scratch" Perry is celebrated for his pioneering contributions to the development of dub music.

Trivia Tidbits

- Bob Marley's Real Name: Bob Marley's full name was Robert Nesta Marley. He was born on February 6, 1945, in Nine Mile, Jamaica.
- Peter Tosh's Activism: Beyond music, Peter Tosh was a vocal advocate for equal rights and justice, often clashing with Jamaican authorities.
- The Origin of "Reggae": The term "reggae" reportedly comes from the 1968 Toots and the Maytals song "Do the Reggay," which is one of the earliest popular songs to use the word.
- Burning Spear's Real Name: Burning Spear, known for his powerful Rastafarian-influenced music, was born Winston Rodney.
- "Redemption Song" Statue: A bronze statue of Bob Marley, located in Emancipation Park in Kingston, Jamaica, depicts him playing guitar, a tribute to his song "Redemption Song."

- Jimmy Cliff's Breakthrough: Jimmy Cliff's role in "The Harder They Come" was a breakthrough for both his acting and music career, helping to introduce reggae to a global audience.
- Toots and the Maytals' Guinness Record: In 1972, Toots and the Maytals made the Guinness Book of World Records for the shortest time between recording a song and its release with "Reggae Got Soul."
- Bunny Wailer's Heritage: Bunny Wailer, born Neville Livingston, was not only a bandmate of Bob Marley but also his stepbrother.
- Lee "Scratch" Perry's Studio: Perry was known for his Black Ark studio, a cradle of reggae and dub music innovation during the 1970s.
- Rastafarianism and the Lion: The lion is a significant symbol in Rastafarianism, often associated with Haile Selassie I of Ethiopia, revered as a messianic figure in the faith.
- Bob Marley's Attempted Assassination: In 1976, Bob Marley survived an assassination attempt at his home in Jamaica, which was politically motivated.
- The Wailers' Early Days: Before international fame, The Wailers had a ska and rocksteady sound and were known as The Teenagers and The Wailing Rudeboys.
- "No Woman, No Cry" Misinterpretation: The title "No Woman, No Cry" is often misinterpreted. In Jamaican Patois, it means "No, woman, don't cry."
- The Clash's Reggae Influence: The punk band The Clash was heavily influenced by reggae and covered several reggae songs, including "Police and Thieves" by Junior Murvin.
- Peter Tosh's Grammy Award: Posthumously, Peter Tosh won a Grammy Award in 1987 for "No Nuclear War," his last recorded album.

Marijuana Use in Relation to Reggae and Rastafarian Influence

Marijuana, often referred to as "ganja" in the Rastafarian tradition, holds significant cultural and spiritual importance in Rastafarianism and, by extension, has become closely associated with reggae music.

In Rastafarian culture, marijuana is considered a sacred herb and is used as part of religious ceremonies. The Rastafari view ganja as a means to spiritual enlightenment, a way to attain a deeper sense of self-awareness, and a tool for meditation. It is often used during "reasoning sessions" where Rastas gather to discuss philosophical and religious ideas while smoking marijuana.

The use of marijuana in Jamaica, which predates Rastafarianism, has roots in the African traditions of the enslaved people brought to the island. Rastafarians adopted marijuana use as a part of their rebellion against colonial and post-colonial systems of oppression. They regard the use of ganja as a rejection of materialistic and unjust societal norms.

Many reggae artists, including Bob Marley, Peter Tosh, and Bunny Wailer, were devout Rastafarians and used their music as a platform to express their religious and philosophical beliefs, including the use of marijuana. Songs like Peter Tosh's "Legalize It" not only advocate for the legalization of marijuana but also reflect the cultural and spiritual importance of ganja in Rastafarianism.

The association between reggae music, Rastafarianism, and marijuana has sometimes led to stereotyping. While marijuana use is indeed a part of Rastafarian religious practice and a recurring theme in reggae music, it is essential to understand it within its complex cultural and spiritual context rather than through a simplified or exoticized lens.

Reggae music played a significant role in popularizing Rastafarian culture and its practices, including marijuana use, on a global scale. Artists like Bob Marley became de facto ambassadors of this culture, bringing its messages to an international audience. This has contributed to a broader discourse on marijuana, encompassing issues of spirituality, decriminalization, and medicinal use.

Bob Marley's Life

- Born in Nine Mile, Jamaica, in 1945, Bob Marley's biracial heritage profoundly influenced his early life. His mixed ancestry often subjected him to ridicule and exclusion, shaping his perspective on racial issues, evident in his later music.
- Despite facing these challenges, Marley's resilience and strength of character earned him the nickname "Tuff Gong," a testament to his toughness in the face of adversity. This nickname would later become an integral part of his brand.
- Marley's musical journey began with the formation of The Teenagers, which later became The Wailers. This group, which included Peter Tosh and Bunny Wailer, laid the foundation for what would become a revolutionary force in music.
- The Wailers' early music was influenced heavily by American rhythm and blues, but they soon developed their unique style, blending local musical traditions with the socio-economic themes of their upbringing.
- Marley's conversion to Rastafarianism in the 1960s significantly influenced his music and public persona. His songs began to reflect Rastafarian beliefs, emphasizing peace, unity, and a connection to African roots.

- The Rastafarian influence extended to his appearance, most notably his iconic dreadlocks, symbolizing a lion's mane and representing strength, defiance, and a natural way of life.
- Marley's work with producer Chris Blackwell and Island Records catapulted him to international fame. Albums like "Catch A Fire" and "Natty Dread" introduced reggae to a global audience, and Marley became its most famous ambassador.
- His music, especially tracks like "Get Up, Stand Up" and "One Love," resonated worldwide, highlighting issues of social injustice, love, and unity.
- Beyond his musical achievements, Marley was a vocal advocate for social justice. His efforts were recognized in 1978 when he received The United Nations Peace Medal of the Third World in New York.
- Marley's influence extended beyond music into social and political spheres, making him a symbol of resistance and empowerment for oppressed communities worldwide
- Despite his untimely death in 1981, Marley's legacy endures. He remains an influential figure in music, and his messages of peace and unity continue to inspire new generations.
- Marley's estate, managed by his family, continues to release music and maintain his presence in popular culture, preserving his status as a timeless icon.

Peter Tosh: Musical Revolutionary and Activist

Peter Tosh, born Winston Hubert McIntosh, was not just a reggae musician but a fervent activist for equal rights and justice. Co-founding The Wailers with Bob Marley and Bunny Wailer, Tosh was instrumental in shaping the sound and message of early reggae music. His solo career, marked by albums like "Legalize It" and "Equal Rights," showcased his commitment to tackling issues such as apartheid and the legalization of marijuana. Tosh's music was often more overtly political than Marley's, reflecting his radical views and unyielding stance against oppression. His tragic death in 1987 cut short a career that was as much about activism as it was about music, but his legacy as a fighter for social justice lives on through his songs.

Bunny Wailer: Keeping the Roots Alive

Bunny Wailer, born Neville Livingston, was a founding member of The Wailers and the only one to have spent his entire career focused on reggae's roots and Rastafarianism. Known as the "keeper of the roots," Wailer's music stayed true to the traditional reggae sound. His solo work, including the critically acclaimed album "Blackheart Man," is revered for its spiritual depth and adherence to Rastafarian beliefs. Despite being less internationally famous than Marley, Wailer's impact on reggae is profound. His commitment to the genre's roots and Rastafarian culture helped preserve the essence of reggae music, influencing generations of artists.

Burning Spear: The Voice of Cultural Heritage

Burning Spear, or Winston Rodney, is a figure synonymous with roots reggae and Rastafarianism. His music, characterized by profound spiritual and cultural messages, has been a staple of reggae since the early 1970s. Albums like "Marcus Garvey" and "Man in the Hills" are not just collections of songs but are cultural artifacts, reflecting Rodney's deep connection to his African heritage and Rastafarian beliefs. His haunting vocals and repetitive, hypnotic rhythms create a meditative quality in his music, inviting listeners to reflect on themes of history, identity, and liberation.

Gregory Isaacs: The Cool Ruler of Lovers Rock

Gregory Isaacs was a reggae musician who brought a unique, romantic flair to the genre. Known as the "Cool Ruler," Isaacs' smooth voice and romantic ballads brought him fame in the 1970s and 80s. While he delved into roots reggae, Isaacs was predominantly known for lovers rock, a sub-genre focusing on tender, romantic reggae. His most famous album, "Night Nurse," remains a classic, showcasing his ability to blend the rhythmic elements of reggae with soulful, romantic lyrics. Despite struggles with drug addiction and legal issues, Isaacs left an indelible mark on reggae, offering a softer, more intimate perspective on the genre.

Lee "Scratch" Perry: The Dub Innovator

Lee "Scratch" Perry is a towering figure in reggae, known for his pioneering work in the development of dub music. As a producer and musician, Perry's innovations in the studio transformed the sound of reggae. His work at the legendary Black Ark studio produced some of the genre's most influential records. Perry's eccentric and experimental approach to music production, including the use of groundbreaking studio effects and remixing techniques, had a profound impact on the evolution of reggae and electronic music. Despite his quirky persona, Perry is revered as a musical genius whose contributions to reggae and dub are unparalleled.

Did You Know Damian Marley, youngest son of reggae legend Bob Marley, carries on his father's musical legacy? His music blends reggae, dancehall, and hip-hop, often exploring themes of social justice and spirituality

Queen: Rock Royalty of the 1970s and Beyond

Queen, formed in London in 1970, emerged as one of the most innovative and iconic rock bands of the 20th century. Comprising Freddie Mercury, Brian May, Roger Taylor, and John Deacon, the band is celebrated for its eclectic musical style, flamboyant stage presence, and unforgettable anthems that have stood the test of time.

Formation and Early Days

The story of Queen, one of the most iconic rock bands in history, begins in the late 1960s with a lesser-known band named Smile. Smile was formed at Imperial College London, comprising guitarist Brian May and drummer Roger Taylor. They played predominantly at college events and small venues, laying the groundwork for what would eventually become Queen. Their sound at this stage was a blend of hard rock and progressive styles, reflective of the era's musical trends.

Enter Freddie Mercury, born Farrokh Bulsara, a dynamic personality and a fan of Smile, who frequented their gigs. Mercury saw potential in Smile that perhaps even its members hadn't fully realized. In 1970, with his flamboyant style and theatrical flair, Mercury joined the band and suggested a name change to Queen. His rationale behind the name was its simplicity, universal appeal, and a touch of royalty and grandeur, which he felt suited the band's image and music style. Mercury's inclusion brought a new dimension to the band, not only in terms of vocals but also in stage presence and aesthetic vision.

"I won't be a rockstar. I will be a legend."

The final piece of the puzzle was John Deacon, who joined the band in 1971 as the bass guitarist. Deacon's musicality and quiet demeanor provided a balance to the otherwise flamboyant and dynamic group. With his addition, Queen's classic lineup was complete, and they started to forge a unique identity. This period was crucial as the band members began to merge their individual influences and styles, ranging from hard rock and heavy metal to progressive rock and even opera.

The band's early years were marked by a rigorous rehearsal schedule and songwriting sessions, with each member contributing to the creative process. Their diverse musical influences converged to create a sound that was both eclectic and cohesive. Mercury's penchant for theatrics and showmanship started to influence their performances, making them a visual and auditory spectacle.

Queen's initial struggle to secure a record deal was a significant hurdle. They faced rejection from multiple labels, with industry executives often failing to see the potential in their unique sound and style. However, their persistence paid off when they signed with EMI Records in 1973. Their debut album, "Queen," released the same year, was a significant first step, showcasing their range and setting the stage for what was to become a meteoric rise to fame.

In these formative years, Queen laid the foundation for a career that would see them become one of the most influential bands in rock history. Their journey from a college band to international stardom was marked by a blend of musical innovation, theatricality, and an unwavering commitment to their unique vision of what rock music could be.

Freddie Mercury: As the lead vocalist of Queen, Freddie Mercury was renowned for his remarkable vocal range and flamboyant stage presence. His ability to connect with audiences and his flair for theatrics made him an unforgettable showman. Mercury's songwriting was diverse, ranging from hard rock to ballads, and he was known for infusing his music with a unique blend of genres. He once stated, "I won't be a rock star. I will be a legend." This statement encapsulates his ambition and the indelible mark he left on the music world.

Brian May: Brian May, the lead guitarist of Queen, is celebrated for his distinctive guitar sound, created using his homemade 'Red Special' guitar. His intricate playing and ability to craft melodic, multi-layered guitar solos are hallmarks of Queen's music. May, who holds a Ph.D. in astrophysics, brought a level of intellectual depth to his music and lyrics. He once said, "I like to be surrounded by splendid things." This reflects his approach to music - rich, detailed, and profound.

Roger Taylor: As the drummer of Queen, Roger Taylor was known for his powerful and dynamic drumming style that added an energetic pulse to their music. Beyond his drumming, Taylor contributed significantly to the band's vocal harmonies and occasionally took lead vocals. His songwriting skills added a raw, rockier edge to some of Queen's tracks. Taylor, known for his outspoken nature, once remarked, "I'd rather be dead than singing 'Satisfaction' when I'm forty-five."

John Deacon: The bassist of Queen, John Deacon, was the quiet, reserved member of the band, often letting his music speak for him. His bass lines were inventive yet unobtrusive, providing a solid foundation for many of Queen's hits. Deacon also contributed to the band's songwriting, penning hits like "Another One Bites the Dust" and "I Want to Break Free." Despite his quieter demeanor, his musical contributions were integral to Queen's sound and success.

"Bohemian Rhapsody" (1975)
- A six-minute suite combining rock, ballad, opera, and hard rock, and is often considered Queen's magnum opus.
- The song topped UK charts for nine weeks and re-entered the charts after Mercury's death, becoming the UK's third best-selling single of all time.
- Accompanied by a groundbreaking music video that helped popularize the format.
- Its complex structure, with no chorus, was unprecedented in rock music.

"We Will Rock You" (1977)
- Known for its iconic stomp-stomp-clap beat, easily recognizable and widely used in sports events worldwide.
- Written by Brian May, the song was intended to engage the audience and has become a universal stadium anthem.
- The song is part of the album "News of the World" and reflects the band's experimentation with simpler compositions.
- It's often paired with "We Are the Champions," as they run consecutively on the album.

"We Are the Champions" (1977)
- A powerful ballad that has become an anthem for victories at sporting events.
- Freddie Mercury wrote the song to create a bond with the audience, and it's known for its message of resilience and triumph.
- Voted the world's favorite song in a global music poll conducted by Sony Ericsson in 2005.
- The song is known for its memorable and sing-along chorus.

"Another One Bites the Dust" (1980)
- One of Queen's best-selling singles, with over 7 million copies sold.

- Features a distinctive bassline and a fusion of disco and funk, showcasing the band's versatility.
- Written by John Deacon, it became the band's only single to sell a million copies in the United States.
- Was used in various media and sporting events, cementing its place in pop culture.

"Killer Queen" (1974)
- The song was Queen's first international hit, reaching the top 20 in several countries.
- Known for its sophisticated melody and Mercury's versatile vocal performance.
- The lyrics reflect Mercury's wit and were inspired by high-class call girls.
- The song showcases Queen's musical range, blending rock with a more cabaret style.

"Somebody to Love" (1976)
- A complex piece that draws inspiration from gospel music with its choir-like harmonies.
- Freddie Mercury's exploration of his struggles with life and love, mirrored in the powerful and emotive vocals.
- The song was a top 20 hit in the UK and the US and remains one of Queen's most beloved tracks.
- Live performances of the song were particularly notable for their intensity and emotional depth.

"Under Pressure" (1981)
- A collaboration with David Bowie, this song is known for its distinctive bassline and vocal performances.
- The lyrics deal with themes of pressure and societal issues, showcasing the songwriting prowess of both Queen and Bowie.
- The song marked a departure from Queen's typical sound, featuring a more funk and R&B style.

- Became a lasting hit, acclaimed for its musical fusion and powerful message.

"Radio Ga Ga" (1984)
- Written by Roger Taylor, the song was a commentary on television overtaking radio's popularity.
- Known for its catchy chorus and synthesizer-driven melody, reflecting the music trends of the 1980s.
- The music video, paying homage to Fritz Lang's film "Metropolis," was acclaimed for its innovative use of imagery.
- The song's title inspired Lady Gaga's stage name, showing its influence on the next generation of artists.

"Don't Stop Me Now" (1978)
- Featured on their album "Jazz," this song is a lively celebration of freedom and joy, showcasing Freddie Mercury's love for life.
- Known for its upbeat tempo and Mercury's exuberant vocal performance, the song has become a feel-good anthem for many.
- The lyrics, written by Mercury, reflect his hedonistic lifestyle and unapologetic pursuit of pleasure.
- Despite a lukewarm initial reception, it has grown in popularity over the years, often featured in movies, commercials, and ranked as one of the greatest songs in rock history.

"Love of My Life" (1975)
- Appearing on the album "A Night at the Opera," this ballad is one of Queen's most tender and emotionally resonant songs.
- Written by Freddie Mercury about his then-girlfriend Mary Austin, the song features beautiful, poignant lyrics paired with a complex, classical-influenced arrangement.

- Often performed live with just Mercury on piano and Brian May on guitar, the song became a favorite at Queen concerts, with audiences frequently singing along.
- "Love of My Life" showcased Queen's versatility, proving their ability to master both hard-hitting rock and delicate, heartfelt ballads.

"I Want to Break Free" (1984)
- Known for its iconic music video where the band members famously dressed in drag, parodying the British soap opera "Coronation Street."
- The song, featured on the album "The Works," has a distinctive synth-pop sound, indicative of Queen's adaptability to the music trends of the 1980s.
- Written by bassist John Deacon, the song is an anthem of liberation and self-expression.
- Although the video was controversial at the time, particularly in the United States, the song remains a beloved classic, symbolizing the band's creative boldness and sense of humor.

Queen: The Latter Years and Freddie Mercury's Legacy

As Queen progressed through the 1980s, their sound evolved, reflecting the changing musical landscape. Albums like "The Works" and "A Kind of Magic" showcased a synthesis of rock, pop, and even elements of disco and funk, exemplifying the band's ability to adapt and remain relevant. Their performance at Live Aid in 1985 was a pivotal moment, reaffirming their status as one of the greatest live bands in rock history. This concert, held at Wembley Stadium, is often hailed as one of the best live performances ever, with Freddie Mercury's commanding presence captivating the global audience.

The late 1980s saw Queen continuing to tour and produce music, although Freddie Mercury's health was beginning to decline. Despite growing concerns and rumors about his health, Mercury and the band maintained a busy schedule, releasing "The Miracle" in 1989 and "Innuendo" in 1991. These albums, particularly "Innuendo," were reflective and introspective, hinting at Mercury's personal struggles. The title track, "Innuendo," with its complex orchestration and profound lyrics, is often seen as a testament to Mercury's perseverance in the face of his illness.

Freddie Mercury's battle with AIDS was kept private until the very end of his life. On November 23, 1991, he publicly acknowledged his illness, issuing a statement about his AIDS diagnosis. Tragically, just over 24 hours later, on November 24, 1991, Freddie Mercury passed away at the age of 45. His death was a profound loss to the music world and brought increased attention to the AIDS epidemic, which at the time was still shrouded in stigma and misunderstanding.

Mercury's death marked the end of an era for Queen in its original form. The remaining members of Queen - Brian May, Roger Taylor, and John Deacon - organized a tribute concert for Mercury at Wembley Stadium in April 1992, featuring performances by many of the era's leading artists and bands. This event not only celebrated Mercury's life and legacy but also raised significant funds and awareness for AIDS research.

In the years following Mercury's death, Queen's legacy continued to grow. The band members pursued solo projects and occasionally came together for performances and recordings. John Deacon retired from the music industry in the late 1990s, while May and Taylor continued to keep the spirit of Queen alive through various collaborations and tours, including performing with vocalists such as Paul Rodgers.

Queen's influence on music and popular culture is immense. Their innovative approach to music and performance, blending rock with other genres and embracing theatricality, has inspired countless artists. Mercury, in particular, is remembered for breaking social and cultural barriers with his flamboyant style and open expression of his identity.

In recent years, the band's story and music have reached new audiences through the biographical film "Bohemian Rhapsody," which brought renewed attention to their music and the extraordinary life of Freddie Mercury. The film, while criticized for some historical inaccuracies, was a commercial and critical success, winning several awards and introducing Queen's music to a new generation.

- Name Origin: The band's name, "Queen," was chosen by Freddie Mercury who loved its regal sound and believed it conveyed a sense of royalty and grandeur.
- Freddie Mercury's Cats: Mercury adored cats, having as many as ten at one time, and dedicated his solo album "Mr. Bad Guy" to his cats.
- Brian May's Astrophysics: Aside from his musical talent, Brian May is also an astrophysicist. He completed his Ph.D. in astrophysics in 2007, over 30 years after he started it.
- Roger Taylor's Vocal Range: Taylor is known for his high vocal range, showcased in songs like "Bohemian Rhapsody," where he hits some of the highest notes.
- John Deacon's Retirement: After Mercury's death, John Deacon retired from music and has mostly stayed out of the public eye, declining to participate in Queen reunions.
- The Red Special: Brian May's iconic guitar, the Red Special, was hand-built by him and his father out of wood from an old fireplace.

- Live Aid Performance: Queen's 1985 Live Aid performance at Wembley Stadium is often ranked as one of the greatest live performances in the history of rock music.
- "Bohemian Rhapsody" Recording: The operatic section of "Bohemian Rhapsody" took over 70 hours to record.
- First Band to Open Stadium Rock: Queen was the first band to play in South American stadiums, breaking world records for concert attendance in the 1981 tour.
- "I Want to Break Free" Video Controversy: The music video for "I Want to Break Free," where the band dressed in drag, was banned by MTV in the United States.
- "We Will Rock You" Musical: The song "We Will Rock You" inspired a musical of the same name, which includes the band's songs.
- Freddie's Unique Microphone Stand: Mercury's signature half-microphone stand was a result of a stage accident where the stand broke, and he decided to keep using it.
- Original Band Members: Before Queen, Brian May and Roger Taylor played in a band called Smile, which Freddie Mercury was a fan of.
- Guinness World Record: Queen holds the Guinness World Record for the longest-running fan club for a rock group.
- "Another One Bites the Dust" Success: "Another One Bites the Dust" is one of the best-selling singles of all time, with sales of over 7 million copies worldwide.
- First Music Video: Queen's first music video was for their song "Bohemian Rhapsody," considered one of the first true music videos.
- Influencing Lady Gaga: The song "Radio Ga Ga" inspired singer Stefani Germanotta to adopt the stage name Lady Gaga.

- Freddie's Teeth: Mercury was self-conscious about his prominent overbite but refused to have dental surgery, fearing it would affect his vocal ability.
- Rock Hall of Fame: Queen was inducted into the Rock and Roll Hall of Fame in 2001.
- "These Are the Days of Our Lives": The last song Mercury recorded with Queen was "These Are the Days of Our Lives." The song's video features a frail Mercury, in his final appearance in a music video.

Questions

1. Which song was inspired by Freddie Mercury's love for his cats?
    - A) "Love of My Life"
    - B) "Delilah"
    - C) "Somebody to Love"

2. Brian May's Red Special guitar was made from:
    - A) An old fireplace mantel
    - B) A piece of driftwood
    - C) An antique table

3. The iconic "Bohemian Rhapsody" music video is considered one of the first true music videos. It was directed by:
    - A) Bruce Gowers
    - B) Freddie Mercury
    - C) Roger Taylor

4. Which Queen song was banned by MTV in the United States due to its music video?
    - A) "I Want to Break Free"
    - B) "Bohemian Rhapsody"
    - C) "Radio Ga Ga"

5. "We Will Rock You" inspired a musical by the same name. Who is credited with writing the musical?
   - A) Ben Elton
   - B) Brian May
   - C) Roger Taylor

6. Queen's performance at Live Aid in 1985 is often ranked as one of the greatest live performances in the history of rock music. Where did this performance take place?
   - A) Madison Square Garden
   - B) Wembley Stadium
   - C) The Forum

Answers

1. Answer: B) "Delilah"
   - Trivia Snapshot: "Delilah" is a tribute to one of Freddie Mercury's favorite cats. He often referred to his cats as his "children" and had a deep affection for them, showcasing his softer side.

2. Answer: A) An old fireplace mantel
   - Trivia Snapshot: Brian May and his father handcrafted the Red Special from wood taken from an old fireplace mantel. This unique origin contributes to the guitar's distinctive sound and is a testament to May's ingenuity.

3. Answer: A) Bruce Gowers
   - Trivia Snapshot: Bruce Gowers directed the music video for "Bohemian Rhapsody," utilizing then-innovative visual effects to create a captivating experience that set a new standard for music videos.

4. Answer: A) "I Want to Break Free"
   - Trivia Snapshot: The music video for "I Want to Break Free," featuring the band members in drag, was controversial at the time and led to its ban by MTV. Despite this.

5. Answer: A) Ben Elton
   - Trivia Snapshot: The musical "We Will Rock You" was written by Ben Elton in collaboration with Queen members Brian May and Roger Taylor. The musical integrates Queen's hits into a dystopian story, celebrating the band's legacy in a theatrical format.

6. Answer: B) Wembley Stadium
   - Trivia Snapshot: Queen's legendary Live Aid performance took place at Wembley Stadium in London 1985. Queen's performance at Wembley Stadium in 1986, a year after Live Aid, was part of their "Magic Tour." The setlist for that concert included a selection of their classic hits, along with some tracks from their then-current album.

One Vision
Tie Your Mother Down
In the Lap of the Gods... Revisited
Seven Seas of Rhye
Tear It Up
A Kind of Magic
Under Pressure
Another One Bites the Dust
Who Wants to Live Forever
I Want to Break Free
Impromptu
Guitar Solo (Brian May)
Now I'm Here
Love of My Life
Is This the World We Created...?
(You're So Square) Baby I Don't Care
Hello Mary Lou (Ricky Nelson cover)
Tutti Frutti (Little Richard cover)
Bohemian Rhapsody
Hammer to Fall
Crazy Little Thing Called Love
Radio Ga Ga
We Will Rock You
Friends Will Be Friends
We Are the Champions
God Save the Queen (Traditional, played over the PA)

Glam Rock and Theatricality

The term "Glam Rock" is derived from "Glamour Rock," emphasizing a style of rock music that incorporated outrageous costumes, flamboyant stage personas, and theatrical performances. It emerged in the early 1970s in the UK.

David Bowie's creation of the Ziggy Stardust persona is a landmark in glam rock. This alter ego, a fictional androgynous rock star from outer space, embodied the genre's blend of music, theater, and visual art. Bowie's album "The Rise and Fall of Ziggy Stardust and the Spiders from Mars" (1972) is a quintessential glam rock work.

Glam rock artists often wore platform shoes, glitter, and outlandish outfits as a form of artistic expression and to challenge traditional gender norms. This fashion trend was influential beyond music, impacting the broader 70s fashion scene.

Glam rock was heavily influenced by theatre and cinema, particularly by the work of artists like Andy Warhol and films like "A Clockwork Orange." These influences brought a sense of drama and narrative to their performances.

Marc Bolan of T. Rex, with his trademark glitter and satin, was one of the pioneers of glam rock. Hits like "Bang a Gong (Get It On)" and "20th Century Boy" exemplify the glam rock sound - catchy, guitar-driven rock with a hint of rebellion.

This American band was integral to the glam rock movement, with their raucous style and androgynous appearance. They were a bridge between early glam rock and the later punk movement.

By the late 1970s, glam rock began to fade, evolving into or being overshadowed by other genres like punk rock, disco, and new wave. However, its influence is seen in the theatrical elements of artists like Lady Gaga and in genres like glam metal.

Glam rock transformed live music performances, making them more visually oriented and theatrical. This shift paved the way for future artists to create more elaborate and spectacle-driven concerts.

Glam rock played a crucial role in challenging and redefining gender norms in rock music, with artists often embracing androgyny and flamboyance, thereby influencing societal perceptions of gender and sexuality.

Elements of glam rock, like theatricality and flamboyant fashion, eventually crossed over into mainstream pop, influencing artists and bands outside the rock genre.

David Bowie
- Songs: "Ziggy Stardust," "Starman," "Rebel Rebel"
- Impact: Bowie's Ziggy Stardust persona redefined the boundaries between music, art, and theater. His music and style had a profound influence on both the glam rock movement and popular culture.

Marc Bolan & T. Rex
- Songs: "Bang a Gong (Get It On)," "20th Century Boy," "Children of the Revolution"
- Impact: Marc Bolan's electric performances and distinctive style set the stage for many glam rock artists. T. Rex's music combined catchy rock with fantasy themes, making them glam rock icons.

Alice Cooper
- Songs: "School's Out," "Billion Dollar Babies," "I'm Eighteen"
- Impact: Known for his theatrical shock-rock shows, Alice Cooper blended horror and glam, influencing both glam and later heavy metal genres.

New York Dolls
- Songs: "Personality Crisis," "Trash," "Jet Boy"
- Impact: The New York Dolls' raw sound and outrageous fashion influenced both the glam and punk scenes, bridging a crucial gap in rock music.

Roxy Music
- Songs: "Virginia Plain," "Love is the Drug," "More Than This"
- Impact: Roxy Music's sophisticated, art-rock style brought a new level of visual and musical experimentation to glam rock.

Slade
- Songs: "Cum On Feel the Noize," "Mama Weer All Crazee Now," "Skweeze Me Pleeze Me"
- Impact: Slade's foot-stomping anthems and outrageous fashion sense made them one of the most successful bands in the UK during the early 70s.

Gary Glitter
- Songs: "Rock and Roll (Part 2)," "I'm the Leader of the Gang (I Am)"
- Impact: Gary Glitter's music, characterized by its stomping beats and shout-along choruses, became anthems of the glam rock era.

Sweet
- Songs: "Ballroom Blitz," "Fox on the Run," "Teenage Rampage"
- Impact: Sweet combined catchy pop hooks with hard rock, creating some of the era's most memorable hits.

Trivia Tidbits

- David Bowie's iconic lightning bolt makeup for Ziggy Stardust was inspired by a rice bowl Elvis Presley wore in a promotional photo for the film "Flaming Star."
- Marc Bolan of T. Rex appeared on BBC's "Top of the Pops" with glitter on his cheekbones, a look that ignited the glam rock fashion trend among British youth.
- Alice Cooper's onstage theatrics once included a live chicken being thrown into the audience, leading to widespread controversy and enhancing his shock rock reputation.
- The New York Dolls' debut album cover featured the band in exaggerated drag, challenging gender norms and shocking the early 1970s rock audience.
- Roxy Music's debut album cover was shot by fashion photographer Karl Stoecker and featured model Kari-Ann Muller, who later said she only received £20 for the shoot.
- Slade's "Cum On Feel the Noize" was covered by Quiet Riot in 1983, whose version became an American heavy metal anthem, despite Slade's glam rock origins.
- Gary Glitter's "Rock and Roll (Part 2)" has become a staple in sports arenas around the world, often played to rally crowds despite his later legal issues.
- Sweet's "Ballroom Blitz" was inspired by an actual incident in 1973 when the band was driven offstage by a barrage of bottles from the audience in Scotland.
- The Ziggy Stardust character was retired by Bowie in a dramatic fashion at the end of a concert in 1973, surprising even his band members who were unaware of his decision.
- Marc Bolan and David Bowie shared a rivalry and friendship, with Bolan appearing on Bowie's TV special "Marc" in 1977, just before Bolan's untimely death.

Fleetwood Mac: A Story of Success and Turmoil

Fleetwood Mac's journey through the annals of rock history is a saga marked by soaring highs, tumultuous lows, and an indelible impact on music and culture. Formed in 1967 by drummer Mick Fleetwood, bassist John McVie, guitarist Peter Green, and later joined by Christine McVie, Stevie Nicks, and Lindsey Buckingham, Fleetwood Mac evolved from a British blues band to rock legends, crafting some of the most enduring songs in the genre.

The early years saw the band navigating the British blues scene with hits like "Black Magic Woman," showcasing Green's haunting guitar work. However, it was the addition of Buckingham and Nicks in 1974 that catapulted Fleetwood Mac into rock superstardom, altering the band's sound and dynamic forever. This lineup change marked the beginning of a new chapter, blending rock, pop, and folk into a unique sound that resonated globally.

The recording of their eleventh studio album, "Rumours" (1977), amid personal turmoil, became a defining moment for Fleetwood Mac. Relationships within the band were fracturing; the McVies were divorcing, Nicks and Buckingham's tumultuous relationship was coming to an end, and Fleetwood was going through his own marital issues. Yet, it was this very turmoil that fueled the album's emotional depth, leading to its monumental success. "Rumours" not only captured the tumult of the time but also became one of the best-selling albums of all time.

> *"And if you don't love me now*
> *You will never love me again"*

Despite their success, the band's journey was far from smooth. The subsequent years were marked by lineup changes, personal struggles, and shifts in musical direction. Yet, Fleetwood Mac's resilience and ability to evolve musically ensured their place in rock history. Albums like "Tusk" (1979) and "Mirage" (1982) continued to showcase the band's musical diversity and willingness to experiment, even as they navigated the challenges of fame and personal conflict.

The band's influence extends beyond their music; they have become symbols of the power of transformation, the beauty that can emerge from pain, and the enduring nature of creativity and collaboration. Fleetwood Mac's story is not just one of success and turmoil but a reminder of the transcendent power of music to reflect, heal, and connect us.

Biggest Songs:

"Go Your Own Way" (1977): Written by Lindsey Buckingham, this anthem of separation was a direct reflection of his tumultuous relationship with Stevie Nicks. Its candid lyrics and catchy melody made it a standout track on "Rumours."

"Dreams" (1977): Penned by Stevie Nicks, "Dreams" was inspired by her breakup with Buckingham. Its ethereal tone and hopeful message of moving on became Fleetwood Mac's only number-one hit in the US.

"The Chain" (1977): Known for its distinctive bass line and group vocals, "The Chain" is the only song credited to all five members of the classic lineup. It symbolizes the band's unity despite personal conflicts.

"Rhiannon" (1975): This Stevie Nicks-written song introduced the world to her mystical songwriting. Inspired by a novel, it showcases Nicks' fascination with Welsh mythology and became a signature Fleetwood Mac song.

"Landslide" (1975): Another Nicks classic, "Landslide" reflects on personal change and vulnerability. Its introspective lyrics and simple melody have made it a beloved ballad.

"Tusk" (1979): The title track from their experimental album, "Tusk" features the USC Trojan Marching Band. Its unconventional sound demonstrated the band's willingness to push musical boundaries.

"Gypsy" (1982): Written by Stevie Nicks, "Gypsy" is a nostalgic look back at her pre-Fleetwood Mac days and her relationship with Buckingham. Its evocative lyrics and melody capture a sense of longing and reflection.

"Sara" (1979): Another Stevie Nicks composition, "Sara" is a complex song rumored to be about her relationship with Don Henley and the child they never had. Its flowing melody and cryptic lyrics have intrigued fans for decades.

"Don't Stop" (1977): Written by Christine McVie, "Don't Stop" is an optimistic anthem about looking forward to the future. Its upbeat message and melody resonated with listeners, making it one of the band's most popular songs.

"Silver Springs" (1977): Originally a B-side to "Go Your Own Way," this Stevie Nicks song was about her relationship with Buckingham. Its emotional depth and Nicks' powerful performance have made it a fan favorite, later gaining recognition as a key Fleetwood Mac track.

- Mick Fleetwood, the band's namesake, was born in Cornwall, England, and is the only member to have been in the band continuously since its formation in 1967.
- The band was named after Mick Fleetwood and John McVie, combining their last names; initially, without McVie's participation, he joined shortly after its formation.
- Fleetwood Mac's first album was a blues record, purely reflecting their roots, before they transitioned to a more pop/rock sound.

- "Rumours" has sold over 40 million copies worldwide, making it one of the best-selling albums of all time.
- Stevie Nicks was the first woman to be inducted into the Rock and Roll Hall of Fame twice: once with Fleetwood Mac and once as a solo artist.
- The iconic cover of the "Rumours" album features Mick Fleetwood and Stevie Nicks, with Fleetwood holding a pair of balls hanging from his belt, symbolizing a sense of humor amidst the band's turmoil.
- "Go Your Own Way," a hit from "Rumours," was one of the first songs recorded for the album and set the tone for its emotional intensity.
- Fleetwood Mac has had 18 different members over its history, showcasing a revolving door of talent and change.
- The band's song "The Chain" is unique for its use in Formula 1 broadcasting; it's been the theme song for the BBC and Sky Sports coverage of F1 races.
- Before joining Fleetwood Mac, Stevie Nicks and Lindsey Buckingham were in a band called Buckingham Nicks; their album flopped, leading to financial struggles before their Fleetwood Mac fame.
- Christine McVie wrote "Songbird," one of the band's most beloved tracks, in just half an hour after waking up in the middle of the night with the melody in her head.
- The band members often recorded their vocals separately for "Rumours" due to the tension between them, coming together only to mix the tracks.
- Mick Fleetwood filed for bankruptcy in 1984, despite the band's massive success, due to poor financial management and investments.
- The penguin is a recurring theme for Fleetwood Mac, with Mick Fleetwood's fondness for the bird leading to its appearance on album artwork and the name of their record label, Penguin Records.

- Fleetwood Mac was originally formed after the disbandment of John Mayall & the Bluesbreakers, which included both John McVie and Mick Fleetwood.
- "Silver Springs" was intended for the "Rumours" album but was cut due to space limitations; it later became a revered track, especially after its inclusion in the 1997 live album "The Dance."
- Lindsey Buckingham's unique fingerpicking guitar style was self-taught and became a defining characteristic of Fleetwood Mac's sound.
- The band's tumultuous relationships and personal dynamics were often reflected in their lyrics, with songs serving as messages between members.
- Fleetwood Mac's "Tusk" album was one of the most expensive rock albums ever produced at the time of its release in 1979.
- Despite their British origins, Fleetwood Mac found its greatest success and artistic identity after reshaping itself into a more American-sounding band with the addition of Buckingham and Nicks.

- "Guardians of the Galaxy Vol. 2" (2017): Fleetwood Mac's "The Chain" is prominently featured in this Marvel superhero film, underscoring a climactic battle scene and adding a powerful and nostalgic touch to the moment.
- "Jerry Maguire" (1996): The film's soundtrack includes Fleetwood Mac's classic hit "Don't Stop," which perfectly captures the uplifting and optimistic tone of the movie's resolution.
- "Forrest Gump" (1994): "Go Your Own Way" by Fleetwood Mac is featured in this iconic film, adding to the rich tapestry of music that accompanies Forrest Gump's journey through decades of American history.

Songs of the Decade (1970s)

The 1970s was a diverse and transformative decade in music, marked by the rise of rock, disco, and the continuation of soul and funk. Here are ten songs that not only define the era but have also left a lasting impact on music and culture

"Stairway to Heaven" by Led Zeppelin (1971) - Often considered one of the greatest rock songs of all time, "Stairway to Heaven" showcases Led Zeppelin's range from folk to hard rock.

"Bohemian Rhapsody" by Queen (1975) - A groundbreaking track that defies genre classification, combining rock, ballad, opera, and hard rock elements, and showcasing Queen's musical versatility and Freddie Mercury's vocal range.

"Hotel California" by The Eagles (1976) - Known for its distinctive guitar riff and mysterious lyrics, "Hotel California" is a classic rock staple that tells a story of excess and illusion.

"What's Going On" by Marvin Gaye (1971) - A poignant reflection on the social issues of the time, including the Vietnam War, this soulful track marked a significant moment in Motown and popular music.

"Imagine" by John Lennon (1971) - A timeless anthem for peace and unity, "Imagine" showcases Lennon's songwriting prowess and his vision for a world without division.

"Superstition" by Stevie Wonder (1972) - With its funky clavinet riff and socially conscious lyrics, "Superstition" is one of Stevie Wonder's most popular and influential songs.

"Stayin' Alive" by Bee Gees (1977) - A disco anthem that became synonymous with the genre, "Stayin' Alive" features the Bee Gees' signature falsetto and a groove that's impossible to resist.

"Born to Run" by Bruce Springsteen (1975) - An epic tale of escape and aspiration, "Born to Run" captures the essence of Springsteen's storytelling and the dreams of a generation.

"Wish You Were Here" by Pink Floyd (1975) - A poignant reflection on absence and the music industry, this title track is celebrated for its emotional depth and instrumental brilliance.

Let's Get It On" by Marvin Gaye (1973) - A sensual soul classic, "Let's Get It On" broke new ground for its overtly sexual themes and remains one of Gaye's most iconic tracks.

"Marvin Gaye was a groundbreaking artist whose music transcended genres and generations. Born Marvin Pentz Gay Jr. on April 2, 1939, in Washington, D.C., he developed a passion for music at an early age, honing his skills as a singer and performer. Signed to Motown Records in the 1960s, Gaye initially found success as a session drummer before emerging as a solo artist. His smooth and soulful voice, coupled with his introspective lyrics and innovative musical arrangements, set him apart in the R&B and pop music landscape.

Gaye's career reached new heights with timeless hits like "I Heard It Through the Grapevine," "What's Going On," and "Sexual Healing." However, his personal life was marked by turmoil, including a turbulent relationship with his father and struggles with addiction. Tragically, Marvin Gaye's life was cut short when he was shot and killed by his father on April 1, 1984, just one day before his 45th birthday. Despite his untimely death, Gaye's music continues to resonate with audiences worldwide, leaving an indelible mark on the music industry and cementing his legacy as one of the greatest soul singers of all time.

1980s

Step into the 1980s, an electrifying era where MTV reshaped the music scene, visuals became as crucial as sound, and stars like Michael Jackson ascended to new heights. This decade witnessed the global unity of Live Aid, the raw power of Heavy Metal, and the revolutionary beats of Hip-Hop and Rap. Synth-Pop introduced futuristic sounds, while icons like Madonna and Bruce Springsteen told stories that echoed across the globe. Through it all, "We Didn't Start the Fire" captured the spirit of the times, making the 80s a period of unmatched musical diversity and innovation. Join us as we delve into the decade that forever altered the landscape of music.

The 1980s, as a whole, was a decade of contrasts and contradictions, where the glitz and glamour of pop culture collided with the gritty realities of social and political unrest. It was an era of excess and ambition, fueled by economic prosperity and technological advancement, yet marred by social inequalities and geopolitical tensions.

Music served as both a reflection of and escape from the complexities of the time. From the infectious melodies of New Wave to the rebellious anthems of Punk, each genre offered a unique lens through which to view the world. The decade saw the rise of iconic artists like Prince, Whitney Houston, and U2, whose music transcended boundaries and defined the sound of a generation.

Yet, amid the neon lights and synthesizer sounds, there were darker undercurrents at play. The AIDS crisis, the Cold War, and economic downturns cast a shadow over the decade, reminding us that progress often comes with its own set of challenges. And yet, in the face of adversity, music provided solace and solidarity, bringing people together in shared experiences of joy, sorrow, and resilience.

MTV and the Music Video Era

The advent of MTV in the early 1980s revolutionized the music industry and transformed the way music was consumed and appreciated worldwide. Launched on August 1, 1981, with the prophetic words "Ladies and gentlemen, rock and roll," MTV heralded the beginning of the music video era, turning the channel into a cultural phenomenon that would leave an indelible mark on pop culture.

Before MTV, music was primarily experienced through audio mediums like radio and vinyl records, with visuals limited to album covers, concert performances, and occasional TV appearances. MTV changed all that by offering a platform where music and visuals were intertwined, allowing artists to express their music through the innovative medium of music videos. This fusion of sound and image not only enhanced the musical experience but also broadened the artists' creative horizons, enabling them to tell stories, convey messages, and create iconic images that would define their careers.

The impact of MTV on the music industry was profound. It transformed unknown artists into international stars overnight and became a crucial marketing tool for the industry. The channel's influence was such that the visuals of a music video could catapult a song to the top of the charts, with the visual appeal sometimes overshadowing the music itself. Artists like Madonna, Michael Jackson, and Duran Duran became synonymous with the MTV generation, using the platform to launch their careers to unprecedented heights. Michael Jackson's "Thriller," with its groundbreaking narrative and special effects, exemplified the potential of music videos as an art form, proving that they could be as compelling and influential as the music itself.

MTV also played a pivotal role in the promotion of genres like rap and hip-hop to mainstream audiences, with shows like "Yo! MTV Raps" breaking cultural and racial barriers, showcasing the rich diversity of musical talent across the United States and beyond. The channel's influence extended beyond music, influencing fashion, language, and lifestyle, becoming a voice for the youth of the 1980s and 1990s.

However, MTV's rise was not without its controversies. Accusations of gender and racial bias in its early years prompted criticism, pushing the channel to diversify its playlist and embrace a wider array of musical genres and artists. The advent of reality TV in the late 1990s and early 2000s marked a shift in MTV's programming, moving away from its music video roots to become a broader entertainment channel.

Despite these changes, MTV's legacy as the pioneer of the music video era remains undisputed. It transformed the music landscape, ushering in a new era where visuals were as integral to an artist's success as the music itself. The channel's influence can still be felt today, in the era of digital streaming and social media, where music videos continue to play a vital role in how music is marketed and consumed.

Trivia Tidbits

- MTV's first music video was "Video Killed the Radio Star" by The Buggles, symbolizing the dawn of the music video age.
- The channel initially struggled to get cable providers to carry MTV, leading to the famous "I want my MTV" marketing campaign, featuring stars like Mick Jagger and David Bowie.
- Michael Jackson's "Thriller" was the first music video to resemble a short film, changing the expectations for production value in music videos.

- Madonna's "Like a Virgin" performance at the first MTV Video Music Awards in 1984 became one of the most iconic performances in the history of the channel.
- MTV was criticized in its early years for featuring few artists of color. The inclusion of Michael Jackson's "Billie Jean" broke this barrier and opened doors for a more diverse range of artists.
- "Yo! MTV Raps" premiered in 1988, significantly contributing to the mainstream acceptance of hip-hop.
- MTV launched several successful shows that had little to do with music videos, including "The Real World" and "Jersey Shore," marking a shift towards reality and scripted programming.
- The channel introduced the MTV Unplugged series in 1989, offering artists a platform to perform acoustic versions of their hits, influencing the music scene of the early '90s.
- MTV's Video Music Awards (VMAs) became a cultural phenomenon, known for memorable performances, controversies, and moments that often overshadowed the awards themselves.
- In response to declining viewership of music videos due to the internet, MTV2 was launched in 1996 to cater to music video fans, though it too eventually broadened its content.

Modern Day MTV

Today, MTV continues to be a prominent force in the music and entertainment industry, although its focus has shifted over the years. While still featuring music videos, MTV has expanded its programming to include reality shows, scripted dramas, and documentaries, catering to a diverse audience. The network remains a platform for emerging artists to showcase their work and connect with fans, while also providing a space for important social and cultural discussions.

Michael Jackson: The King of Pop

Michael Jackson, often hailed as the King of Pop, stands as one of the most significant cultural figures of the 20th century. His career, spanning over four decades, was a blend of record-breaking achievements, groundbreaking musical innovation, and unprecedented global influence. Born on August 29, 1958, in Gary, Indiana, Jackson's musical journey began at a tender age, showcasing his prodigious talents in the family band, the Jackson 5, before soaring to unprecedented heights as a solo artist.

Jackson's impact on music, dance, and fashion, coupled with his publicized personal life, made him a global figure in popular culture. His 1982 album "Thriller" remains the best-selling album of all time, with estimated sales of over 66 million copies worldwide. It was a masterpiece that broke racial barriers on MTV, transforming the music video from a promotional tool into an art form, and making Jackson a pivotal figure in the music video revolution.

Jackson's music career was marked by his innovative approach to music, video, and live performances. He was a pioneer in using music videos as an integral part of promoting his music, with his videos for "Billie Jean," "Beat It," and especially "Thriller" becoming iconic. "Thriller," a 14-minute horror-themed music video, was a cultural phenomenon that merged filmmaking and music, showcasing Jackson's flair for storytelling and his unparalleled dance abilities.

His contributions to music were not just limited to his records and performances. Jackson pushed the boundaries of the pop genre, integrating rock, funk, soul, and disco into his songs, creating a unique sound that appealed to a wide audience.

His vocal style, characterized by his distinctive voice, emotive delivery, and innovative use of the vocal hiccup, became his signature.

Jackson's influence extended beyond music to his pioneering dance moves. His moonwalk, first performed during the "Motown 25: Yesterday, Today, Forever" television special in 1983, became a global dance phenomenon, imitated by millions. His dance style, a mix of complex footwork, body isolations, and effortless fluidity, changed the landscape of dance within popular music, influencing artists across various genres.

Despite his unparalleled success, Jackson's life was not without controversy. His appearance, personal life, and legal troubles were a constant source of media speculation and public debate. Nevertheless, his humanitarian efforts, including his philanthropy and advocacy for children's rights and against racism, painted a picture of a complex individual committed to making a positive impact on the world.

Jackson's legacy is a testament to his profound impact on music and culture. He broke numerous records, including most Grammy Awards won in a single year (eight in 1984) and was inducted into the Rock and Roll Hall of Fame twice. His influence on subsequent artists across diverse music genres is immeasurable, with many citing him as a major inspiration for their own careers.

Michael Jackson's death on June 25, 2009, sent shockwaves around the world, marking the end of an era. However, his music, dance, and influence continue to resonate with millions, cementing his status as the King of Pop. Through his artistic innovations and humanitarian efforts, Jackson's legacy endures, immortalizing him as a pivotal figure in the history of music and popular culture.

Trivia Tidbits on Michael Jackson:

- Jackson won 8 Grammy Awards in 1984, the most anyone had won in a single year at the time.
- He was known for his philanthropy, donating millions of dollars to various charities throughout his life.
- Jackson's 1993 Super Bowl halftime performance is one of the most watched in the event's history.
- The "Moonwalk" dance move was not invented by Jackson, but he popularized it globally.
- He purchased the rights to the Beatles' song catalog in 1985, a move that was controversial at the time.
- Jackson's "Thriller" jacket became a fashion icon and has been replicated countless times.
- He had two ceremonies inducted into the Rock and Roll Hall of Fame: once with the Jackson 5 and once as a solo artist.
- The music video for "Scream," a duet with his sister Janet, is one of the most expensive ever made.
- Jackson's album "Bad" produced five consecutive number one singles, a record at the time.
- He was awarded the Presidential Medal of Freedom posthumously in 2021.
- "Thriller" was the first music album to use music videos as successful promotional tools.
- Jackson's influence extended beyond music to break racial barriers on MTV with his videos.
- He was known for his extensive humanitarian work, including his "Heal the World" Foundation.
- Jackson's 1987 album "Bad" was the first album to have five number one singles on the Billboard Hot 100.
- His signature single, "Billie Jean," was the first video by a black artist to be played in heavy rotation on MTV.
- Jackson's estate has continued to release music and documentaries posthumously.

- He was deeply interested in film and made several attempts to star in movies throughout his career.
- Jackson's Neverland Ranch was famous for its amusement park rides and petting zoo, reflecting his love for childhood innocence.
- He was awarded 13 Grammy Awards from a total of 39 nominations over his career.
- Jackson's influence is evident in the work of countless artists across genres, from pop and R&B to hip hop and beyond.

Exploring some of Michael Jackson's biggest hits reveals the depth and diversity of his musical legacy. Each song not only showcases his exceptional talent but also the innovative approach he brought to music and performance.

"Billie Jean"
- Release: 1983
- Album: Thriller
- The song's distinct bassline was inspired by Jackson's desire to mix complexity with compelling simplicity, becoming one of the most recognizable in music history.
- "Billie Jean" was one of the first videos by a black artist to receive heavy rotation on MTV, breaking down racial barriers in the music industry.

"Thriller"
- Release: 1982
- Album: Thriller
- The "Thriller" music video set a new standard for music video production, featuring a movie-like approach and elaborate dance sequences directed by John Landis.
- The iconic red jacket worn by Jackson influenced fashion trends and has been widely replicated.

"Beat It"
- Release: 1983
- Album: Thriller
- Eddie Van Halen provided the guitar solo for "Beat It" for free, blending rock and pop in a groundbreaking way.
- The video featured real gang members alongside professional dancers, promoting a message of unity and reconciliation.

"Smooth Criminal"
- Release: 1987
- Album: Bad
- The anti-gravity lean was achieved using specially designed shoes that locked into the stage, showing Jackson's innovative spirit.
- "Smooth Criminal" was part of the "Moonwalker" film, showcasing Jackson's interest in blending music with storytelling and cinema.

"Man in the Mirror"
- Release: 1988
- Album: Bad
- Reflects Jackson's humanitarian efforts with its message of self-improvement and making a change in the world.
- Nominated for Record of the Year at the Grammy Awards and has been covered by numerous artists.

"Black or White"
- Release: 1991
- Album: Dangerous
- Famous for its use of morphing technology to promote a message of global unity and racial harmony.
- Became one of the fastest songs to reach number one on the Billboard Hot 100 chart at the time.

"Human Nature"
- The song showcases Jackson's softer, more introspective side, differing from the more upbeat tracks on the "Thriller" album.
- It was a last-minute addition to the album, replacing another song called "Carousel."

"Dirty Diana"
- The track features hard rock elements and was a departure from Jackson's usual pop and R&B style, showcasing his versatility as an artist.
- Steve Stevens, known for his work with Billy Idol, played the distinctive guitar solo on the track.

"Remember the Time"
- Set in ancient Egypt, the music video for "Remember the Time" featured groundbreaking visual effects and appearances by Eddie Murphy, Iman, and Magic Johnson.
- The song's production, led by Teddy Riley, was a testament to Jackson's ability to blend contemporary R&B with his unique pop sensibility.

"Heal the World"
- The song emphasized Michael Jackson's humanitarian concerns, aiming to spread a message of peace and care for the planet.
- Jackson founded the Heal the World Foundation in 1992, demonstrating his commitment to improving the lives of children worldwide.

"They Don't Care About Us"
- The music video was filmed in Brazil and directed by Spike Lee, highlighting social issues and injustices.
- The song faced controversy due to its lyrics, which led Jackson to issue an apology and re-record certain lines to address concerns of antisemitism.

Michael Jackson's discography is filled with songs that broke barriers, set records, and left an indelible mark on the music industry and popular culture. His innovative use of technology in music videos, messages of peace and unity, and groundbreaking achievements in music and dance continue to inspire artists and fans worldwide.

Lyric Based Multiple-Choice Questions on Michael Jackson

1. "The way she came into the place I knew right then and there" is from which Michael Jackson song?
   - A) "Dirty Diana"
   - B) "Billie Jean"
   - C) "Smooth Criminal"

2. "She was more like a beauty queen from a movie scene" refers to which song?
   - A) "Remember the Time"
   - B) "Billie Jean"
   - C) "Thriller"

3. "But if you're thinkin' about my baby, it don't matter if you're black or white" is from which song?
   - A) "Black or White"
   - B) "Heal the World"
   - C) "Man in the Mirror"

4. "Every day create your history" is a lyric from which Michael Jackson song?
   - A) "History"
   - B) "You Are Not Alone"
   - C) "Earth Song"

5. "You knock me off of my feet now baby" is from which song?
   - A) "The Way You Make Me Feel"
   - B) "Rock with You"
   - C) "Bad"

Answers

1. Answer: C) "Smooth Criminal"
   - Trivia Snapshot: The song "Smooth Criminal" is notable for its music video, which features Michael Jackson performing the anti-gravity lean. This move was achieved using special shoes that locked into the stage floor, a patented design that Jackson co-invented.

2. Answer: B) "Billie Jean"
   - Trivia Snapshot: "Billie Jean" was a groundbreaking track for its time, both musically and visually. Its music video was among the first by a black artist to be played in heavy rotation on MTV, helping to break down racial barriers in the music industry.

3. Answer: A) "Black or White"
   - Trivia Snapshot: "Black or White" was celebrated for its use of morphing technology in its music video, which was cutting-edge at the time. The video featured faces of various ethnicities blending into one another, emphasizing the song's message of racial harmony.

4. Answer: A) "History"
   - Trivia Snapshot: "HIStory" is from Michael Jackson's ninth studio album, "HIStory: Past, Present and Future, Book I." The song, like much of the album, touches on the themes of reflection, status, and the scrutiny Jackson felt from the media and public.

5. Answer: A) "The Way You Make Me Feel"
   - Trivia Snapshot: "The Way You Make Me Feel" is known for its upbeat rhythm and was a departure from the more serious tones of some of Jackson's other work. Its music video features a lengthy street chase scene, showcasing Jackson's signature dance moves and storytelling through dance.

Live Aid

Live Aid was a groundbreaking dual-venue benefit concert held on July 13, 1985, organized by Bob Geldof and Midge Ure to raise funds for the relief of the ongoing Ethiopian famine.

Spanning across Wembley Stadium in London and John F. Kennedy Stadium in Philadelphia, it was one of the largest-scale satellite link-ups and television broadcasts of all time, with an estimated global audience of 1.9 billion across 150 nations, nearly 40% of the world population.

The event was conceived in the wake of the success of the charity single "Do They Know It's Christmas?" released by Band Aid in 1984. Geldof, moved by the harrowing BBC news reports of the famine, was determined to raise more awareness and funds. Live Aid transformed that ambition into a 16-hour music marathon, featuring performances by some of the biggest names in music. The event showcased the power of music to unite people worldwide for a common cause, setting a precedent for future charity events in the music industry.

The planning of Live Aid was a monumental task, involving coordination between musicians, event planners, and broadcasters on an unprecedented scale. Despite the logistical challenges, the enthusiasm and goodwill of everyone involved ensured its success. The concert's line-up read like a who's who of rock and pop royalty from that era, including Queen, U2, Led Zeppelin (in their first live performance since the death of their drummer John Bonham), Madonna, David Bowie, Bob Dylan, and Paul McCartney, among others.

Financially, Live Aid was a triumph, raising over £150 million (approximately $245 million) for famine relief in Ethiopia. Beyond the monetary impact, it raised awareness about the plight of those affected by the famine and highlighted the potential for global events to foster solidarity and prompt action on humanitarian issues.

Lineup Highlights

London, Wembley Stadium

- Queen: Delivered what is often heralded as one of the greatest live performances ever. Their set included hits like "Bohemian Rhapsody," "Radio Ga Ga," and "We Are the Champions," captivating the audience and setting a gold standard for live performances.

- David Bowie: One of the day's most anticipated acts, Bowie's set was powerful and emotive, including memorable performances of "Heroes" and a poignant video introduction highlighting the famine in Africa.

- U2: Solidified their place as rock superstars with a performance that extended beyond their allocated time, particularly during an emotional rendition of "Bad." Bono's interaction with the audience became a defining moment of their career.

- Elton John: Brought his characteristic flair and a string of hits to the stage, performing songs like "Rocket Man" and "Don't Go Breaking My Heart" with Kiki Dee, showcasing his dynamic showmanship and musical talent.

- Wham!: Featuring George Michael and Andrew Ridgeley, gave one of their final performances together, including the energetic "Wake Me Up Before You Go-Go" and "Everything She Wants," capturing the essence of 80s pop.

- The Who: Despite technical difficulties that temporarily disrupted the satellite broadcast, delivered a thrilling set that reaffirmed their status as rock icons, including "Won't Get Fooled Again."

Philadelphia, John F. Kennedy Stadium

- Madonna: At the peak of her early fame, Madonna's performance was energetic and defiant, featuring hits like "Holiday" and "Into the Groove," and marked by her statement, "I ain't taking off shit," in defiance of media speculation.
- Bob Dylan: Joined by Keith Richards and Ronnie Wood for an acoustic set that included "Blowin' in the Wind," his performance was symbolic, albeit marred by sound issues, reminding the audience of the day's philanthropic purpose.
- Mick Jagger and Tina Turner: Collaborated for a high-energy duet that was one of the day's most electrifying moments, including a memorable performance of "It's Only Rock 'n Roll (But I Like It)."
- Hall & Oates: Teamed up with Eddie Kendricks and David Ruffin of The Temptations for a set that bridged the gap between 70s soul and 80s pop, highlighting their smooth harmonies and catchy tunes.

5 Biggest Moments from Live Aid

Often cited as one of the greatest live performances in the history of rock music, Queen's 20-minute set at Wembley Stadium was a masterclass in live performance, showcasing Freddie Mercury's extraordinary stage presence and the band's musical prowess.

The band's first live performance since 1980, albeit with Phil Collins and Tony Thompson on drums, was a highly anticipated and memorable moment, despite the band members' later criticisms of their performance.

U2's performance, particularly an extended rendition of "Bad," is often credited with elevating the band's status to global superstars. Bono's impromptu decision to dance with a fan from the audience highlighted the band's connection with their fans.

Phil Collins performed at both Wembley and JFK stadiums, flying on the Concorde to make it possible. His appearance at both venues symbolized the global nature of the event.

The finale saw artists in London and Philadelphia join together to sing "Do They Know It's Christmas?" and "We Are the World," highlighting the event's message of global unity and cooperation.

Bob Geldof

Bob Geldof, the Irish singer, songwriter, and philanthropist, was the driving force behind the monumental Live Aid concerts in 1985. Motivated by a deep sense of urgency and compassion, Geldof's journey to organizing one of the most iconic charity events in music history began after he watched a BBC news report on the devastating famine in Ethiopia. The harrowing images of suffering and the sheer scale of the humanitarian crisis struck a chord with Geldof, compelling him to use his influence and resources to make a difference.

Geldof, then lead singer of the Boomtown Rats, first responded by rallying fellow musicians to record the charity single "Do They Know It's Christmas?" under the banner of Band Aid in 1984. The record's success, both critically and financially, was a testament to the potential of music to mobilize people for a cause. However, Geldof realized that more could be done to alleviate the suffering in Ethiopia. This realization led to the conception of Live Aid, a dual-venue concert that would leverage global satellite technology to connect audiences around the world in a shared experience of music and philanthropy.

The ambition behind Live Aid was unprecedented. It wasn't just about raising funds; it was about raising awareness and uniting people across continents in a common cause. Geldof's tenacity and persuasive abilities were crucial in bringing together a lineup of stars that spanned genres and generations. He was known for his relentless pursuit of artists, famously convincing many to join the cause with his impassioned pleas.

Live Aid's success set a new benchmark for charity events, proving that music had the power to bridge divides and bring tangible change to the world's most pressing issues. The event raised over £150 million for famine relief, a figure that far exceeded initial expectations and contributed significantly to relief efforts in Ethiopia.

Beyond the financial impact, Live Aid altered the public's perception of celebrities and their potential to influence global humanitarian efforts. It inspired a wave of charity events in the following years, cementing music's role as a powerful tool for social change. Geldof's knighthood in 1986, while he is not entitled to be known as "Sir Bob Geldof" as he is not a citizen of a Commonwealth realm, and his continued activism, including the organization of Live 8 in 2005, are testaments to his enduring commitment to leveraging music for the greater good.

Bob Geldof's legacy, shaped significantly by Live Aid, is a powerful reminder of how passion, creativity, and determination can come together to make a difference in the world. His efforts have not only provided aid to those in dire need but have also inspired countless individuals to take action in their communities, demonstrating the enduring impact of compassion and collective action.

Heavy Metal Mania

The 1980s heralded a seismic shift in the music landscape, with heavy metal bursting into the mainstream, riding a wave of louder, faster, and more aggressive tunes that captured the imagination of a generation. This era was characterized by its defiance of the status quo, featuring anthemic guitar solos, thunderous drumming, and vocalists who could soar with power and grit. The heavy metal mania of the 1980s wasn't just a musical movement; it was a cultural phenomenon that embodied the spirit of rebellion, individualism, and a quest for identity amidst the backdrop of cold war tensions and economic upheaval.

At the heart of this movement was the New Wave of British Heavy Metal (NWOBHM), which emerged in the late 1970s and early 1980s. Bands like Iron Maiden, Judas Priest, and Motorhead redefined the genre with their speed, technical skill, and thematic complexity, combining the hard rock of the 1970s with punk's energy and ethos. This fusion created a sound that was both accessible and decidedly heavy, laying the groundwork for the metal genres that would follow.

Across the Atlantic, American bands took note and contributed their unique flavors to the metal cauldron. Metallica, Slayer, Megadeth, and Anthrax, collectively known as the "Big Four," pushed the boundaries further with thrash metal, a subgenre marked by its fast tempos, intricate guitar work, and politically charged lyrics. These bands, with their relentless touring and groundbreaking albums, played a crucial role in heavy metal's international proliferation.

The 1980s metal scene was also notable for its visual aesthetics, with bands donning leather, chains, and elaborate stage outfits that complemented their larger-than-life personas. Music videos became a vital tool for promotion, with MTV serving as a critical platform for bands to reach a global audience. The theatricality of bands like Kiss and the shock rock tactics of Alice Cooper set the stage for acts like Mötley Crüe and Twisted Sister, who embraced glam metal's flashy and androgynous appeal, blending catchy hooks with an edgy image.

However, heavy metal was not without its controversies. The genre often found itself at the center of moral panics, with critics linking it to various social ills, from delinquency to satanism. Despite, or perhaps because of, these controversies, heavy metal's appeal only grew, with bands harnessing the media backlash to bolster their outsider status and deepen their connection with fans.

The legacy of the 1980s heavy metal era is its lasting impact on music and culture. It was a time of innovation and experimentation, where metal diversified into a myriad of subgenres, from the melodic power metal to the extreme death and black metal. Bands like Guns N' Roses and Metallica became household names, headlining arenas and selling millions of albums worldwide.

As the decade closed, heavy metal had firmly established itself as a dominant force in music, its influence permeating beyond the genre into mainstream pop culture. The 1980s may have been the golden age of heavy metal, but the foundations laid during this period ensured that metal's spirit of defiance and its quest for intensity would endure, inspiring new generations of musicians and fans alike.

Biggest Artists

Metallica: With their fast tempos, intricate guitar work, and aggressive energy, Metallica became one of the leading forces of the thrash metal movement.

Iron Maiden: Known for their epic narratives and complex compositions, Iron Maiden became synonymous with the NWOBHM, influencing countless bands.

Judas Priest: Pioneers of the metal genre, Judas Priest defined the sound and aesthetic of heavy metal with dual guitar leads and Rob Halford's powerful vocals.

Slayer: Slayer's fast, aggressive style contributed significantly to the development of thrash metal and its darker subgenres.

Megadeth: Founded by ex-Metallica guitarist Dave Mustaine, Megadeth was known for its technical prowess and politically charged lyrics.

Anthrax: Part of the "Big Four" of thrash, Anthrax stood out for incorporating elements of punk and rap into their music.

Mötley Crüe: Emblematic of the glam metal scene, Mötley Crüe's hedonistic lifestyle and catchy tunes epitomized the excesses of 80s metal.

Guns N' Roses: Blending hard rock with a punk ethos, Guns N' Roses became one of the last decade's most successful and influential bands.

Ozzy Osbourne: After parting ways with Black Sabbath, Ozzy's solo career took off in the 80s, establishing him as a metal icon.

Def Leppard: With their polished sound and massive hooks, Def Leppard brought metal to the pop charts, blending hard rock with a pop sensibility.

Biggest Songs

Metallica - "Master of Puppets" (1986): This song is a critical examination of addiction and control, metaphorically portraying how substances can become the master of one's life, featuring complex arrangements and aggressive musicianship that became a hallmark of thrash metal.

Iron Maiden - "The Number of the Beast" (1982): Inspired by a nightmare of the band's bassist, this track delves into themes of apocalypse and the occult, with its narrative lyricism and powerful melodies, it became an anthem in the heavy metal genre.

Judas Priest - "Breaking the Law" (1980): With its iconic opening riff and anthemic chorus, this song speaks to the frustration and desperation felt by the youth of the era, becoming a symbol of rebellion against societal constraints.

Slayer - "Angel of Death" (1986): Tackling the atrocities committed by Nazi physician Josef Mengele at Auschwitz, this song's relentless speed and graphic lyrics sparked controversy while solidifying Slayer's place in the thrash metal pantheon.

Megadeth - "Peace Sells" (1986): This track critiques societal hypocrisy and political disillusionment, underpinned by intricate guitar work and sharp lyrics, becoming an anthem for the politically disenfranchised and showcasing Megadeth's technical prowess.

Anthrax - "Indians" (1987): Combining thrash metal's aggression with a message about the mistreatment of Native Americans, this song is noted for its socially conscious lyrics and energetic riffs, reflecting Anthrax's willingness to tackle serious issues.

Mötley Crüe - "Girls, Girls, Girls" (1987): Celebrating the band's love for motorcycles, strip clubs, and the hedonistic lifestyle, this song epitomizes glam metal's excess and party atmosphere, with catchy hooks and a memorable music video.

Guns N' Roses - "Sweet Child o' Mine" (1987): A serendipitous love ballad that became one of the band's biggest hits, featuring iconic guitar work and heartfelt lyrics that showcased a softer side to the hard rock scene of the 1980s.

Ozzy Osbourne - "Crazy Train" (1980): This song, dealing with the Cold War fears and the possibility of annihilation, is highlighted by Randy Rhoads' revolutionary guitar playing, combining catchy melodies with a message of peace and stability.

Def Leppard - "Pour Some Sugar on Me" (1987): With its blend of hard rock and pop elements, this track became a defining song of the era, known for its anthemic chorus and polished production, embodying the band's crossover appeal between heavy metal and mainstream audiences.

Trivia Tidbits

- Metallica's "Kill 'Em All" was originally titled "Metal Up Your Ass," but was changed due to label pressure.
- Iron Maiden's mascot, Eddie, has appeared on almost all of their album covers, evolving visually with each release.
- Judas Priest is credited with introducing the leather and studs look that became synonymous with the metal genre.
- Slayer's "Reign in Blood" album was financed by Rick Rubin, a well-known hip-hop producer, marking an unusual crossover of production talent.
- Megadeth's Dave Mustaine was famously kicked out of Metallica for substance abuse and personal conflicts, leading to a longstanding rivalry.

- Anthrax is named after a bacterial disease; the band members thought it sounded sufficiently 'metal' without fully understanding its implications.
- Mötley Crüe's Nikki Sixx once had a near-death experience due to a heroin overdose, inspiring their song "Kickstart My Heart."
- Guns N' Roses' "Appetite for Destruction" is one of the best-selling debut albums of all time, despite initially slow sales.
- Ozzy Osbourne was banned from San Antonio, Texas, for 10 years after urinating on the Alamo while wearing a dress.
- Def Leppard's drummer, Rick Allen, lost his left arm in a car accident but continued to play with a specially designed electronic drum kit.
- Iron Maiden's Bruce Dickinson is not only a rock vocalist but also a licensed commercial pilot, aviation entrepreneur, and beer brewer.
- Metallica's James Hetfield has been a major contributor to the custom car scene, with several of his creations featured in magazines.
- Judas Priest's "Painkiller" album marked a significant comeback with a faster, heavier sound after the band had been declared irrelevant by some critics.
- Slayer's Kerry King made a guest appearance on the Beastie Boys' song "No Sleep till Brooklyn," a nod to the crossover between metal and other music genres.
- Megadeth's "Peace Sells... but Who's Buying?" album cover features the band's mascot, Vic Rattlehead, in front of a UN building with flags flying upside down, signaling distress.
- Anthrax teamed up with Public Enemy to create a groundbreaking rap-metal version of "Bring the Noise," bridging two seemingly disparate musical genres.
- Mötley Crüe's Tommy Lee was known for his gravity-defying drum solos, which included his drum kit flying over the audience during concerts.

- Guns N' Roses once went on tour with a carny game called "The Robbie Knievel Bike Jump Challenge" backstage, involving miniature motorcycles and fire.
- Ozzy Osbourne's "No More Tears" was one of the first albums to be remastered for the then-new CD format, showcasing the industry's shift towards digital music.
- Def Leppard's "Hysteria" album produced seven hit singles, a rare achievement for a rock album, demonstrating their crossover appeal.
- Metallica's "One" was their first music video ever, breaking their previous stance against music videos. It featured footage from the anti-war film "Johnny Got His Gun."
- Iron Maiden's plane, piloted by Bruce Dickinson, is named "Ed Force One," a play on Air Force One and their mascot's name.
- Judas Priest's Rob Halford is one of the first openly gay icons in the heavy metal community, coming out in a 1998 interview.
- Slayer's Tom Araya is a devout Catholic, contrasting with the band's often dark and controversial lyrical themes.
- Megadeth's mascot, Vic Rattlehead, represents the phrase "See no evil, hear no evil, speak no evil" with metal twists: his eyes are covered with a visor, his mouth is clamped shut, and his ears are closed with metal caps.

Questions

Which band's original name for their debut album was "Metal Up Your Ass" before changing due to label pressure?
- A. Anthrax
- B. Slayer
- C. Metallica

Iron Maiden's mascot, Eddie, has appeared on almost all of their album covers. What is Eddie's role in the band's imagery?
- A. A symbol of rebellion
- B. A visual representation of the band's themes
- C. The band's lead singer

Judas Priest is credited with introducing which iconic look to the metal genre?
- A. Glam and glitter
- B. Leather and studs
- C. Flannel and denim

Who financed Slayer's "Reign in Blood" album, marking an unusual crossover of production talent from a different music genre?
- A. Dr. Dre
- B. Rick Rubin
- C. George Martin

Dave Mustaine founded Megadeth after being kicked out of which band?
- A. Anthrax
- B. Slayer
- C. Metallica

Anthrax is named after a bacterial disease. What was the reason behind choosing this name?
- A. It sounded sufficiently 'metal'
- B. It represents their music's infectious nature
- C. A tribute to scientific achievements

"Girls, Girls, Girls" by Mötley Crüe celebrates what aspects of the band's lifestyle?
- A. Peace and love
- B. Motorcycles, strip clubs, and hedonism
- C. Political activism

Guns N' Roses' "Appetite for Destruction" became one of the best-selling debut albums of all time after initially slow sales. What genre does this album primarily belong to?
- A. Glam metal
- B. Thrash metal
- C. Hard rock

Which incident led to Ozzy Osbourne being banned from San Antonio, Texas, for 10 years?
- A. Performing without a permit
- B. Urinating on the Alamo
- C. Stage diving into the crowd

How did Def Leppard's drummer, Rick Allen, continue his music career after losing his left arm?
- A. By becoming a singer
- B. Using a specially designed electronic drum kit
- C. Switching to play bass guitar

What was the original title of Metallica's "Kill 'Em All" album?
- A. Fight Fire With Fire
- B. Metal Militia
- C. Metal Up Your Ass

Which band is known for the hit song "Master of Puppets"?
- A. Slayer
- B. Metallica
- C. Megadeth

Who is the frontman of Iron Maiden known for his skills as a commercial pilot?
- A. Dave Mustaine
- B. Bruce Dickinson
- C. Rob Halford

Judas Priest's "Painkiller" album is noted for what significant shift in their music?
- A. Acoustic to electric transition
- B. A faster, heavier sound
- C. Introduction of synthesizers

Slayer's Kerry King made a guest appearance on which Beastie Boys' song, highlighting the crossover between metal and other music genres?
- A. Fight For Your Right
- B. Sabotage
- C. No Sleep till Brooklyn

Answers

Metallica (C)
- Trivia: Metallica's debut album was initially titled "Metal Up Your Ass," featuring a provocative cover art. Due to label pressure for a more marketable title, it was changed to "Kill 'Em All," a nod to their frustration with the music industry.

A visual representation of the band's themes (B)
- Trivia: Eddie, Iron Maiden's iconic mascot, serves as a visual keystone for the band, embodying the themes and stories told in their music. Eddie's evolution over the years has seen him take on numerous forms, from an Egyptian pharaoh to a futuristic cyborg.

Leather and studs (B)
- Trivia: Judas Priest popularized the leather and studs look, which became synonymous with the heavy metal genre. This fashion choice underscored the music's intensity and rebellion, influencing countless bands and fans worldwide.

Rick Rubin (B)
- Trivia: Rick Rubin, known for his work across various music genres, financed Slayer's "Reign in Blood" album. His involvement was pivotal in its production, helping to shape it into a seminal thrash metal record.

Metallica (C)
- Trivia: Dave Mustaine was originally a member of Metallica but was ousted from the band due to personal and professional conflicts. He went on to form Megadeth, another influential thrash metal band, turning his dismissal into a catalyst for success.

It sounded sufficiently 'metal' (A)
- Trivia: Anthrax chose their name because it sounded "sufficiently metal," reflecting the band's desire to stand out with a strong, impactful name. The choice underlines metal's fascination with themes of destruction and resilience.

Motorcycles, strip clubs, and hedonism (B)
- Trivia: "Girls, Girls, Girls" by Mötley Crüe is an ode to the band's hedonistic lifestyle, celebrating motorcycles, strip clubs, and their rock and roll way of life. The song reflects the era's excess and the band's notorious reputation.

Hard rock (C)
- Trivia: "Appetite for Destruction" by Guns N' Roses, while incorporating elements of glam and punk, is primarily considered a hard rock album. Its raw energy and attitude helped redefine rock music in the late '80s and remains a landmark record.

Urinating on the Alamo (B)
- Trivia: Ozzy Osbourne was banned from San Antonio, Texas, for a decade after an incident where he urinated on the Alamo monument while wearing his future wife Sharon's dress, an act that outraged locals and led to his temporary exile from the city.

Using a specially designed electronic drum kit (B)
- Trivia: After losing his left arm in a car accident, Rick Allen of Def Leppard continued his career using a custom-designed electronic drum kit that allowed him to play using his remaining arm and legs. His resilience and adaptation have inspired many.

Metal Up Your Ass (C)
- Trivia: The original title for Metallica's "Kill 'Em All" album was "Metal Up Your Ass," a title that reflected the band's aggressive, no-compromise attitude. The change to "Kill 'Em All" came after distributors refused to stock the album with such a controversial name.

Metallica (B)
- Trivia: "Master of Puppets" is one of Metallica's most celebrated songs, showcasing the band's complex compositions and lyrical depth. The song and the album of the same name are considered masterpieces of the thrash metal genre.

Bruce Dickinson (B)
- Trivia: Bruce Dickinson, the lead singer of Iron Maiden, is also a licensed commercial pilot. He has flown the band around the world on tour in a Boeing 757 nicknamed "Ed Force One," which he pilots himself.

A faster, heavier sound (B)
- Trivia: Judas Priest's "Painkiller" album marked a significant shift towards a faster, heavier sound, incorporating double-bass drumming and speed metal elements. This evolution solidified their place in metal history and influenced the genre's development.

No Sleep till Brooklyn (C)
- Trivia: Kerry King of Slayer made a guest appearance on the Beastie Boys' song "No Sleep till Brooklyn," delivering a fiery guitar solo. This collaboration highlighted the crossover appeal between metal and other music genres, particularly hip hop.

Hip-Hop and Rap: From the Streets to Mainstream

Hip-hop emerged in the 1970s as a cultural movement from the economically disadvantaged neighborhoods of New York City, particularly the Bronx. It started as a form of expression for African-American and Latino youth, channeling their frustrations and aspirations through graffiti, breakdancing, DJing, and, most notably, rap. Rap music, characterized by its rhythmic, spoken delivery of rhymes and wordplay, quickly became the voice of a generation marginalized by mainstream society.

The roots of hip-hop are deeply intertwined with social and political activism, with early artists using their music to address issues like poverty, racism, police brutality, and inequality. Grandmaster Flash and the Furious Five's "The Message" (1982) is one of the earliest examples, vividly depicting the struggles of living in the inner city. This track laid the groundwork for hip-hop as a tool for social commentary, setting a precedent for future artists.

As hip-hop evolved through the 1980s and 1990s, it began to diversify in sound and geographical influence. Artists from Los Angeles, such as N.W.A., brought the West Coast into the spotlight, introducing gangsta rap, which highlighted the gang violence and police harassment in their communities. Meanwhile, the East Coast continued to innovate with artists like Public Enemy, who infused their music with politically charged messages, and The Notorious B.I.G., who offered a cinematic portrayal of his life in Brooklyn.

The 1990s also saw the rise of the "Golden Age" of hip-hop, a period marked by its incredible creativity, diversity, and innovation. This era brought forth a variety of styles, from the jazz-infused sounds of A Tribe Called Quest to the hardcore realism of Wu-Tang Clan. The late 1990s and early 2000s witnessed the commercial explosion of hip-hop, with artists like Jay-Z, Eminem, and Missy Elliott achieving massive success, both critically and commercially.

In the 21st century, hip-hop has become the most influential and popular genre in music, dominating charts worldwide. Its reach has extended far beyond its original confines, influencing fashion, language, and lifestyle globally. Artists like Kanye West, Drake, and Kendrick Lamar have pushed the boundaries of the genre, incorporating new sounds and addressing complex themes such as fame, mental health, and racial injustice.

Pioneers of the Rap Game

Grandmaster Flash and the Furious Five - "The Message" (1982)
- Pioneers of Political and Social Commentary: Their lyrics provided a gritty, realistic view of urban life, setting a precedent for socially conscious rap.
- Innovative Use of Turntablism: Grandmaster Flash was known for his innovative DJ techniques, which revolutionized hip-hop music production.
- Rock and Roll Hall of Fame: They were the first hip-hop group ever inducted, acknowledging their foundational role in the genre.
- Influence: Inspired Kendrick Lamar's narrative technique and focus on social issues.

Run-D.M.C. - "Walk This Way" (1986)
- Bridging Rock and Hip-Hop: Their collaboration with Aerosmith on "Walk This Way" was groundbreaking, bringing hip-hop to a wider audience.
- Street Fashion Pioneers: They popularized the Adidas sneakers and tracksuits look, impacting hip-hop fashion.

- Music Video Innovators: Their music videos were among the first for hip-hop acts on MTV, increasing the genre's visibility.
- Influence: Influenced Linkin Park and Kid Rock's fusion of rock and rap.

LL Cool J - "I Need Love" (1987)
- Romantic Hip-Hop: One of the first to introduce a softer, more romantic side to rap music.
- Longevity in Music and Acting: Successfully transitioned to acting, maintaining relevance across decades.
- Def Jam Recordings: Played a crucial role in the success of Def Jam, one of hip-hop's most influential labels.
- Influence: Paved the way for artists like Drake who blend rap with R&B themes.

Public Enemy - "Fight the Power" (1989)
- Political Activism: Their music tackled issues of racism, social injustice, and the need for change, making them icons of political rap.
- Innovative Production: The Bomb Squad, their production team, was known for its dense, chaotic soundscapes that were revolutionary.
- Impact on Culture: Their message inspired a generation of activists and musicians alike.
- Influence: Influenced politically conscious artists like J. Cole.

Eric B. & Rakim - "Paid in Full" (1987)
- Lyrical Complexity: Rakim's complex flows and layered metaphors elevated the standard for MCing.
- Sampling Innovators: Their use of James Brown samples in "Paid in Full" set a template for hip-hop production.
- Quiet Influence: While never achieving the commercial success of some contemporaries, their artistic impact is unmatched.

Beastie Boys - "(You Gotta) Fight for Your Right (To Party!)" (1986)
- Punk and Hip-Hop Fusion: They started as a punk band before transitioning to hip-hop, blending the two genres.
- Cultural Icons: Became one of the few acts to successfully cross over to a mainstream audience while maintaining their hip-hop credibility.
- Innovative Music Videos: Their video work, particularly with director Spike Jonze, was groundbreaking.
- Influence: Inspired Travis Scott's genre-bending work.

Salt-N-Pepa - "Push It" (1986)
- Female Empowerment: Among the first female groups to achieve success in the male-dominated world of hip-hop.
- Sexual Liberation: Their lyrics often touched on themes of sex and love from a female perspective, breaking taboos.
- Grammy Winners: They were one of the first female rap artists to win a Grammy Award, paving the way for future generations.
- Influence: Paved the way for Nicki Minaj and other female rappers.

N.W.A. - "Straight Outta Compton" (1988)
- Gangsta Rap Pioneers: Their raw portrayal of life in Compton introduced gangsta rap to a wide audience.
- Controversy and Impact: Their explicit lyrics and social commentary on police brutality brought them both acclaim and scrutiny.
- Solo Successes: Members like Dr. Dre, Ice Cube, and Eazy-E went on to have successful solo careers and significant impacts on music and culture.
- Influence: Influenced Kendrick Lamar and the acting and musical career of Ice Cube's son, O'Shea Jackson Jr.

Electronic and Synth-Pop Revolution

The 1980s witnessed the electronic and synth-pop revolution, a transformative era in music that introduced the world to a new sonic landscape. This period marked a significant shift from traditional rock and acoustic sounds to music characterized by synthesizers, drum machines, and digital production techniques. The impact of this revolution was profound, influencing not just the soundscapes of the decade but also the future of music production, performance, and consumption.

At the heart of the electronic and synth-pop revolution was the advent of affordable synthesizers and drum machines. Instruments like the Roland TR-808, the Yamaha DX7, and the Moog synthesizer became staples in music studios, allowing musicians to create sounds that were previously unimaginable. This technological innovation gave rise to a new genre of music known as synth-pop, characterized by its heavy use of electronic instruments and futuristic themes.

Often hailed as the pioneers of electronic music, this German band's use of robotic and machine-like sounds in the late '70s laid the groundwork for the synth-pop explosion. Their album "The Man-Machine" is a seminal work that influenced countless artists across various genres.

With their dark, industrial take on synth-pop, Depeche Mode brought a new depth to electronic music, exploring themes of love, religion, and politics. Albums like "Violator" and "Music for the Masses" showcased their ability to blend catchy melodies with complex, layered synth arrangements.

Rising from the ashes of Joy Division, New Order became one of the most influential synth-pop bands by merging post-punk with electronic dance music.

Their hit "Blue Monday" remains one of the best-selling 12-inch singles of all time, demonstrating the commercial viability of electronic music.

Their album "Dare" is a landmark in synth-pop, featuring hits like "Don't You Want Me." The Human League's success proved that electronic bands could achieve mainstream popularity, paving the way for future acts.

New Order - "Blue Monday" (1983)
Innovative Production: Utilized cutting-edge technology, including the Oberheim DMX drum machine and Moog Source synthesizer, to create its groundbreaking sound.

Inspirational Artwork: The sleeve design, inspired by floppy disks, didn't feature the band's name or the single title, emphasizing the music's primacy.

Cultural Impact: Its influence extends beyond music into fashion, art, and design, symbolizing the 80s' electronic music's aesthetic.

Live Performances: "Blue Monday" remains a centerpiece in New Order's live performances, often extended with improvisational synth and bass sections.

Depeche Mode - "Just Can't Get Enough" (1981)
Early Success: This track was one of Depeche Mode's first major hits, establishing their place in the new wave and synth-pop scenes.

Fan Favorite: Despite the band's darker evolution, "Just Can't Get Enough" remains a beloved classic among fans for its upbeat tempo and catchy melody.

Innovative Synthesis: The song's use of the Roland Jupiter-4 and Moog synthesizers helped define the sound of early 80s synth-pop.

Legacy: The song has been covered by numerous artists across various genres, illustrating its wide-reaching influence.

The Human League - "Don't You Want Me" (1981)
Chart-Topping Hit: Became the Christmas number one single in the UK for 1981 and has sold over 1.5 million copies in the UK alone.

Synthesizer Pioneers: The Human League utilized the Linn LM-1 Drum Computer, one of the first drum machines to use digital samples.

Crossover Appeal: "Don't You Want Me" helped synth-pop music achieve mainstream success, appealing to both pop and alternative audiences.

Music Video Innovation: The song's music video was ahead of its time, utilizing narrative storytelling that paralleled the song's lyrics, enhancing its appeal.

Soft Cell - "Tainted Love" (1981)
Record-Breaking: Holds the record for spending the longest time on the Billboard Hot 100 chart without reaching number one.

Synth Arrangement: Marc Almond's vocal performance combined with Dave Ball's innovative synth arrangements created a new sound that defined an era.

Global Phenomenon: "Tainted Love" became a global hit, topping charts around the world and becoming one of the best-selling singles of its time.

Enduring Legacy: The song's popularity has endured, with its inclusion in films, TV shows, and commercials, showcasing its timeless appeal.

Gary Numan - "Cars" (1979)

Pioneering Sound: "Cars" is often credited with popularizing the synth-pop genre, with its pioneering use of electronic instruments.

Autobiographical Influence: Numan has mentioned that the song was inspired by an incident of road rage, reflecting the dehumanization of modern life.

Innovative Music Video: The music video for "Cars" was one of the early examples of computer-generated imagery in music videos.

Chart Success: "Cars" reached the top of the charts in several countries, including the UK and Canada, and became a top 10 hit in the US.

Pet Shop Boys - "West End Girls" (1984)

Critical and Commercial Success: The song won the Brit Award for Best British Single in 1987 and has been critically acclaimed for its production and reflective lyrics.

Unique Composition: "West End Girls" features a distinctive low-pitched vocal delivery, which became a signature style for lead singer Neil Tennant.

Lyrical Depth: The lyrics discuss class and the pressures of inner-city life, showcasing the Pet Shop Boys' ability to blend catchy pop music with thoughtful social commentary.

Music Video: The music video's portrayal of London's West End and East End helped visualize the song's themes of class disparity and urban life.

Eurythmics - "Sweet Dreams (Are Made of This)" (1983)
Global Stardom: The song catapulted Eurythmics to international fame, becoming a number one hit in the US and reaching the top 10 in various countries.

Iconic Synth Riff: The song's main synth riff is one of the most recognizable in music history, instantly evoking the 80s era.

Versatile Duo: Annie Lennox's powerful vocals and Dave Stewart's innovative production techniques showcased the duo's musical versatility.

Music Video: The music video, featuring Annie Lennox in a boardroom and wandering through a field with a cow, is memorable for its surreal imagery, contributing to the song's mystique.

Bronski Beat - "Smalltown Boy" (1984)
Social Commentary: "Smalltown Boy" is renowned for its poignant commentary on the challenges faced by LGBTQ+ individuals, particularly in conservative environments.

Innovative Sound: The song combines Jimmy Somerville's distinctive falsetto with synthesizers to create a sound that was both emotive and danceable.

Music Video: The accompanying music video was groundbreaking for its explicit portrayal of homophobia and the journey of coming out.

Enduring Influence: The song remains an anthem for the LGBTQ+ community and is celebrated for its contribution to raising awareness and fostering acceptance.

A-ha - "Take On Me" (1984)

Revolutionary Music Video: The music video, featuring a blend of live-action and pencil-sketch animation, won six awards at the 1986 MTV Video Music Awards and is considered one of the best music videos of all time.

Chart Success: "Take On Me" reached number one on the Billboard Hot 100 in the United States and was a top 10 hit in many other countries.

Enduring Popularity: The song's catchy melody and innovative video continue to resonate with audiences, making it a staple of 80s pop culture.

Musical Complexity: Despite its pop veneer, "Take On Me" features complex time signatures and a challenging vocal range, showcasing A-ha's musicianship.

Trivia Tidbits

- Kraftwerk's founders originally met while studying classical music, which influenced their pioneering approach to electronic music.
- Depeche Mode's name was inspired by a French fashion magazine, reflecting the band's interest in fashion and design.
- New Order was formed by the remaining members of Joy Division after the tragic suicide of lead singer Ian Curtis.

- The Human League was originally formed as an all-male group, but after a split, they added two female vocalists, which significantly changed their sound and image.
- Gary Numan's "Cars" was influenced by his love for machines and his feelings of isolation, symbolized through the metaphor of being safe inside a car.
- Soft Cell's version of "Tainted Love" is a cover; the original was recorded by Gloria Jones in 1965.
- The iconic music video for A-ha's "Take On Me" took four months to complete due to its pioneering use of rotoscope animation.
- Pet Shop Boys named their band after friends who worked in a pet shop, reflecting their sense of humor and penchant for the ordinary.
- Eurythmics' name comes from the term "eurythmy," an art form involving harmonious body movements, reflecting Annie Lennox and Dave Stewart's intention to create harmonious music.
- Bronski Beat's "Smalltown Boy" was inspired by lead singer Jimmy Somerville's own experiences growing up gay in Glasgow.
- Before achieving fame with Depeche Mode, Martin Gore worked as a bank teller, and Dave Gahan was a window dresser for a fashion retailer.
- New Order's "Blue Monday" is the best-selling 12-inch single of all time, yet the band famously lost money on each copy sold due to the elaborate sleeve design.
- The Human League's "Don't You Want Me" was nearly left off their album "Dare" because the band members didn't think it was good enough.
- Gary Numan is also a licensed pilot and once flew around the world in his own aircraft.

- Soft Cell's "Tainted Love" holds the Guinness World Record for the longest consecutive stay on the US Billboard Hot 100 chart without reaching number one.
- Kraftwerk's Ralf Hütter and Florian Schneider were avid cyclists, even releasing a song titled "Tour de France" inspired by the famous bicycle race.
- A-ha's "Take On Me" initially flopped upon its first release; it only became a hit after the music video was produced and the song was re-released.
- The Pet Shop Boys have written and produced songs for a wide range of artists, including Dusty Springfield and Liza Minnelli.
- Eurythmics' Annie Lennox and Dave Stewart were previously members of a band called The Tourists before forming Eurythmics.
- Bronski Beat's "Smalltown Boy" music video was one of the first to include a clear narrative about gay experience, making it groundbreaking for its time and contributing significantly to the dialogue around LGBTQ+ issues in the mainstream media.

Madonna: Queen of Pop

Madonna, the undisputed Queen of Pop, rose to prominence in the 1980s, leaving an indelible mark on the music industry and pop culture. Her ascent was not just a series of hit songs; it was a revolution that challenged societal norms, fashion, and the very fabric of the music video era. Madonna's influence in the 1980s can be encapsulated by her innovative music, iconic style, and groundbreaking music videos, which together forged a path for future female artists in the industry.

Madonna's journey to stardom began with her move to New York City in 1978, armed with nothing but ambition and a unique vision for her future. By 1983, she had released her debut album, "Madonna," which featured hits like "Holiday," signaling the arrival of a new force in pop music. However, it was her follow-up album, "Like a Virgin" (1984), that catapulted her into superstardom. The title track, "Like a Virgin," became an anthem of the era, reaching the top of the Billboard charts and remaining there for six weeks. The performance of "Like a Virgin" at the first MTV Video Music Awards, where Madonna famously writhed on stage in a wedding dress, exemplified her knack for creating controversial, yet unforgettable moments.

Madonna's impact in the 1980s extended beyond her music. She was a cultural icon who influenced fashion with her distinctive style—lace gloves, crucifix necklaces, and the famous "Boy Toy" belt. Her look was emulated by millions of young fans worldwide, symbolizing a blend of street savvy with glamorous reinvention. This era saw Madonna not just as a music star but as a style icon, setting trends that defined the decade's fashion.

Moreover, Madonna utilized the burgeoning platform of music videos to elevate her artistry and message. The video for "Like a

Prayer" (1989) is a prime example, blending religious symbolism with social commentary and sparking widespread controversy and discussion. It underscored her ability to use pop music as a vehicle for challenging societal norms and pushing boundaries.

Madonna's contributions to the 1980s music scene were also marked by her relentless innovation. She consistently reinvented her music and image, a testament to her versatility and understanding of the pop landscape. Albums like "True Blue" (1986) and "Like a Prayer" (1989) showcased her ability to evolve, featuring hits such as "Papa Don't Preach," "Open Your Heart," "La Isla Bonita," and the titular "Like a Prayer." These works solidified her status as a pop icon capable of exploring deep emotional and societal issues within the framework of mainstream music.

The 1980s concluded with Madonna firmly established as the Queen of Pop, but her legacy was only beginning. She had not only dominated the charts but also shaped the pop music landscape, influencing fashion, music video production, and the role of women in the music industry. Madonna's 1980s oeuvre left a lasting legacy, setting the stage for her continued evolution and impact on pop culture in the decades to follow.

Madonna's Biggest Stories
"Like a Virgin" Performance at the MTV VMAs (1984)

Madonna's 1984 MTV Video Music Awards performance of "Like a Virgin" stands as a watershed moment in live music history. Dressed in a wedding gown and a "Boy Toy" belt, she provocatively rolled on stage, challenging the conventional norms of female sexuality in popular culture. This performance not only solidified her image as a pop provocateur but also demonstrated her masterful understanding of visual symbolism and its impact on audiences. Madonna's bold expression of female sexuality and autonomy was groundbreaking, setting the tone for her career as an artist unafraid to push societal boundaries.

The "Like a Prayer" Controversy (1989)

The "Like a Prayer" controversy stands as a testament to Madonna's fearless approach to intertwining social commentary with her music, becoming a pivotal moment in her career and in pop culture at large. Released in 1989, the music video for "Like a Prayer" was a bold exploration of themes of race, religion, and sexuality, all of which were hot-button issues at the time. Directed by Mary Lambert, the video featured imagery that was daring and provocative, including stigmata, burning crosses, and a black saint, pushing the boundaries of what was considered acceptable in mainstream media.

Madonna's artistic intention was to challenge societal norms and provoke thought among her audience. The video's narrative, which included a black man wrongfully accused of a crime and Madonna seeking solace and guidance in a church, was a commentary on racial injustice and the power of faith. However, the religious imagery, especially the burning crosses and the depiction of a black saint resembling Jesus, was met with fierce backlash from religious groups and the public, who viewed these elements as blasphemous and disrespectful.

This controversy was not just a momentary scandal; it was a cultural flashpoint that highlighted the power of pop music to engage with complex social issues. Madonna used the video to blur the lines between the sacred and the profane, suggesting that spirituality and sexuality are not mutually exclusive. This approach was groundbreaking, challenging viewers to reconsider their preconceived notions about religion and morality.

The "Like a Prayer" video also underscored Madonna's role as a cultural provocateur and a champion of artistic freedom. By refusing to shy away from controversial topics, she opened the door for future artists to express their creativity without fear of censorship. The video's impact went beyond its initial controversy, contributing to the dialogue around censorship, artistic expression, and the role of pop stars in shaping public discourse.

Despite the immediate backlash, "Like a Prayer" became one of Madonna's most acclaimed works, praised for its ambitious vision and its ability to provoke discussion on important issues. The song and the video were commercial successes, further cementing Madonna's status as the Queen of Pop and a fearless advocate for change. Through the "Like a Prayer" controversy, Madonna not only demonstrated her artistic genius but also her unwavering commitment to challenging societal norms, making it a defining moment in her career and in the history of pop music.

Role in "Desperately Seeking Susan" (1985)

Madonna's role in "Desperately Seeking Susan" marked a pivotal moment in her career, blurring the lines between her music persona and film acting. Playing the free-spirited Susan, Madonna's on-screen wardrobe became iconic, inspiring fashion trends and making her a style icon for the decade. The film not only showcased her acting talents but also amplified her status in pop culture, demonstrating her versatility and ability to influence fashion and film alike.

The Pepsi Commercial Controversy (1989)

In 1989, Madonna starred in a Pepsi commercial that premiered her "Like a Prayer" music video. The ad, devoid of the video's controversial religious imagery, was met with anticipation and excitement. However, the subsequent release of the full music video led to a global controversy, resulting in Pepsi pulling the ad and canceling their sponsorship deal with Madonna. This incident highlighted the burgeoning power of music videos as cultural statements and Madonna's unapologetic artistic expression, despite commercial partnerships.

First Female Artist to Sell Over 5 Million Copies of an Album (1984)

Madonna's "Like a Virgin" achieving sales of over 5 million copies in the U.S. was a monumental achievement, marking her as the first female artist to reach such a milestone. This record-breaking success shattered industry ceilings and redefined the commercial potential for female pop artists. "Like a Virgin's" commercial triumph, coupled with its cultural impact, paved the way for future female artists, demonstrating that they could achieve both critical and commercial success on a grand scale.

True or False

True or False: Madonna's first job in New York City was working at Dunkin' Donuts.

True or False: "Like a Prayer" was Madonna's first song to reach number one on the Billboard Hot 100.

True or False: Madonna originally studied biology at the University of Michigan before dropping out to pursue her music career.

True or False: Madonna has written children's books, with one of them reaching the New York Times bestseller list.

True or False: Madonna's birth name is Madonna Louise Ciccone, without any middle names.

True or False: In addition to her music career, Madonna has a patent for a design of a backpack.

True or False: Madonna's performance at the 1990 MTV Video Music Awards featured a live lion on stage.

True or False: Madonna has won more Grammy Awards than any other female artist.

True or False: Madonna once owned an English pub located in London.

True or False: The music video for "Vogue" was directed by Quentin Tarantino.

True or False: Madonna was considered for the role of Catwoman in Tim Burton's "Batman Returns."

True or False: Madonna has a twin sister.

True or False: Madonna's "Ray of Light" album includes a track that features her daughter Lourdes singing.

True or False: Madonna has climbed Mount Everest as part of a charity event.

True or False: The "Material Girl" music video was inspired by Marilyn Monroe's performance of "Diamonds Are a Girl's Best Friend" in the film "Gentlemen Prefer Blondes."

Answers

True: Madonna's first job in New York City was indeed at a Dunkin' Donuts, where she reportedly was fired for squirting jelly filling at customers.

False: While "Like a Prayer" was a number one hit, it was not her first. Madonna's first Billboard Hot 100 number one was "Like a Virgin" in 1984.

False: Madonna attended the University of Michigan on a dance scholarship, not to study biology, before leaving to pursue her career in New York.

True: Madonna has written a series of children's books, including "The English Roses," which indeed reached the New York Times bestseller list.

False: Madonna's birth name is Madonna Louise Ciccone, indicating she does have middle names.

False: There's no public record of Madonna holding a patent for a backpack or any other invention related to her music career.

False: While Madonna's performances have been iconic and sometimes controversial, there was no live lion on stage during her 1990 MTV VMAs performance.

False: Madonna has won numerous Grammy Awards, but she does not hold the record for the most wins by a female artist; that distinction goes to artists like Beyoncé.

True: Madonna did own a pub in London called The Punchbowl, located in Mayfair, during her marriage to Guy Ritchie.

False: The music video for "Vogue" was directed by David Fincher, not Quentin Tarantino.

True: Madonna was indeed considered for the role of Catwoman in Tim Burton's "Batman Returns" before Michelle Pfeiffer was cast.

False: Madonna does not have a twin sister. She is the third of six children in her family.

False: While Lourdes Leon, Madonna's daughter, has been involved in her mother's career, there is no track on the "Ray of Light" album featuring her singing.

False: Madonna has not climbed Mount Everest. She is known for her fitness and adventurous spirit, but climbing Everest is not among her achievements.

True: The "Material Girl" music video was indeed inspired by Marilyn Monroe's performance of "Diamonds Are a Girl's Best Friend" from the film "Gentlemen Prefer Blondes."

Bruce Springsteen

Bruce Springsteen, affectionately known as "The Boss," is a monumental figure in American music, whose storied career has deeply influenced rock music and the cultural landscape for over five decades. Born on September 23, 1949, in Long Branch, New Jersey, Springsteen's passion for rock 'n' roll ignited at an early age, particularly after witnessing Elvis Presley on "The Ed Sullivan Show." This early inspiration would drive him to become a prolific storyteller, whose music chronicles the lives, struggles, and dreams of working-class Americans.

At the heart of Springsteen's musical journey is his collaboration with the E Street Band, a group of musicians renowned for their dynamic performances and instrumental prowess. Members like Clarence Clemons on the saxophone and Max Weinberg on drums have become almost as iconic as Springsteen himself, helping to produce a sound that is both powerful and evocative. Together, they achieved breakthrough success with the 1975 album "Born to Run," a masterpiece that cemented Springsteen's place in the pantheon of rock legends. This album, with anthems like "Thunder Road" and "Jungleland," showcased Springsteen's skill in weaving intricate narratives with unforgettable melodies.

Over the years, Springsteen's discography has expanded to include a wide array of albums that reflect his diverse musical influences and lyrical themes. From the raw, haunting tones of "Nebraska" to the commercial juggernaut that was "Born in the U.S.A.," Springsteen has demonstrated a remarkable ability to capture the essence of the American spirit. His music delves into social and political issues, personal introspection, and tales of love and loss, resonating with audiences around the world. His accolades, including 20 Grammy Awards and an Academy Award for Best Original Song for "Streets of Philadelphia," underscore his profound impact on music and culture.

Springsteen's influence extends beyond his recordings and performances. His Broadway show, "Springsteen on Broadway," offered a more intimate glimpse into his life and creative process, further solidifying his status as a master storyteller. Beyond his artistic contributions, Springsteen has been an outspoken advocate for various social issues, from veterans' rights to marriage equality, showcasing his commitment to using his platform for positive change.

The legacy of Bruce Springsteen is not just in the songs he has written or the concerts he has performed, but in the way he has touched the hearts and minds of millions. His ability to connect with his audience, to articulate the joys and sorrows of the human experience, and to remain a relevant and compassionate voice through changing times, cements his status as one of rock's most enduring icons. As he continues to write, perform, and inspire, Springsteen's legacy as "The Boss" is assured, a testament to the enduring power of rock 'n' roll.

Bruce Springsteen's 5 Biggest Songs

1. "Born to Run" (1975, Album: Born to Run)
   - Became an anthem for youthful aspiration and a quest for freedom.
   - The song took six months to record, showcasing Springsteen's perfectionism.
   - Helped the album become a commercial success, solidifying Springsteen's career.
   - Features a prominent saxophone solo by Clarence Clemons, a signature of the E Street Band's sound.

2. "Thunder Road" (1975, Album: Born to Run)
   - Opens with a harmonica solo, setting a tone of hopeful escape.
   - Lyrics tell the story of a young couple's decision to flee their hometown for a better life.
   - Widely regarded as one of Springsteen's greatest songs, encapsulating the essence of his storytelling.
   - The song's name was inspired by the 1958 movie "Thunder Road."

3. "Born in the U.S.A." (1984, Album: Born in the U.S.A.)
   - A critical examination of the treatment of Vietnam veterans upon their return to America.
   - The album and song became one of the best-selling records of all time.
   - Often misunderstood as a patriotic anthem, the lyrics convey a critique of American policies.
   - The iconic synthesizer riff and Springsteen's powerful vocals made it an 80s rock staple.

4. "Dancing in the Dark" (1984, Album: Born in the U.S.A.)
   - Became Springsteen's highest-charting single, peaking at No. 2 on the Billboard Hot 100.
   - Lyrics express frustration and the desire for change, resonating with a wide audience.
   - The music video introduced Courteney Cox, who dances on stage with Springsteen.
   - Synthesizer-driven sound marked a shift to a more mainstream, pop-oriented direction.

5. "The River" (1980, Album: The River)
   - A poignant ballad that narrates the story of a couple's struggle with life's hardships.
   - Inspired by Springsteen's sister and her life in the early 1980s.
   - Features harmonica and piano, emphasizing its melancholic tone.
   - The song's narrative style and emotional depth highlight Springsteen's songwriting prowess.

These songs not only define Bruce Springsteen's illustrious career but also capture the heart and soul of American life, making him a beloved figure in rock music history.

Trivia Tidbits

- Rock and Roll Hall of Fame: Bruce Springsteen was inducted into the Rock and Roll Hall of Fame in 1999, a testament to his enduring influence on the genre and his significant contributions to music.

- Super Bowl Halftime Show: Springsteen performed at the Super Bowl XLIII halftime show in 2009, delivering a memorable 12-minute set that included hits like "Born to Run," "Glory Days," and "Dancing in the Dark."

- Podcast with Barack Obama: Springsteen co-hosted a podcast with former U.S. President Barack Obama titled "Renegades: Born in the USA." The series featured deep conversations about their lives, music, and enduring love for America amidst its challenges.

- Kennedy Center Honors: In 2009, Springsteen was honored at the Kennedy Center Honors, recognizing his contributions to American culture through the performing arts. President Obama praised him for his storytelling ability and the profound impact of his work.

- Best-Selling Memoir: In 2016, Springsteen published his autobiography, "Born to Run," which became a best-seller. The book offers an intimate look at his life, his struggles with depression, and the behind-the-scenes stories of his music.

- Tony Award: Springsteen was awarded a Special Tony Award in 2018 for his critically acclaimed "Springsteen on Broadway" show, which combined music and personal stories in a unique performance format.

- Presidential Medal of Freedom: In 2016, President Barack Obama awarded Springsteen the Presidential Medal of Freedom, the nation's highest civilian honor, citing his contributions to music and American culture.

- Environmental Advocacy: Springsteen has been a vocal advocate for environmental issues, including participating in benefit concerts and supporting initiatives aimed at combating climate change and preserving natural landscapes.

- Charity Work: Throughout his career, Springsteen has been involved in various charitable efforts, including donating proceeds from concerts and recordings to food banks, veterans' organizations, and disaster relief efforts.

- Collaboration with Other Artists: Aside from his work with the E Street Band, Springsteen has collaborated with a wide range of artists across different genres, including Sting,

U2, and John Mellencamp, showcasing his versatility and deep respect for the broader music community.

Questions - Test Your Bruce Knowledge

Lyric Interpretation:
- Question: In Bruce Springsteen's "Atlantic City," what event is alluded to with the line "Well, they blew up the chicken man in Philly last night"?
- A) A gang rivalry
- B) A political scandal
- C) A casino heist

Early Career:
- Question: Before achieving fame, Bruce Springsteen was a member of several bands. Which of the following was NOT one of those bands?
- A) Steel Mill
- B) The Castiles
- C) The Sundowners

Music Video Cameos:
- Question: In which music video did Bruce Springsteen pull a then-unknown Courteney Cox onto the stage to dance, launching her into the public eye?
- A) "Glory Days"
- B) "Dancing in the Dark"
- C) "Born in the U.S.A."

Song Inspiration:
- Question: Bruce Springsteen's song "My Hometown" reflects on the changes in a town affected by economic downturns. What inspired Springsteen to write this song?
- A) His childhood experiences in Freehold, New Jersey
- B) A news article about factory closures
- C) Conversations with Vietnam veterans

Unique Performances:
- Question: Bruce Springsteen performed an entire album live in concert for the first time during the 2009 Working on a Dream Tour. Which album was it?
- A) "Born in the U.S.A."
- B) "Darkness on the Edge of Town"
- C) "Born to Run"

Answers

Lyric Interpretation:
- Answer: A) A gang rivalry
- Trivia Snapshot: The line from "Atlantic City" references the real-life bombing death of mobster Philip Testa, who was known as "The Chicken Man," in Philadelphia in 1981. This event is reflective of the organized crime influence in the area, which Springsteen often alludes to in his songs to highlight themes of struggle and redemption.

Early Career:
- Answer: C) The Sundowners
- Trivia Snapshot: Bruce Springsteen was never a member of a band called The Sundowners. His early bands included The Castiles and Steel Mill, among others. These early experiences were crucial in shaping his musical style and in honing his skills as a performer and songwriter, laying the foundation for his future success.

Music Video Cameos:
- Answer: B) "Dancing in the Dark"
- Trivia Snapshot: The music video for "Dancing in the Dark" was directed by Brian De Palma and shot at the Saint Paul Civic Center in Minnesota in 1984. The moment when Springsteen pulls Courteney Cox onto the stage became iconic, significantly boosting her career before she became famous for her role on "Friends."

Song Inspiration:
- Answer: A) His childhood experiences in Freehold, New Jersey
- Trivia Snapshot: "My Hometown" is deeply influenced by Springsteen's own upbringing in Freehold, New Jersey. The song reflects the economic challenges and changes his hometown faced, mirroring the broader American experience of towns affected by industrial decline and economic shifts during the latter half of the 20th century.

Unique Performances:
- Answer: C) "Born to Run"
- Trivia Snapshot: During the 2009 Working on a Dream Tour, Bruce Springsteen and the E Street Band performed the "Born to Run" album in its entirety for the first time live, to celebrate the 35th anniversary of its release. This was a significant event, as "Born to Run" is one of Springsteen's most beloved and critically acclaimed albums, capturing the essence of his musical and thematic ambitions.

We Didn't Start the Fire

Billy Joel's "We Didn't Start the Fire" is more than just a catchy tune; it's a historical journey set to music. Released in 1989, the song remains a unique piece of cultural commentary, encapsulating the tumultuous journey of the latter half of the 20th century. Here's a deeper look into the song, its impact, and the inspiration behind its creation.

Decades of History: The song's lyrics are a rapid-fire enumeration of notable events, figures, and cultural phenomena from 1949 (Joel's birth year) to 1989. It covers a wide range of topics from the Cold War, civil rights movements, space exploration, to pop culture icons.

Surprisingly, "We Didn't Start the Fire" has been used in educational settings as a novel way to teach post-World War II history, encouraging students to explore the events mentioned in the song.

The song resonated with listeners who had lived through the decades it covered, serving as a reminder of how much had occurred in just 40 years.

While the song was a commercial success, critics were divided. Some praised its catchiness and historical references, while others critiqued it for its rapid pacing and surface-level treatment of complex events.

Billy Joel was inspired to write the song after a conversation with a younger person who was unaware of many historical events. Joel realized the breadth of change he had witnessed in his lifetime and decided to condense it into a song.

Crafting the lyrics was a challenge due to the vast amount of history Joel wanted to include. The song's structure required fitting these events into a rhythmic and rhyming format without losing their essence.

- "Harry Truman, Doris Day, Red China, Johnnie Ray": This line from the beginning of the song mentions U.S. President Harry Truman, singer-actress Doris Day, the rise of Communist China under Mao Zedong (referred to as "Red China"), and popular 50s singer Johnnie Ray.

- "Joe McCarthy, Richard Nixon, Studebaker, television": This snippet refers to Senator Joseph McCarthy, known for his anti-communist pursuits, U.S. President Richard Nixon and the emergence of television as a mass medium.

- "North Korea, South Korea, Marilyn Monroe": These lyrics touch upon the Korean War that resulted in the division of Korea into North and South, and the iconic status of actress Marilyn Monroe.

- "Einstein, James Dean, Brooklyn's got a winning team": Albert Einstein, iconic actor James Dean, and a nod to the Brooklyn Dodgers' success in baseball are covered here.

- "Hemingway, Eichmann, Stranger in a Strange Land": References to author Ernest Hemingway, Nazi war criminal Adolf Eichmann, and Robert A. Heinlein's science fiction novel "Stranger in a Strange Land."

Song's Legacy

We Didn't Start the Fire" remains popular, often played on radio and in pop culture references. It's seen as a snapshot of an era, capturing the spirit of the late 20th century. Even a podcast was based on the song, giving listeners a lyric each week to explore.

A Launchpad for Discussion: The song continues to spark conversations about history and the events that shape our world. It encourages listeners to reflect on how these events are interconnected and how they've shaped the current socio-political landscape.

> *"JFK, blown away, what else do I have to say?"*

Billy Joel, with a career spanning several decades, has given us an array of hits beyond "We Didn't Start the Fire." Each song not only showcases his musical versatility but also offers insight into different aspects of life, history, and emotion. Here are some of his other significant songs.

"Piano Man" (1973)
- Autobiographical: Inspired by Joel's own experiences playing at a piano bar, capturing the stories of the people he met.
- Signature Song: Often considered Joel's signature song, it's a staple in his live performances, illustrating his storytelling prowess.
- Cultural Impact: Has become an anthem for piano players and singers, encapsulating the essence of the performer's life.

"Uptown Girl" (1983)
- Music Video: Featured Christie Brinkley, Joel's then-wife, which helped catapult the song to greater popularity through visual media.
- Pop Hit: Marked a shift towards a more pop-oriented sound for Joel in the early '80s.
- Inspiration: Inspired by the music of Frankie Valli and the Four Seasons, showcasing Joel's ability to blend contemporary music with classic influences.

"The Longest Time" (1983)
- Doo-Wop Style: A tribute to the doo-wop genre of the '50s and '60s, showcasing Joel's diverse musical influences.
- Vocal Harmony: Features Joel's multi-tracked vocal harmonies, highlighting his vocal talent and production skills.
- Nostalgic: Lyrics reflect on a past love, evoking a sense of nostalgia and longing.

"Just the Way You Are" (1977)
- Grammy Winner: Won the Grammy for Record of the Year and Song of the Year, solidifying Joel's place in music history.
- Dedication: Originally written for Joel's first wife, Elizabeth Weber, as a testament to unconditional love.

"New York State of Mind" (1976)
- Tribute to New York: An ode to Joel's home state of New York, capturing the city's essence.
- Jazz Influences: Features rich saxophone solos and a jazz-inspired arrangement, showcasing Joel's versatility.
- Live Favorite: A favorite in Joel's live performances, often seen as a unifying song for New Yorkers and beyond.

Trivia Tidbits
- Billy Joel has never learned to read music traditionally, relying instead on his innate musical talents.
- He holds the record for the most live performances by any artist at Madison Square Garden.
- Joel is an accomplished motorcycle enthusiast and collector, owning an extensive collection of bikes.
- He was once a successful boxer during his high school years, winning 22 out of 24 fights.
- Joel's song "Allentown" reflects the economic decline of American manufacturing cities in the early 1980s.
- He was inducted into the Rock and Roll Hall of Fame in 1999.
- Joel has received honorary doctorates from several universities, including Berklee College of Music and Hofstra University.
- His daughter, Alexa Ray Joel, is also a musician and has performed with her father on several occasions.
- Joel's music has been featured in numerous films, TV shows, and theater productions.
- He has performed at the White House for several U.S. Presidents.
- Joel decided to stop writing new pop/rock music after his 1993 album "River of Dreams."
- The Library of Congress awarded him the Gershwin Prize for Popular Song in 2014.
- Despite his success, Joel has been open about his struggles with depression and substance abuse.
- He has a longstanding residency at Madison Square Garden, performing monthly since 2014.

Bonus Section
Legendary Music Venues

The Cavern Club - Liverpool, England

A legendary venue where The Beatles' early performances ignited Beatlemania, The Cavern Club is a historic site for music lovers worldwide.

The Beatles - February 9, 1961
- Debut Performance: Marking the start of an era, The Beatles began their extensive residency.
- Cultural Phenomenon: Their shows contributed to the global frenzy known as Beatlemania.
- Historic Venue: Became a pilgrimage site for Beatles fans.

The Beatles - August 3, 1963
- Final Show: Marked the end of their legendary performances at The Cavern Club.
- Rise to Stardom: The Beatles were on the brink of international fame.
- Legacy: The last Cavern show underscored their evolution from local heroes to global icons.

CBGB - New York City, USA

The cradle of punk rock, CBGB's stage was graced by iconic bands like The Ramones, Blondie, and Talking Heads.

The Ramones - August 16, 1974
- Punk Birthplace: Their debut at CBGB is often hailed as the launch of punk rock in the U.S.
- Setlist Legends: Featured songs like "Blitzkrieg Bop" and "Judy Is a Punk."

- Influential Audience: Inspired future punk and new wave bands.

Blondie - May 17, 1975
- Emerging Icons: Blondie's early performance at CBGB showcased their unique blend of punk, disco, and pop.
- Cultural Impact: Helped define the New York City music scene and the global new wave movement.
- Fashion Forward: Debbie Harry's style became as influential as their music.

The Fillmore - San Francisco, USA

A central figure in the psychedelic music scene, The Fillmore hosted groundbreaking performances by Jefferson Airplane and Jimi Hendrix.

Jefferson Airplane - February 4, 1966
- Psychedelic Pioneers: Their performance is considered a cornerstone of psychedelic rock.
- Cultural Shift: Symbolized the counterculture movement's rise.
- Innovative Sound: Blended rock with electronic experimentation.

Jimi Hendrix - February 1, 1968
- Guitar God: Hendrix's performance showcased his revolutionary guitar techniques.
- Sonic Landmarks: Featured iconic songs like "Purple Haze" and "Foxy Lady."
- Live Legacy: Cemented The Fillmore's status as a musical mecca.

Whisky a Go Go - Los Angeles, USA

An emblem of rock 'n' roll, hosting landmark performances by The Doors and other rock legends.

The Doors - July 25, 1966
- Residency Kickoff: Their performances propelled them to stardom.
- Musical Innovation: Merged rock with poetry and theatricality.
- Cultural Icon: The venue and band became symbols of the LA rock scene.

Van Halen - March 3, 1977
- Eruption: Van Halen's explosive performance showcased their groundbreaking sound.
- Guitar Hero: Eddie Van Halen's techniques influenced countless guitarists.
- Rise to Fame: Their performance helped secure their place in rock history.

Royal Albert Hall - London, England

A prestigious venue hosting iconic concerts by Bob Dylan and Led Zeppelin, marking significant moments in rock history.

Bob Dylan - May 26, 1966
- Folk-Rock Fusion: Dylan's electric set was a pivotal moment in music.
- Audience Division: Sparked controversy among folk purists.
- Historic Transition: Marked Dylan's shift from folk to rock.

Led Zeppelin - January 9, 1970
- Rock Titans: Showcased the band at their peak.
- Setlist Classics: Included "Whole Lotta Love" and "Dazed and Confused."
- Musical Mastery: Demonstrated their virtuosity and stage presence.

The Apollo Theater - New York City, USA

A cornerstone of African-American music and culture, The Apollo Theater has launched the careers of countless music legends.

James Brown - October 24, 1962
- Dynamic Performance: James Brown's live recording at The Apollo is one of the most acclaimed live albums in music history.
- Showmanship: Showcased Brown's extraordinary energy and stage presence.
- Cultural Impact: Cemented his status as a soul and funk pioneer.

Aretha Franklin - June 12, 1971
- Queen of Soul: Franklin's performance solidified her role in soul music and civil rights movement.
- Vocal Power: Demonstrated her unparalleled singing talent and emotional depth.
- Historical Venue: The Apollo's reputation as a launchpad for African-American artists was further enhanced.

Budokan Hall - Tokyo, Japan

Originally a martial arts hall, Budokan Hall became a key venue for international artists breaking into the Japanese market.

The Beatles - June 30, 1966
- Historic Concert: Marked the first appearance of a Western rock band at Budokan, challenging traditional cultural norms.
- Fan Frenzy: Unleashed Beatlemania in Japan, with thousands of fans gathering outside.
- Cultural Exchange: Opened the door for future Western acts in Japan.

Bob Dylan - February 28, 1978
- Folk Ambassador: Dylan's performance at Budokan was a significant moment in his career, showcasing his evolution as an artist.
- Setlist Diversity: Featured a wide range of Dylan's repertoire, reimagined with a large band.
- Recording Legacy: The concert was recorded and released as "Bob Dylan at Budokan," capturing a unique phase of his musical journey.

Red Rocks Amphitheatre - Morrison, USA

A naturally formed amphitheater that has hosted some of the most memorable concerts in rock history, set against a stunning geological backdrop.

The Beatles - August 26, 1964
- Historical Performance: The Beatles' concert at Red Rocks was part of their first U.S. tour, marking a significant moment in rock history.

- Natural Acoustics: The venue's unique setting provided an unforgettable sonic experience.
- Cultural Phenomenon: Represented the global reach of Beatlemania and the band's influence on American culture.

U2 - June 5, 1983
- Iconic Recording: U2's performance at Red Rocks was filmed and released as "Live at Red Rocks: Under a Blood Red Sky," a pivotal release in their career.
- Atmospheric Show: The concert took place under a stormy sky, adding to the dramatic setting and performance.
- Career Milestone: Helped establish U2 as one of the world's biggest bands and showcased Red Rocks as a premier concert venue.

Madison Square Garden - New York City, USA

An iconic venue known for hosting some of the biggest names in music, sports, and entertainment.

Elton John - October 1974
- Record-Setting Performances: Elton John's numerous sell-outs at Madison Square Garden underscore his massive popularity and the venue's importance in popular culture.
- Showmanship: Known for his flamboyant stage presence and costumes, John's performances at MSG have been pivotal in his career.
- Historical Significance: His concerts have contributed to the Garden's reputation as a "mecca" for live music.

Led Zeppelin - February 12, 1975
- Epic Shows: Part of Led Zeppelin's legendary North American tours, their MSG performances were known for their incredible energy and musicianship.
- Musical Mastery: Showcased the band's prowess across a wide spectrum of their catalog.
- Cultural Impact: These concerts solidified Led Zeppelin's status as rock icons and Madison Square Garden's place in rock history.

Wembley Stadium - London, England

Wembley Stadium has been a focal point for significant musical events, particularly known for its concerts that have global significance.

Queen - July 12, 1986
- Queen's performance is often conflated with their triumphant return to Wembley in 1986 for their own concert, which is equally legendary.
- Freddie Mercury's Charisma: Mercury's ability to engage the entire audience of tens of thousands is often cited as one of the greatest live performances.
- Legacy: This concert, especially Mercury's performance, is regularly referenced in discussions about the greatest live performances in rock history.

Live Aid - July 13, 1985
- Global Impact: A dual-venue concert held simultaneously at Wembley Stadium and JFK Stadium in Philadelphia, aimed at raising funds for famine relief in Ethiopia.
- Star-Studded Lineup: Featured performances by some of the biggest names in music, including U2, Madonna, and David Bowie.

- Historical Significance: Live Aid is one of the largest-scale satellite link-up and television broadcasts of all time, with an estimated global audience of 1.9 billion across 150 nations.

Sydney Opera House - Sydney, Australia

An architectural marvel and UNESCO World Heritage Site, the Sydney Opera House is a multi-venue performing arts center known for its unique design and acoustics.

Dame Joan Sutherland - 1973
- Opera Legend: The Australian soprano, known as "La Stupenda," gave memorable performances at the Opera House, celebrating her incredible vocal talent and contribution to opera.
- Homecoming: Her performances at the Sydney Opera House were seen as a homecoming for the internationally acclaimed soprano.
- Cultural Icon: Sutherland's performances helped cement the Opera House's status as a premier venue for opera globally.

The Sydney Symphony Orchestra - Ongoing
- Resident Orchestra: The Sydney Symphony Orchestra regularly performs at the Opera House, showcasing classical music to audiences from around the world.
- Acoustic Excellence: The performances highlight the venue's world-class acoustics and its ability to host a wide range of musical genres.
- Cultural Beacon: The ongoing presence of the Sydney Symphony Orchestra at the Opera House underscores the venue's importance in Australia's cultural landscape.

One-Hit Wonders Through the Decades

Ah, the fascinating world of one-hit wonders! Picture this: an artist climbs the charts, captures hearts, and fills the airwaves with a tune so catchy, so unforgettable, that... well, that's it. They shine brightly like a comet across the musical night sky, leaving behind a single, indelible mark on the tapestry of pop culture before fading into the annals of trivia and "Where are they now?" segments. A one-hit wonder is that rare gem—a song that achieves massive popularity, often becoming more famous than the artist who performed it. Now, let's dive into a playful exploration of these ephemeral stars of the music world, from the 1950s to the 1989, highlighting one for each decade.

1950s
- "Rockin' Robin" - Bobby Day (1958): Peaked at No. 2 on the Billboard Hot 100. This catchy tune has been covered by numerous artists, including Michael Jackson, making it a timeless classic that still gets people tapping their feet.
- "At the Hop" - Danny & the Juniors (1957): Reached No. 1 on the Billboard Hot 100. An anthem of the rock and roll era, it captured the spirit of teenage dance parties, or "hops," and remains a staple of 50s nostalgia.
- "Sea of Love" - Phil Phillips (1959): Climbed to No. 2 on the Billboard Hot 100. Its haunting melody has made it a favorite for use in films and TV shows, echoing the longing and romance of the late 1950s.

1960s
- "Spirit in the Sky" - Norman Greenbaum (1969): Reached No. 3 on the Billboard Hot 100. Its inclusion in major films and commercials has cemented its status as an iconic track of the era.

- "Hey Baby" - Bruce Channel (1962): Hit No. 1 on the Billboard Hot 100. This song's simple, catchy chorus and harmonica riff have made it a beloved oldie.
- "Sugar, Sugar" - The Archies (1969): Topped the Billboard Hot 100. Originally by a fictional band from the Archie comics, this sweet tune is one of the most memorable hits of the 60s.

1970s
- "Play That Funky Music" - Wild Cherry (1976): Topped the Billboard Hot 100. Its funky beat and catchy chorus have kept it alive on playlists and at parties decades later.
- "Kung Fu Fighting" - Carl Douglas (1974): Reached No. 1 on the Billboard Hot 100. This song capitalized on the mid-70s kung fu craze and remains a fun, novelty classic.
- "Afternoon Delight" - Starland Vocal Band (1976): Peaked at No. 1 on the Billboard Hot 100. Known for its close harmony and sexually suggestive lyrics, it's a quintessential 70s soft rock hit.

1980s
- "Take On Me" - a-ha (1984): Reached No. 1 on the Billboard Hot 100. Its groundbreaking music video and catchy synth melody make it an enduring 80s classic.
- "Tainted Love" - Soft Cell (1981): Climbed to No. 8 on the Billboard Hot 100. A synth-pop reimagining of a soul classic, it's celebrated for its catchy hook and innovative sound.
- "Come on Eileen" - Dexys Midnight Runners (1982): Hit No. 1 on the Billboard Hot 100. This mix of Celtic folk and pop, with its infectious chorus, has become a sing-along favorite at parties and weddings.

Trivia Tidbits

- Bobby Day, known for "Rockin' Robin" (1958), was a founding member of the Hollywood Flames.
- "At the Hop" (1957) by Danny & the Juniors was initially titled "Do the Bop" before Dick Clark suggested changing it.
- Phil Phillips was paid only $6,800 for "Sea of Love" (1959) and received no further royalties.
- Norman Greenbaum purchased a unique fuzz box for the distinctive guitar sound in "Spirit in the Sky" (1969).
- Delbert McClinton taught John Lennon some harmonica tricks after playing on "Hey Baby" (1962) by Bruce Channel.
- The Archies were the first fictional band to have a No. 1 hit on the Billboard Hot 100 with "Sugar, Sugar" (1969).
- "Play That Funky Music" (1976) by Wild Cherry was inspired by a shout from the audience: "Play some funky music, white boy."
- Carl Douglas recorded "Kung Fu Fighting" (1974) in just 10 minutes at the end of a studio session.
- The title "Afternoon Delight" (1976) by Starland Vocal Band was inspired by a menu item at a restaurant in Washington, D.C.
- The sketch animation for a-ha's "Take On Me" (1984) video took four months to complete.
- Soft Cell's "Tainted Love" (1981) holds the Guinness World Record for the longest consecutive stay on the US Billboard Hot 100 by a British artist.
- "Come on Eileen" (1982) by Dexys Midnight Runners prevented Michael Jackson from having back-to-back No. 1 hits in the UK.
- Many one-hit wonders gain new popularity through movie soundtracks or commercials.

Famous Music Festivals Through Time

Beyond the iconic Woodstock and Live Aid, the rich tapestry of music history is dotted with festivals that have not only captured the spirit of their times but continue to resonate today. These gatherings have evolved from simple concerts to elaborate celebrations of music, culture, and community, showcasing a diverse range of genres and attracting audiences from around the globe. Let's explore some of the other monumental music festivals that have left an indelible mark on the industry and continue to thrive.

The Glastonbury Festival, held in Somerset, England, is a beacon of music and performing arts. Starting in 1970, the day after Jimi Hendrix's death, Glastonbury has grown from a humble gathering at Michael Eavis's farm to one of the most famous festivals worldwide. Renowned for its eclectic lineup, the festival spans genres from rock and pop to electronic, world music, and beyond, all while promoting environmental awareness and charity. Its iconic Pyramid Stage has hosted unforgettable performances by the world's biggest artists, making it a pilgrimage site for music lovers.

Another festival that has significantly impacted the music scene is Coachella. Held annually in the Colorado Desert of California since 1999, Coachella has become synonymous with groundbreaking musical performances, art installations, and celebrity sightings. Its influence extends beyond the music, with fashion trends and live-streaming milestones marking its modern cultural significance. Coachella's ability to blend genres and showcase both established and emerging artists across its sun-drenched stages has cemented its place as a trendsetter in the festival circuit.

Outside the United States and the UK, Tomorrowland in Belgium has emerged as the world's largest electronic music festival. Since its inception in 2005, Tomorrowland has become a global phenomenon, celebrated for its extravagant stages, intricate themes, and a lineup that includes the biggest names in electronic dance music. The festival's ethos of unity and love, coupled with its innovative use of technology in production, creates an immersive experience that draws fans from every corner of the planet, underscoring the universal language of music.

Trivia Tidbits about Music Festivals

Glastonbury was initially called the Pilton Festival and charged £1 for entry, including free milk from the farm.

The first Coachella festival lost $800,000 despite its groundbreaking lineup.

Tomorrowland sells out within minutes, with tickets for recent editions gone in as little as one hour.

Glastonbury takes a "fallow year" every five years to give the land, local residents, and organizers a break.

Coachella's iconic Ferris wheel has become one of the festival's most recognizable symbols.

The 1971 Glastonbury Festival featured the first use of a pyramid stage, inspired by the Great Pyramid of Giza.

Coachella expanded to two weekends in 2012 due to high demand.

Tomorrowland bridges the physical and digital worlds with its "Unite with Tomorrowland" events, live-streaming performances to global audiences.

David Bowie's 2000 performance at Glastonbury is often hailed as one of the greatest in the festival's history.

Coachella was one of the first major festivals to embrace live streaming, offering performances to a global audience via YouTube.

Tomorrowland's main stage designs are themed, with past themes including "The Book of Wisdom" and "The Elixir of Life."

A portion of Coachella's profits is donated to local community organizations in Indio, California.

Glastonbury has its own newspaper, The Glastonbury Free Press, printed on-site during the festival.

In 2017, Tomorrowland held two weekends themed "Amicorum Spectaculum," celebrating the spectacle of friendship.

The largest crowd in Coachella history was in 2012 for Dr. Dre and Snoop Dogg's performance, featuring a hologram of Tupac Shakur.

Glastonbury's Pyramid Stage was powered by 100% renewable energy for the first time in 2010.

Coachella's grounds are on a polo field, which is part of the Empire Polo Club.

Tomorrowland's "DreamVille" is a vibrant camping city that hosts festival-goers from over 200 countries.

Glastonbury's "Shangri-La" area focuses on contemporary music and immersive art installations.

Coachella initially started as a protest by Pearl Jam against ticket service fees, leading to the selection of the Empire Polo Club as a venue

Welcome to the Ultimate Countdown of Record-Breaking Album Sales!

As we journey through the golden era of vinyl and cassettes, we uncover the albums that not only defined their time but also broke sales records, leaving an indelible mark on the music industry. From rock 'n' roll revolutions to pop phenomenons, the period between 1950 and 1989 was a time of musical innovation and expansion. These albums became the soundtrack to generations, influencing countless artists and fans alike. As we prepare to dive into this countdown, let's celebrate the incredible achievements of these legendary records, which continue to resonate with music lovers around the world.

Before we unveil the iconic number one spot, let's take a moment to appreciate the journey we've embarked on. From the initial beats of the 10th entry to the unforgettable melodies that have graced our list, each album has contributed uniquely to the tapestry of music history. Their stories, from studio struggles to groundbreaking production techniques, have become as legendary as the tracks themselves. As anticipation builds, remember that the number one spot represents more than just sales—it symbolizes a moment in time that captured the hearts and ears of the world.

#10: "Hotel California" - Eagles (1976)
- Introduced the iconic title track with its unforgettable guitar solo.
- Themes of materialism, disillusionment, and the excesses of the American dream.

- Won the Grammy for Record of the Year.
- A mix of rock, country, and folk influences.
- Album cover art is a photograph of the Beverly Hills Hotel.
- "New Kid in Town" and "Life in the Fast Lane" were also hit singles.
- The title track's solo is ranked among the greatest guitar solos ever.
- The term "Hotel California" has become synonymous with critiques of Hollywood.
- Rumors persist about hidden meanings in the lyrics, though the band insists it's more metaphorical.

#9: "Back in Black" - AC/DC (1980)
- First album with Brian Johnson as the lead vocalist after Bon Scott's death.
- "You Shook Me All Night Long" and the title track are rock anthems.
- Recorded in the Bahamas during a tropical storm.
- The all-black cover was a tribute to Bon Scott.
- Known for its solid rock production by Mutt Lange.
- Revitalized AC/DC's career and rock music in the early '80s.
- "Hells Bells" features a 2,000-pound bronze bell.
- AC/DC's comeback story, overcoming the tragedy of losing their lead singer.

#8: "Saturday Night Fever" - Bee Gees (Soundtrack) (1977)
- Soundtrack to the film starring John Travolta, defining the disco era.
- Hits include "Stayin' Alive," "How Deep Is Your Love," and "Night Fever."
- Won five Grammy Awards, including Album of the Year.
- Iconic album cover featuring Travolta in his famous white suit pose.

- Music composed before the movie was filmed, influencing its scenes.
- "Stayin' Alive" became an anthem for the disco dance movement.
- Played a crucial role in popularizing disco music worldwide.
- Led to a disco boom in the late '70s.

#7: "Rumours" - Fleetwood Mac (1977)
- Born out of personal turmoil, featuring songs about the band members' relationships.
- Includes timeless hits like "Go Your Own Way," "Dreams," and "The Chain."
- "Dreams" became Fleetwood Mac's only No. 1 hit in the U.S.
- Won the Grammy Award for Album of the Year in 1978.
- The making was fraught with tension, fueled by breakups and substance abuse.
- Considered a masterpiece of production and songwriting.
- Stevie Nicks' "Dreams" was written in a single day.
- Album cover features Mick Fleetwood and Stevie Nicks in a peculiar pose.

#6: "The Dark Side of the Moon" - Pink Floyd (1973)
- A concept album exploring themes of conflict, greed, time, death, and mental illness.
- Remained on the Billboard charts for 937 weeks, more than any other album in history.
- Features the iconic prism cover art by Storm Thorgerson.
- Includes the hit "Money," known for its cash register and coin sound effects.
- Engineered by Alan Parsons, known for the Alan Parsons Project.
- Praised for its complex sonic landscape and pioneering use of synthesizers and sound effects.
- A favorite for audiophiles due to its high production quality.

- Inspired countless musicians and bands across various genres.

#5: "Born in the U.S.A." - Bruce Springsteen (1984)
- Contains seven top-10 hit singles, tying with another iconic album.
- Lyrics explore the disillusionment with the American Dream and hardships of working-class Americans.
- The title track is often misunderstood as a patriotic anthem.
- Cover photo features Springsteen's backside in front of an American flag.
- "Dancing in the Dark" was Springsteen's highest-charting single.
- Made Springsteen a global superstar.
- Features the E Street Band at the peak of their powers.
- Received critical acclaim for storytelling ability.
- Recorded on analog tape, contributing to its warm, distinctive sound.

#4: "Abbey Road" - The Beatles (1969)
- The last album recorded by The Beatles, though not their last released.
- Famous cover of the band crossing the street outside Abbey Road Studios.
- Known for its second side medley, a series of connected songs.
- Includes classics like "Come Together," "Something," and "Here Comes the Sun."
- Cover sparked the "Paul is dead" conspiracy theory.
- "Something" and "Here Comes the Sun" are considered some of George Harrison's best work.
- Groundbreaking production techniques and sound engineering.
- One of the first mainstream pop music uses of a Moog synthesizer.

- Often cited as one of the greatest albums in music history.

#3: "Thriller" - Michael Jackson (1982)
- Broke racial barriers on MTV with the "Billie Jean" music video.
- Won a record-breaking eight Grammy Awards.
- Features collaborations with Paul McCartney and Eddie Van Halen.
- Groundbreaking use of music videos for "Thriller," "Billie Jean," and "Beat It."
- Produced by Quincy Jones, blending pop, post-disco, funk, and rock.
- "Thriller" music video was a landmark in music video production.
- Album's success transformed Jackson into a dominant figure in global pop culture.
- Influenced countless artists across various music genres.

#2: "Sgt. Pepper's Lonely Hearts Club Band" - The Beatles (1967)
- Pioneered the concept album format, influencing the structure of future music albums.
- Features an elaborate cover with the Beatles in costume among historical figures.
- Won four Grammy Awards, including Album of the Year.
- Songs like "Lucy in the Sky with Diamonds" and "A Day in the Life" became anthems of the era.
- Utilized innovative studio techniques, including multi-track recording and tape loops.
- The album's release marked the beginning of the Summer of Love.
- Widely regarded as one of the most important albums in music history, influencing both music and culture.
- Helped to legitimize popular music as a genuine art form.

#1: "Pet Sounds" - The Beach Boys (1966)
- Considered Brian Wilson's masterpiece, with elaborate arrangements and innovative production.
- Inspired The Beatles' "Sgt. Pepper's Lonely Hearts Club Band."
- Features hits like "Wouldn't It Be Nice" and "God Only Knows."
- Utilized unconventional instruments and studio techniques.
- Lyrics reflect themes of love, innocence, and disillusionment.
- Praised for its emotional depth and sophistication in songwriting.

The Beach Boys, an American rock band formed in Hawthorne, California, in 1961. Initially gaining fame for their vocal harmonies and lyrics reflecting Southern California's youth culture of surfing, cars, and romance, the group's creative direction shifted under the leadership of Brian Wilson.
- The band, consisting of brothers Brian, Dennis, and Carl Wilson, their cousin Mike Love, and friend Al Jardine, initially formed during their high school years.
- Often cited as one of the greatest pop songs ever written, "Good Vibrations" was a technical marvel of its time, costing an unprecedented amount of money and taking months to record, showcasing Wilson's genius as a producer.
- Dennis Wilson was the only actual surfer in the band.
- The band originally performed under the name The Pendletones.
- The original lyrics for "California Girls" were written on a napkin by Brian Wilson while in bed.
- They were the first major rock band to play a live concert in the Soviet Union in 1988.
- The Beach Boys' song "Never Learn Not to Love" was co-written by Charles Manson. The infamous cult leader! The song is an altered version of "Cease to Exist"

Influential Music Producers

1950s

Sam Phillips

Artists & Songs: Discovered and produced early recordings of Elvis Presley, including "That's All Right." Also worked with Johnny Cash ("Folsom Prison Blues"), Jerry Lee Lewis ("Great Balls of Fire"), and Carl Perkins ("Blue Suede Shoes").

- Founded Sun Records, which played a crucial role in the birth of rock 'n' roll.
- Phillips is credited with discovering Elvis Presley when he was just an 18-year-old truck driver.
- He famously sold Elvis Presley's contract to RCA for $35,000 to finance his label, a move he never regretted.

George Martin

Artists & Songs: While George Martin's most influential work came in the 1960s with The Beatles, his career began in the 1950s. He produced comedy and novelty records for artists like Peter Sellers and Spike Milligan.

- Known as the "Fifth Beatle" for his extensive involvement in The Beatles' albums.
- Pioneered studio techniques that transformed music production.
- His classical background brought unique orchestral arrangements to rock music.

1960s

Phil Spector

Artists & Songs: Created the "Wall of Sound" production technique. Worked with The Ronettes ("Be My Baby"), The Righteous Brothers ("You've Lost That Lovin' Feelin'"), and Ike & Tina Turner ("River Deep - Mountain High").

- Spector's "Wall of Sound" involved dense orchestration, multiple musicians, and innovative studio techniques.
- His tumultuous personal life and legal troubles later overshadowed his musical achievements.
- He was inducted into the Rock and Roll Hall of Fame in 1989.

Berry Gordy

Artists & Songs: Founded Motown Records, launching the careers of The Supremes ("Where Did Our Love Go"), Stevie Wonder ("Fingertips"), Marvin Gaye ("I Heard It Through the Grapevine"), and many others.

- Gordy started Motown with an $800 loan from his family.
- He developed a production line approach to record making, emphasizing quality control.
- Gordy also wrote or co-wrote numerous hits for his artists.

1970s

Quincy Jones

Artists & Songs: Produced Michael Jackson's albums, including "Off the Wall" and "Thriller." Worked with Frank Sinatra ("Fly Me to the Moon"), and produced the soundtrack for "The Wiz."

- Jones has won 28 Grammy Awards, the most by a living person.
- He was the first African American to be nominated for an Academy Award for Best Original Song.
- Jones has worked in various capacities across the entertainment industry, including film, television, and magazines.

Brian Eno

Artists & Songs: Pioneer of ambient music, produced albums for Talking Heads ("Remain in Light"), David Bowie (Berlin Trilogy: "Low," "Heroes," "Lodger"), and U2 ("The Joshua Tree").
- Eno coined the term "ambient music" and was instrumental in its development.
- Developed the Oblique Strategies cards, a set of prompts intended to break creative blocks.
- His influence extends beyond music to visual arts and writing.

1980s

Rick Rubin

Artists & Songs: Co-founded Def Jam Recordings, producing early hip-hop classics like LL Cool J's "Radio" and The Beastie Boys' "Licensed to Ill." Also worked with Run-D.M.C. ("Raising Hell").
- Rubin is known for his minimalist production style, focusing on the essence of the music.
- He has worked across a wide range of genres, from hip-hop to rock to country.
- Rubin's work with Johnny Cash revitalized the country legend's career.

Mutt Lange

Artists & Songs: Produced some of the biggest rock albums of the decade, including AC/DC's "Back in Black," Def Leppard's "Pyromania" and "Hysteria," and Foreigner's "4."
- Lange is known for his meticulous attention to detail and pursuit of perfection in the studio.
- Rarely gives interviews or appears in public, maintaining a mystique around his persona.
- He also had a successful partnership with his then-wife, country singer Shania Twain, producing her best-selling albums.

Daniel Lanois

Artists & Songs: Daniel Lanois is best known for his collaboration with Brian Eno in producing U2's seminal albums of the 1980s, including "The Unforgettable Fire" (1984) and "The Joshua Tree" (1987). His production work helped to define U2's sound, with a focus on ambiance, texture, and emotional depth. Lanois also worked on Peter Gabriel's "So" (1986).
- Production Style: Known for creating atmospheric, mood-driven soundscapes, using the studio as an instrument through innovative sonic experimentation.
- Genre Versatility: Demonstrated ability to produce across genres—rock, ambient, country, folk, and world music—highlighting a broad musical palette.
- Influence on Artists: Recognized for deep, personal connections with artists, nurturing their creativity and vision, leading to critically and commercially successful albums.

Music in Movies: Iconic Soundtracks

Delving into the realm of cinema, certain soundtracks have transcended their films to become iconic in their own right, shaping not just the movies they accompany but also the wider cultural landscape. Here's a look at two standout soundtracks from each era that have left an indelible mark on the world of music and film.

1950s

"Singin' in the Rain" (1952)

- Artists & Songs: Gene Kelly, Debbie Reynolds, and Donald O'Connor bring to life memorable tunes like the title track "Singin' in the Rain" and "Good Morning."

Despite its acclaim today, the film was only a modest hit upon its original release.
The iconic scene of Gene Kelly dancing in the rain was accomplished with a mixture of water and milk to ensure visibility on camera.
Gene Kelly was reportedly running a fever of 103°F (39.4°C) while performing the famous rain-soaked dance sequence.

"Blackboard Jungle" (1955)

- Artists & Songs: Featured Bill Haley & His Comets' "Rock Around the Clock," which became an anthem for rock 'n' roll youth culture.

The film is credited with popularizing rock 'n' roll, using its energy to underscore the themes of teenage angst and rebellion.
"Rock Around the Clock" wasn't originally intended for the

opening credits but was added after its success in test screenings.

The film faced censorship issues in several countries due to its depiction of juvenile delinquency and its association with rock 'n' roll music.

1960s

"The Sound of Music" (1965)

- Artists & Songs: Julie Andrews and the cast perform timeless songs like "Do-Re-Mi," "My Favorite Things," and the title song "The Sound of Music."

The soundtrack was immensely successful, topping the charts worldwide and becoming one of the best-selling albums of the 1960s.

The film's Austrian locations have become pilgrimage sites for fans of the movie.

Julie Andrews performed her own stunts, including the opening hilltop scene, despite adverse weather conditions.

"West Side Story" (1961)

Artists & Songs: Features Leonard Bernstein's music and Stephen Sondheim's lyrics with songs like "Maria," "Tonight," and "Somewhere."

The film won 10 Academy Awards, including Best Picture and Best Music.

The choreography and vibrant use of color in the film have been highly influential in both cinema and theater.

Some of the singing voices were dubbed, a common practice at the time, to achieve the desired musical effect.

1970s

"Saturday Night Fever" (1977)

Artists & Songs: The Bee Gees dominated the soundtrack with hits like "Stayin' Alive," "How Deep Is Your Love," and "Night Fever."
The soundtrack became one of the best-selling albums of all time, epitomizing the disco era.
John Travolta's dance moves and white suit became cultural icons.
The soundtrack's success propelled disco music into mainstream popularity, sparking a global disco fever.

"Grease" (1978)

- Artists & Songs: John Travolta and Olivia Newton-John singing "You're the One That I Want," "Summer Nights," and "Greased Lightnin'."

The film's soundtrack is one of the best-selling of all time, capturing the nostalgic essence of the 1950s.
Olivia Newton-John's pants in the final scene were so tight she had to be sewn into them.
"Grease" sparked a resurgence in interest in 1950s culture and music.

1980s

"Purple Rain" (1984)

- Artists & Songs: Prince and The Revolution brought hits like "When Doves Cry," "Let's Go Crazy," and the iconic "Purple Rain."

The album served as the soundtrack to the film of the same name and won an Academy Award for Best Original Song Score. "Purple Rain" is often hailed as one of the greatest albums of all time, showcasing Prince's genius.
The film and album marked a pivotal moment in Prince's career, cementing his status as a music icon.

"Top Gun" (1986)

- Artists & Songs: Features Berlin's "Take My Breath Away" and Kenny Loggins' "Danger Zone."
- The music of "Top Gun" is not just background noise; it's carefully integrated with key scenes to enhance the emotional impact and storytelling.
- Beyond the success of individual songs, the "Top Gun" soundtrack as a whole became an iconic album of the 1980s. It features a mix of rock, pop, and instrumental score pieces that capture the movie's energy and themes.
- The album achieved massive commercial success, reaching the top of the Billboard 200 chart and earning a 9x Platinum certification from the RIAA, signifying over 9 million copies sold in the United States alone.

The songs "Danger Zone" and "Take My Breath Away" have become anthems of the era, often used in media and events to evoke the 1980s' spirit. The soundtrack's impact extends beyond the film, encapsulating the decade's musical trends and continuing to resonate with audiences both old and new.

The opening sequence of "Top Gun," featuring the song "Danger Zone" by Kenny Loggins, is one of the most iconic in film history. The combination of thrilling aerial footage and adrenaline-pumping music sets the tone for the entire movie, instantly grabbing the audience's attention and immersing them in the world of naval aviation.

Iconic Album Covers and Artwork
1950s

"Elvis Presley" - Elvis Presley (1956)
- Idea Behind Cover: The debut album cover of Elvis Presley aimed to capture his raw energy and emerging rock 'n' roll spirit. It showcases Presley in mid-performance, embodying the youthful rebellion and musical innovation of the era.
- Cover Art: A black-and-white photo of Elvis with his guitar, captured in an animated pose, suggesting movement and excitement, a visual that became synonymous with rock 'n' roll.

"Miles Davis Volume 1" - Miles Davis (1957)
- Idea Behind Cover: This album cover reflects the cool, sophisticated essence of jazz. It portrays Miles Davis as the epitome of the jazz musician: stylish, contemplative, and deeply connected to his art.
- Cover Art: A photo of Davis playing his trumpet, with a blue hue dominating the image, reinforcing the "cool" atmosphere of his music and the jazz genre itself.

1960s

"The Beatles - Sgt. Pepper's Lonely Hearts Club Band" (1967)

- Idea Behind Cover: Designed by Peter Blake and Jann Haworth, the cover was meant to represent a fictional band performance. It reflects the Beatles' shift from pop stars to studio artists, embodying the psychedelic era.
- Cover Art: Features the Beatles in vibrant, satin military-style costumes among a gathering of life-sized cardboard cutouts of famous people, blending reality with fantasy in a colorful collage.

"The Velvet Underground & Nico" (1967)
- Idea Behind Cover: The cover, featuring Andy Warhol's banana artwork, symbolizes the band's connection to the pop art movement and their departure from mainstream music norms.
- Cover Art: A simple, yet striking yellow banana sticker with "Peel slowly and see" instructions, beneath which is a flesh-colored banana, suggesting themes of revelation and the avant-garde.

1970s

"Pink Floyd - The Dark Side of the Moon" (1973)

- Idea Behind Cover: Designed by Storm Thorgerson of Hipgnosis, the cover reflects the album's themes of life, light, and the human experience, using light refraction as a metaphor.
- Cover Art: A prism dispersing light into color spectrum against a black background, symbolizing simplicity, clarity, and the band's exploration of light and sound.

"Led Zeppelin - Led Zeppelin IV" (1971)
- Idea Behind Cover: Intended to contrast the commercialization of music, the album features no mention of the band or album name, aiming to let the music speak for itself.
- Cover Art: A 19th-century rustic oil painting of a dilapidated wall and a framed picture of a man carrying sticks, juxtaposed with modern high-rise buildings in the background, representing the clash between old and new.

1980s

"Michael Jackson - Thriller" (1982)

- Idea Behind Cover: The cover aimed to present Jackson as a larger-than-life figure, capturing his charisma and the album's groundbreaking fusion of pop and music video storytelling.
- Cover Art: A portrait of Jackson lying down in a white suit, smiling, exuding confidence and appeal, signaling his dominance in the pop music landscape.

"The Clash - London Calling" (1979)

- Idea Behind Cover: Inspired by Elvis Presley's debut album design, the cover captures the energy of live performance and the band's punk ethos, signaling a clash with traditional rock norms.
- Cover Art: A photo of Paul Simonon smashing his bass guitar on stage, encapsulated in a stark, impactful design, echoing the rebellious spirit of punk and the album's critique of contemporary issues.

he tradition of featuring artwork on record covers dates back to the 1940s, but it was in the 1950s and beyond that album art truly began to flourish, transforming the vinyl record cover into a canvas for creative expression.

The importance of vinyl covers lies not just in their aesthetic appeal but also in their role in marketing and identity. Iconic album covers can become as memorable as the music itself, creating a visual association with the artist or band and often reflecting the era's cultural and artistic movements. For many music enthusiasts, collecting vinyl is as much about the cover art as it is about the music.

Music and Technology: From Vinyl to Digital

The story of music's evolution from vinyl to digital is a vibrant tapestry woven with innovations, cultural shifts, and an ever-changing landscape of how we consume music. It's a journey that mirrors our own technological advancements and societal changes, transforming not just the medium but the very essence of music listening experiences.

Once upon a time, the warm crackle of a vinyl record was the hallmark of audio fidelity. Introduced in the late 1940s, vinyl records became the standard for music consumption, beloved for their rich sound and tangible connection to the artistry of music. Album covers were art pieces, and liner notes were devoured by eager fans. This era was characterized by the ritual of music listening; dropping the needle on a record was an act of anticipation and reverence.

As the decades rolled on, the 1960s and 1970s saw music and technology dancing closely, with advancements in stereo sound and multi-track recording pushing the boundaries of what music could sound like. The introduction of the compact cassette tape in the 1960s offered a new form of portability and personalization, allowing music lovers to create mixtapes, a curated collection of one's musical tastes, shared between friends, lovers, and generations.

However, it was the digital revolution that would bring the most seismic shift in music consumption. The compact disc (CD), introduced in the early 1980s, promised unparalleled sound clarity and convenience. A silver disc that could hold hours of music with the press of a button felt like science fiction come to life. The CD era also ushered in the age of the album, with artists and labels capitalizing on the format's capacity to craft expansive, thematic works.

But even as CDs dominated, a new digital frontier was on the horizon. The advent of the MP3 in the late 1990s began to challenge the very foundation of the music industry. Music files could now be compressed, shared, and downloaded over the emerging internet, leading to a tumultuous period of adaptation and conflict within the industry. Peer-to-peer sharing sites like Napster disrupted traditional music distribution, sparking debates about copyright, ownership, and the value of music.

The response to this digital upheaval was multifaceted. While the music industry grappled with piracy, it also embraced the potential of the internet as a platform for music distribution. The launch of platforms like iTunes and, later, streaming services such as Spotify and Apple Music, transformed music from a product into a service. These platforms offered unprecedented access to vast libraries of music, changing the listener's relationship with music; from owning to accessing, from albums to playlists, music became more fluid, personalized, and accessible than ever before.

Today, we stand at another interesting juncture in the music and technology saga. Vinyl has seen a resurgence, cherished not just by audiophiles and collectors but by a new generation seeking tangible connections to music in a digital age. Meanwhile, streaming platforms continue to evolve, with algorithms curating personalized listening experiences and artists leveraging technology to release music in innovative formats.

The journey from vinyl to digital is a testament to music's enduring power to adapt, evolve, and continue to capture the human spirit. It reflects our desire for connection, expression, and the endless pursuit of sonic perfection. As we look ahead, the only certainty is that music and technology will continue to dance together, leading us into new realms of auditory experience.

- The first vinyl LP (Long Play) record was introduced by Columbia Records in 1948, revolutionizing the music industry by allowing for up to 22 minutes of music per side, compared to the previous limit of about 3 minutes on a 78 rpm record.
- Cassette tapes, introduced in the 1960s, were initially designed for dictation, not music, until advancements in tape quality and recording techniques made them suitable for music in the late 1970s.
- The iconic "Walkman" portable cassette player was introduced by Sony in 1979, changing the way people listened to music on the go and becoming a cultural phenomenon.
- The first commercially available CD was "52nd Street" by Billy Joel, released in 1982, signaling the beginning of the digital music era.
- Philips and Sony, the developers of the CD, agreed on the standard disc diameter of 120mm based on the capacity to hold Beethoven's Ninth Symphony in its entirety.
- The MP3, developed in the late 1980s and popularized in the 1990s, originally faced skepticism from the music industry due to its compression technique, which some feared would degrade audio quality.
- Napster, founded in 1999, was the first peer-to-peer (P2P) file sharing service that made it easy to download music for free, leading to major legal battles and discussions about copyright in the digital age.
- Apple's iTunes Store, launched in 2003, was the first legal site to sell music downloads on a massive scale, marking a turning point for the digital music industry.

- The Spotify streaming service was launched in October 2008 in Sweden and would eventually revolutionize music consumption again by offering access to millions of songs through a subscription model.
- Vinyl record sales have seen a resurgence since the early 2010s, with sales numbers reaching levels not seen since the 1980s, driven by a desire for tangible music and high-quality sound.
  - The world's largest vinyl record is located on the roof of the Forum Shops at Caesars in Las Vegas. It's a replica of The Beatles' "Sgt. Pepper's Lonely Hearts Club Band" album cover.
- In 2015, the "Golden Record," which was sent into space aboard the Voyager spacecraft in 1977, became the first vinyl record to leave the solar system, carrying sounds and images selected to portray the diversity of life and culture on Earth to any extraterrestrial finders.
  - The most expensive vinyl record ever sold is Wu-Tang Clan's "Once Upon a Time in Shaolin," a unique album of which only one copy was made. It was sold for $2 million in 2015.
- A study in 2014 revealed that the color of vinyl could affect its sound quality, with black vinyl generally providing the best sound due to the carbon added, which strengthens the record.
- The introduction of Auto-Tune in the late 1990s was a technological advancement that changed music production forever, initially designed to correct off-key inaccuracies, it has since become a popular effect for artistic expression in its own right.

International Music: Influences Across Borders

The global exchange of musical styles and influences from the 1950s to the 1989 has been a significant factor in shaping the world's musical landscape, creating a rich mosaic of sounds that defy geographical and cultural boundaries. This period witnessed the emergence and global spread of genres such as reggae, bossa nova, and Afrobeat, each bringing distinct cultural identities to the international stage. These genres not only enriched the global music scene but also highlighted the unique cultural heritages of their countries of origin, fostering a greater appreciation for diversity in music.

During these decades, several artists from outside the English-speaking world left an indelible mark on the international music scene, their songs crossing borders and resonating with audiences worldwide. Their music, often infused with traditional elements, spoke of universal themes, bridging differences and connecting people across continents.

Significant International Artists and Songs (1950s-1989):

- Bob Marley (Jamaica) - "No Woman, No Cry" (1974): This reggae anthem introduced the world to the struggles and resilience of the Jamaican experience, making Bob Marley an international symbol of peace and unity.

- Antônio Carlos Jobim (Brazil) - "The Girl from Ipanema" (1964): Written by Jobim, this bossa nova classic brought the sultry sounds of Brazil to a global audience, becoming one of the most covered songs in the world.

- Fela Kuti (Nigeria) - "Zombie" (1977): Fela's Afrobeat masterpiece, with its potent mix of jazz, funk, and Nigerian traditional music, carried a fierce political message that resonated well beyond Africa.
- Nusrat Fateh Ali Khan (Pakistan) - "Mustt Mustt" (1988): The Qawwali maestro's collaboration with Western musicians introduced the soul-stirring power of Sufi music to a global audience, blending traditional South Asian music with contemporary sounds.
- Serge Gainsbourg and Jane Birkin (France) - "Je t'aime... moi non plus" (1969): This controversial duet captivated audiences worldwide, showcasing the provocative side of French pop music and the cultural liberation of the era.

Trivia Tidbits

- "No Woman, No Cry" became an anthem for resilience and hope, not just in Jamaica but globally, solidifying Bob Marley's status as a musical and cultural icon.
- "The Girl from Ipanema" was a hit both in Brazil and internationally, bringing bossa nova to the forefront of the jazz and pop music scenes in the 1960s.
- "Zombie" was a sharp critique of the Nigerian military regime and became an anthem for resistance against oppression, showcasing the power of music as a form of protest.
- "Mustt Mustt" was groundbreaking in its fusion of Qawwali with Western music, paving the way for future collaborations between South Asian artists and Western musicians.

- "Je t'aime... moi non plus" was banned in several countries due to its explicit content, but it only fueled the song's popularity, highlighting the changing social mores of the late 1960s.

- Bob Marley was posthumously awarded the Grammy Lifetime Achievement Award in 2001, recognizing his everlasting impact on the music industry and his role in spreading reggae music globally.

- "The Girl from Ipanema" is one of the most recorded songs of all time, with hundreds of versions by artists around the world, illustrating its universal appeal and the global influence of bossa nova.

- Fela Kuti's music was heavily influenced by his social and political activism. He founded the Kalakuta Republic, a communal compound that declared independence from the Nigerian state, serving as a hub for his revolutionary ideas and music.

- The recording of "Mustt Mustt" by Nusrat Fateh Ali Khan marked one of the first successful fusions of Pakistani music with Western pop, influencing many artists across genres to explore similar cross-cultural collaborations.

- The controversy surrounding "Je t'aime... moi non plus" led to it being banned from radio play in several countries, yet it still reached number one on the UK singles chart, a testament to its provocative appeal and the changing cultural landscape of the era.

- Bob Marley's "No Woman, No Cry" is actually credited to Vincent Ford, a friend of Marley's who ran a soup kitchen in Trenchtown, the ghetto of Kingston, Jamaica. Marley attributed the song to Ford to ensure the royalty checks would fund the soup kitchen.

- Antônio Carlos Jobim, the composer of "The Girl from Ipanema," is considered one of the primary creators of the bossa nova style, and his music has left a lasting legacy on the international jazz and pop music scene.

- Fela Kuti was not only a musician but also a political maverick. He ran for president in Nigeria's 1979 elections, although his candidacy was ultimately refused. His music continued to challenge the country's military regimes and corrupt politics.

- The collaboration album "Mustt Mustt" by Nusrat Fateh Ali Khan and Michael Brook was one of the first major releases by Real World Records, Peter Gabriel's label dedicated to world music, highlighting the label's mission to bridge cultural gaps through music.

- Serge Gainsbourg and Jane Birkin's collaboration on "Je t'aime... moi non plus" sparked not only controversy but also a real-life romance, with their relationship becoming one of the most talked-about love stories in French pop culture history.

These artists and songs not only brought international attention to their respective genres and cultures but also demonstrated the universal language of music, capable of transcending borders and connecting people across the globe.

The Eurovision Song Contest, widely known simply as Eurovision, is a unique and enduring international song competition held annually among the member countries of the European Broadcasting Union (EBU). It began in 1956, making it one of the longest-running television programs in the world and one of the most watched non-sporting events globally.

Thank You

And just like that, our musical time machine winds down, bringing us back to the present. We hope you've enjoyed this rockin' rollercoaster ride through the decades as much as we've loved guiding you through each twist, turn, and toe-tapping tune.

We're a small publishing company fueled by a passion for music, history, and the stories that connect us across generations. Your support means the world to us—it's what allows us to dive deep into the archives, unearthing the trivia treasures and melodic memories that keep the legacy of these iconic decades alive. So, from the bottom of our vinyl-loving hearts, thank you for tuning in, turning up the volume, and being a part of our musical exploration.

As we close this chapter (or should we say, track?), we hope you'll carry these melodies and moments with you, sharing the trivia, tales, and tunes with fellow music aficionados. The world of music is vast and vibrant, and every song has a story. Perhaps you've discovered a few new favorites or reignited your love for classic hits.

So, keep the records spinning, the playlists playing, and your curiosity for music's rich history alive. Until next time, keep rockin', groovin', and movin' to the rhythm of the beat. Remember, every decade has its melody, and every melody has its moment.

BNW
PUBLISH

Join us on your favourite platform, Scan the QR code on your phone or tablet

Printed in Great Britain
by Amazon